OCR **Citizenship** Studies

Teacher's Resource Book

for GCSE short and full courses

Second Edition

Official Publisher Partnership

OCR **Citizenship** Studies

Teacher's Resource Book

for GCSE short and full courses

Second Edition

Steve Johnson, Rebecca Bentley, Tony Thorpe, Julie Nakhimoff

AN HACHETTE UK COMPANY

Acknowledgements: photo credits
The Publishers would like to thank the following for permission to reproduce copyright material:
p.7 *t* © Kerioak – Fotolia.com, *b* © Aidas Zubkonis – Fotolia.com; **p.10** *bl* ©Photodisc/Getty Images, *tl* ©Stockdisc/Corbis, *tc* Claudia Veja/Alamy, *bc* ©Ryan McVay/Photodisc/Getty Images, *br* © Royalty-Free/Corbis, *tr* © www.purestockX.com; **p.24** *tl* © Design Pics Inc./Alamy, *bl* ©Andrew Holt/Alamy, *tr* ©Ray Tang/Rex Features, *br* ©Sandra Baker/Alamy; **p.72** Reproduced with permission of Traidcraft; **p.73** © PA Archive/Press Association Images.

c = centre, *b* = bottom, *t* = top, *l* = left, *r* = right

Every effort has been made to trace all copyright holders, but if any have been inadvertently overlooked the Publishers will be pleased to make the necessary arrangements at the first opportunity.

Although every effort has been made to ensure that website addresses are correct at time of going to press, Hodder Education cannot be held responsible for the content of any website mentioned in this book. It is sometimes possible to find a relocated web page by typing in the address of the home page for a website in the URL window of your browser.

Hachette UK's policy is to use papers that are natural, renewable and recyclable products and made from wood grown in sustainable forests. The logging and manufacturing processes are expected to conform to the environmental regulations of the country of origin.

Orders: please contact Bookpoint Ltd, 130 Milton Park, Abingdon, Oxon OX14 4SB. Telephone: +44 (0)1235 827720. Fax: +44 (0)1235 400454. Lines are open 9.00a.m.–5.00p.m., Monday to Saturday, with a 24-hour message answering service. Visit our website at www.hoddereducation.co.uk

First published 2003

This second edition published 2009
by Hodder Education, an Hachette UK company
338 Euston Road
London NW1 3BH

Impression number   5 4 3 2 1
Year   2013 2012 2011 2010 2009

Typeset in 10.5 on 12pt Bembo by Phoenix Photosetting, Chatham, Kent
Printed in Great Britain by Hobbs the Printers, Totton, Hants

A catalogue record for this title is available from the British Library

ISBN 978 0 340 98282 2

Contents

Introduction

This Teacher's Book has been written to accompany the Student's Book *OCR Citizenship Studies for GCSE short and full courses Second Edition*. It supports teachers in course organisation and planning as well as providing advice on resources and on how best to tackle the controlled assessments and examinations. Examples of student responses to parts of the controlled assessments and to key examination questions are included and have been designed specifically to promote *assessment for learning*. Revision checklists are included for each of the examinations. As with all of the material in this guide, these resources can be adapted and copied by teachers and students.

■ Section 1: Rationale for the OCR GCSE in Citizenship Studies

This introduction to the specification shows its flexibility and offers advice on how to integrate the different areas of content into a coherent scheme of work. There is also advice on promoting active citizenship through the controlled assessments and on how to market the course to students and parents.

■ Section 2: Organising GCSE Citizenship in your school or college

There are several ways of organising the course to suit the needs of different students and of different schools or colleges. This section considers different models of course organisation to suit different school or college contexts. A sample scheme of work is included to illustrate the advantages of combining content from the Short Course and Full Course, as well as a chart showing how Citizenship Studies links with other parts of the National Curriculum.

■ Section 3: A whole school/college approach to Citizenship

Community cohesion is a priority for many schools and colleges. As well as explaining community cohesion in straightforward, practical terms, this section shows how a well-planned Citizenship course can promote community cohesion as part of a whole school or college approach. The section contains tools for auditing the current state of Citizenship in your school or college and the effectiveness of your school, college or student council. A planning grid is also included to help teachers, governors or school and college leaders plan for the future.

■ Section 4: Success in the Short Course

This section provides practical guidance for teachers and students on how to plan for success in the controlled assessment and examination for the Short Course Units A341 and A342. Mark schemes and model answers enable teachers and students to see exactly what is required to reach grade C and grade A. This section also includes a revision checklist for the Short Course.

■ Section 5: Success in the Full Course

This section is organised in a similar way to section 4 above and offers advice on how to succeed in the controlled assessment and examination for the Full Course Units A343 and A344.

■ Section 6: Answers to questions in the Student's Book

This section contains answers to the questions in the Student's Book.

■ Section 7: Further resources

A comprehensive list of publications and resources.

■ Appendix 1 and Appendix 2

Grids mapping the specification to the Student's Book, and the Student's Book to the programme of study.

Section 1: Rationale for the OCR GCSE in Citizenship Studies

Introduction

OCR now offers short and full GCSE courses in Citizenship Studies. The two courses share the same two themes: *rights and responsibilities*, and *identity, democracy and justice*. These are organised to allow teachers and students considerable flexibility in choosing routes through the courses. As a result, decisions about taking the Short Course or Full Course routes to accreditation need not be made at the outset but can be delayed to meet the needs and aspirations of particular students as they progress through the course.

The OCR GCSE specification in Citizenship Studies covers the National Curriculum Key Stage 4 Programme of Study for Citizenship. It offers a coherent but flexible accreditation for candidates' study of Citizenship within their school or college and the wider community. *Key Concepts* and *Key Processes* from the National Curriculum Programme of Study are cross-referenced in the specification content. Each part of the specification content is linked to an appropriate example to help teachers with their interpretation of the content.

Each section of specification content is cross-referenced with the National Curriculum for Citizenship

Examples are included to help teachers with their interpretation of the specification content

3.2.3 Democracy and voting

Candidates should be able to:

- engage in different democratic decision-making exercises that have an influence on school or community life. (**National Curriculum Key Concept 1.1a. National Curriculum Key Process 2.2b. Range and Content 3d and 3h.**)

Example: through debating and voting on an appropriate focus for an end-of-year celebration or tutor group charity or selecting Student Council representatives.

The OCR specification builds upon the strengths of the previous popular OCR specification for Short Course GCSE Citizenship Studies but the new specification now includes an opportunity for candidates to qualify for a Full Course GCSE.

Specification rationale

- Promote effective advocacy, active citizenship, enquiry and debate.
- Promote community cohesion in line with OFSTED requirements.
- Enable teachers to integrate the Short Course and Full Course content into a single coherent experience for students.
- Enable choices of campaigns and practical actions by teachers and students, and give as much credit as possible for students' actions within an assessment framework that places minimum demands on teacher time.
- Build on the popular features of OCR's market-leading Short Course, such as the emphasis on active citizenship and the quality of the support available to teachers.
- Provide maximum flexibility by offering an exam in January as well as in June and providing computer-based assessment as an option.

OCR Citizenship Studies Teacher's Resource Book for GCSE full and short course
© 2009 Hodder Education

Flexible opportunities

Students can follow the GCSE (Short Course) by completing the two Core Units:
• Unit A341   *Rights and Responsibilities – Getting Started as an Active Citizen*
• Unit A342   *Identity, Democracy and Justice – Understanding our Role as Citizens.*

These two Core Units cover the statutory Programme of Study for Citizenship.

Students can qualify for the GCSE (Full Course) by extending their studies with two Extension Units:
• Unit A343   *Rights and Responsibilities – Extending our Knowledge and Understanding*
• Unit A344   *Identity, Democracy and Justice – Leading the Way as an Active Citizen.*

Teachers can either plan a course that integrates the Core and Extension Units into a single scheme of work from the outset (see further guidance in section 2) or ask students to study the extension material once the Core Units have been completed.

Full Course – all 4 Units	Short Course – 2 Units		
		Unit A341 Rights and Responsibilities – Getting Started as an Active Citizen	**Unit A342** Identity, Democracy and Justice – Understanding our Role as Citizens
		↕ Unit A341 and Unit A343 are linked through the theme *Rights and Responsibilities*	↕ Unit A342 and Unit A344 are linked through the theme *Identity, Democracy and Justice*
		Unit A343 Rights and Responsibilities – Extending our Knowledge and Understanding	**Unit A344** Identity, Democracy and Justice – Leading the Way as an Active Citizen

The specification content

The specification content is arranged so that the sections within the Extension Units (Full Course) match the sections in the Core Units (Short Course). Content in the two Extension Units enables students to broaden and deepen their knowledge and understanding of the two specification themes: *Rights and Responsibilities* and *Identity, Democracy and Justice.*

Core Units for the GCSE Short Course:

Unit A341 *Rights and Responsibilities – Getting Started as an Active Citizen*	Unit A342 *Identity, Democracy and Justice – Understanding our Role as Citizens*
• **3.1.1** Our rights and responsibilities to each other, within families and within the wider community • **3.1.2** Our rights and responsibilities as citizens within the economy and welfare systems • **3.1.3** Our rights and responsibilities as global citizens • **3.1.4** Campaigning to raise awareness and advocate action within the community	• **3.2.1** Citizenship, identity and community in the United Kingdom • **3.2.2** Fairness and justice in decision-making and the law • **3.2.3** Democracy and voting • **3.2.4** The United Kingdom's relationships in Europe, including the European Union (EU), and relationships with the Commonwealth and the United Nations (UN)
Assessment Controlled Assessment – The Citizenship Campaign	**Assessment** Examination – 1 hour

These complementary Extension Units make up the GCSE Full Course:

Unit A343 *Rights and Responsibilities – Extending our Knowledge and Understanding*	Unit A344 *Identity, Democracy and Justice – Leading the Way as an Active Citizen*
• **3.3.1** Our rights and responsibilities at school/college and within the wider community (EXTENSION of Unit A341 3.1.1) • **3.3.2** Our rights and responsibilities as citizens within the economy and welfare systems (EXTENSION of Unit A341 3.1.2) • **3.3.3** Extending understanding of a Global Citizen's rights and responsibilities (EXTENSION of Unit A341 3.1.3)	• **3.4.1** Citizenship, identity and community cohesion in the United Kingdom (EXTENSION of Unit A342 3.2.1) • **3.4.2** Extending understanding of the legal and justice system (EXTENSION of Unit A342 3.2.2) • **3.4.3** Democracy and voting (EXTENSION of Unit A342 3.2.3)
Assessment Examination – 1 hour	**Assessment** Controlled Assessment Part 1 – The Citizenship Enquiry Part 2 – Practical Citizenship Action

Active citizenship

Active citizenship is a key feature of the specification. By following the specification, students will be encouraged to understand and make sense of the legal, political, economic and social aspects of their lives. The specification provides a framework for students to become more interested in citizenship issues by exploring topical controversial issues and problems, taking action to try to influence others and participating actively in decision-making.

Opportunities for active citizenship are highlighted right across the subject content. However, the Controlled Assessments for the Short Course (Unit A341 on *Rights and Responsibilities*) and the Full Course (Unit A344 on *Identity, Democracy and Justice*) offer students the chance to engage in sustained action as part of a group.

Rewards for achievement in the Controlled Assessment are substantial. Sixty per cent of students' final marks come from the Controlled Assessments. Teachers should plan to spend a large proportion of guided learning hours (class work and homework) on the Controlled Assessments. OCR recommends around 37 hours on each.

With this new specification, Citizenship should be seen as an active subject in the same way as Art, Drama and Technology, all of which have a similar proportion of marks for their Controlled Assessments.

The Citizenship Campaign

Students research, plan, manage and produce an evaluation of a *Citizenship Campaign* within a school, college or local community.

The Campaign should seek to promote or extend individual or collective rights or responsibilities.

Students should negotiate with others and manage time and resources appropriately. They must evaluate how they managed their campaign and the extent to which it was successful rather than just describing what they did.

Where does it fit?

Controlled Assessment for Unit A341
Rights and Responsibilities – Getting Started as an Active Citizen

Time recommendation

37 guided learning hours

Value

60% of Short Course marks or
30% of Full Course marks

The Citizenship Enquiry and Practical Citizenship Action

For Part 1 of this Controlled Assessment, the *Citizenship Enquiry*, students use a Source Book (provided each year by OCR) to help them research different viewpoints on a controversial citizenship issue.

For Part 2 of the Controlled Assessment, students plan, manage and evaluate *Practical Citizenship Action* to promote community cohesion or equal opportunity, or to discourage discrimination in the school or local community.

Where does it fit?

Controlled Assessment for Unit A344
Identity, Democracy and Justice – Leading the Way as an Active Citizen

Time recommendation

37 guided learning hours

Value

30% of Full Course marks

Active citizenship: the process

For both Controlled Assessments, students should take part in a similar process which involves research, planning, engagement and evaluation.

In the OCR specification, the *engagement* part of this process has a very high weighting. This enables students to be rewarded for the quality of their teamwork, leadership and organisation and for the impact of their action rather than for how convincingly they can write about it afterwards.

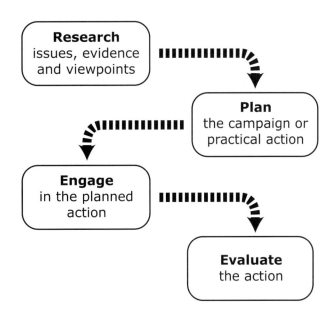

Examining Citizenship

The one-hour Short Course exam assesses Unit A342 *Identity, Democracy and Justice – Understanding our Role as Citizens*. The exam is worth 40 per cent of the total mark for the Short Course and contributes 20 per cent of the total mark to the Full Course. Details of the exam are in section 4 of this book.

The one-hour Full Course exam assesses Unit A343 *Rights and Responsibilities – Extending our Knowledge and Understanding*. The exam is worth 20 per cent of the total mark for the Full Course. Details of the exam are in section 5 of this book.

Ten ways students benefit from taking the OCR GCSE in Citizenship Studies

In taking the OCR GCSE in Citizenship Studies, students benefit by having opportunities to:
- Find out more about their rights and responsibilities in the home and at school and as: consumers; employees; future employers and future tenants; and in relation to criminal and civil law.
- Explore and appreciate the diversity of cultures and traditions within the United Kingdom.
- Find out about power, accountability and decision-making within their school or college, community and country, and on a global scale.
- Explore their role as citizens and decision-makers in our democracy.
- Use accessible case studies to evaluate recognisable issues and dilemmas, and to interpret these in relation to their own social, moral and political ideas.
- Exercise choice over the focus for their *Citizenship Campaign* and, for the Full Course, their *Practical Citizenship Action* so as to take action they feel is worthwhile for their school or wider community, and gain considerable credit for their active citizenship through the OCR assessment framework.
- Develop their skills of research, planning, organisation, evaluation and advocacy, and demonstrate these through the Controlled Assessments.
- Demonstrate initiative and leadership, and work collaboratively as part of a team.
- Gain further experience in research and enquiry that will prepare them for the new Level 3 Project in the sixth form.
- Opt for a computer-based test instead of a paper-based exam for the Short Course.

Many schools have designed a simple brochure to highlight the benefits of the GCSE course in Citizenship. This can be used with parents and students in Year 9 as part of the option choice process for Key Stage 4.

An example of such a brochure is shown on pages 7–10. The template provided can be adapted to suit each school or college's needs.

OCR Citizenship Studies Teacher's Resource Book for GCSE full and short course
© 2009 Hodder Education

Citizenship at Oakfield

Make your point

Get involved

Take action

... with Citizenship GCSE

· ·

???   Try our questionnaire   ???

· ·

Which of these things will happen to you in the next 10 years?

No way	Write 0 in the box
Maybe	Write 1 in the box
Likely	Write 2 in the box
Probably	Write 3 in the box

☐ Get a job

☐ Rent a flat or buy a house

☐ Buy a major item like a holiday or a car

☐ Get married or have a long-term partner

☐ Join the armed forces, the public services (doctor, teacher, police officer, etc) or the legal profession

☐ Start a business

☐ Live or work overseas

☐ Vote in an election

☐ Join a campaign

☐ Raise money on Red Nose Day or for Children in Need or similar

☐ Take action to improve your neighbourhood or community

☐ Get stopped or arrested by the police

☐ Ask for legal advice

☐ Take legal action or appear in court

Now add up your score.

28–42   You should definitely take Citizenship and might even be a bit of an expert already! You'll learn more about important rights and responsibilities as well as having a go at campaigns and practical action.

12–27   Citizenship will help you understand more about the law and how decision-making works in our country. You'll get more interested and involved as you follow the course.

0–11   So you're going to live with your parents and never go out? Start a new outlook on life with Citizenship!

OCR Citizenship Studies Teacher's Resource Book for GCSE full and short course
© 2009 Hodder Education

Citizenship: What will I study? How will I be assessed?

The GCSE Short Course (two units)

Unit 1 Rights and Responsibilities:

- towards each other, within families and within the wider community
- as citizens within the economy and welfare systems
- as global citizens.

Unit 1 includes the chance to research, plan and take part in a *Citizenship Campaign*. This will be assessed by your teacher and is worth 60 per cent of your Short Course mark.

Unit 2 Identity, Democracy and Justice

- Understanding our role as citizens in the United Kingdom, Europe and the World
- Fairness and justice in decision-making and the law
- Democracy and voting.

Unit 2 is assessed with an exam or computer-based test worth 40 per cent of your Short Course mark.

The GCSE Full Course (four units)

You study Units 1 and 2 from the Short Course plus these two units:

Unit 3 Extending our Knowledge and Understanding of Rights and Responsibilities:

- at school and within the wider community
- as citizens within the economy and welfare systems
- as global citizens.

Unit 3 is assessed with an exam worth 20 per cent of your Full Course mark.

Unit 4 Identity, Democracy and Justice – Leading the Way as an Active Citizen

- Citizenship, identity and community cohesion
- Extending our understanding of the legal and justice system
- Democracy and voting.

Unit 4 includes the chance to research an important issue (*Citizenship Enquiry*) and to plan and take part in some *Practical Citizenship Action*. This will be assessed by your teacher and is worth 30 per cent of your Full Course mark.

Why study citizenship?

Citizenship Studies will help you to understand and make sense of important social, legal and political issues that you will encounter throughout your life.

What skills will I develop?

- Research
- Analysis of the law and deciding suitable action
- Constructing arguments and presenting your case (advocacy)
- Evaluation of evidence and viewpoints
- Campaigning
- Planning, team work and leadership

What Next?

Courses: **AS levels or A levels**
Business Studies, Citizenship, Economics, History, Government and Politics, Law, Sociology

Diplomas or other vocational qualifications
Business, Health and Social Care or Public Services, Humanities

Careers: Barrister, solicitor, legal secretary, social worker, doctor, nurse, teacher, politician, campaigner, researcher, community worker, police officer, probation officer, human resources manager, teacher, journalist, investigative reporter, diplomat, business leader, trade union representative, pressure group organiser, and many more

OCR Citizenship Studies Teacher's Resource Book for GCSE full and short course
© 2009 Hodder Education

Benefits for your school or college

Adopting the OCR GCSE Citizenship course will have major benefits not only for students in your school but also for teachers and for members of the wider community.

■ The school or college in the community

- OCR GCSE Citizenship will make a major contribution to the school or college's obligation to promote community cohesion (see page 23).
- Students are encouraged to appreciate the value of living in a culturally diverse society and to understand the interdependence of people locally and globally. Promoting such understanding should be at the heart of the curriculum.
- The course provides the perfect vehicle for promoting *Student Voice* and encouraging information literacy and oral literacy.
- Students are encouraged to understand their rights and responsibilities at home, in school or college and as young citizens, so contributing to a positive school or college ethos.
- The course enables and encourages teachers and students to make positive links with governors, community organisations, local politicians, the police, legal support services, local magistrates, pressure groups, political parties, and many other groups and organisations that help give the school or college an enhanced position in the local community.

■ Flexible course organisation and assessment

- The unitised nature of the course and the links between the Short Course and Full Course units provide considerable flexibility for the school or college in course organisation and delivery. Decisions about whether to accredit students for the Short Course or Full Course can be made during the teaching programme depending on the progress made by students.
- Students who are better at course-based assessment than at examinations will benefit from 60 per cent of the final mark being based on Controlled Assessments.
- The flexibility and choice available in the Controlled Assessments enables students to pursue their own interests and priorities within the *Citizenship Campaign* and *Practical Citizenship Action*.
- The OCR emphasis on the assessment of practical skills will favour students who enjoy active work.
- Concise and manageable assessment criteria enable teachers to spend a greater proportion of their time on supporting students than on assessment activities.
- Short Course exams in January and/or June provide greater flexibility for organising the teaching and learning programme as well as opportunities for students to retake the exam should they need to.
- Computer-based tests, as an alternative to the paper-based exam, are favoured by students.

Section 2: Organising GCSE Citizenship in your school or college

Introduction

There are several ways of organising GCSE Citizenship. Whichever way you choose, be aware of the guided learning hours (class work and independent study) recommended by OCR:

- **Short Course**   60–70 guided learning hours including a maximum of 37 hours for the Controlled Assessment (Unit A341)
- **Full Course**   120–140 guided learning hours including a maximum of 74 hours for the Controlled Assessments (Unit A341 and A344)

Before going too far with your strategic planning, arrange a discussion with members of your school or college's Leadership Team.

It will be helpful to brief Leadership Team members on:

- the huge contribution Citizenship can make to the school or college's obligations to address cultural diversity and community cohesion
- the flexible nature of the course and the links between Short Course and Full Course units and content
- the Controlled Assessment weighting and Citizenship's status as a practical subject
- the interesting and potentially controversial nature of the Controlled Assessments.

Questions to discuss with members of the school or college's Leadership Team include:

- Should all students follow the Short Course GCSE as an entitlement?
- Should we offer the Full Course and, if so, should it be an entitlement for all, an option for all or a guided option for particular students?
- Can we offer the Full Course units to gifted and talented students as an option after school?
- Is it possible to start the teaching and learning programme in Year 9?
- Can we complete the Short Course at the end of Year 10 and then take students forward to the Full Course units in Year 11? If so, can a block of time be made available for the Controlled Assessment (A341)? (See Model 2 on page 14.)
- If we offered the Full Course as an option, how much time would be available for it and would it have equal status with other practical options with a 60 per cent weighting on the Controlled Assessment?
- Would there be support for allowing students to resit the Short Course exam as it is offered in January and June?
- Would there be support for computer-based testing of Unit A341? (For more details of computer-based testing, see page 51.)

Models of organisation

Teachers can organise the OCR course to suit the needs of their students and to fit with the school or college's overall curriculum plan. This section contains five different models of organisation for consideration.

Note that all models are based on a six-term year with five terms in the final year of the course. Terms are of approximately six weeks' duration. Less has been planned for the summer term to accommodate the usual adjustments to the normal school timetable at that time of year. Extra blocks of time, in addition to the normal timetabled hours, may be needed for completion of the Controlled Assessments.

■ Model 1: Short Course for all; no Full Course

- A two-year course starting in Year 9 or 10
- Based on a 1-hour lesson per week plus homework
- Eleven terms of approximately six weeks each (term twelve will be taken up by examinations in Year 11).

EITHER

Terms	Year 9 or 10	Year 10 or 11
1	*Unit A341* Rights and responsibilities to each other, within families and within the wider community (Section 3.1.1)	*Unit A342* Citizenship, identity and community in the UK (Section 3.2.1)
2	*Unit A341* Rights and responsibilities as citizens within the economy and welfare systems (Section 3.1.2)	*Unit A342* Fairness and justice in decision-making and the law (Section 3.2.2)
3	*Unit A341* Rights and responsibilities as global citizens (Section 3.1.3)	*Unit A342* Democracy and voting (Section 3.2.3)
4	**A341 Controlled Assessment** *Unit A341* Campaigning to raise awareness and advocate action within the community (Section 3.1.4)	*Unit A342* The UK's relationships in Europe, including the EU, and relationships with the Commonwealth and the UN (Section 3.2.4)
5	**A341 Controlled Assessment**	Exam preparation A341 Controlled Assessment to OCR
6	**A341 Controlled Assessment**	**A342 Exam**

OR

Terms	Year 9 or 10	Year 10 or 11
1	*Unit A341* Rights and responsibilities to each other, within families and within the wider community (Section 3.1.1)	*Unit A342* Democracy and voting (Section 3.2.3)
2	*Unit A341* Rights and responsibilities as citizens within the economy and welfare systems (Section 3.1.2)	*Unit A342* The UK's relationships in Europe, including the EU, and relationships with the Commonwealth and the UN (Section 3.2.4) Exam preparation
3	*Unit A341* Rights and responsibilities as global citizens (Section 3.1.3)	**A342 Exam** (January) **A341 Controlled Assessment** *Unit A341* Campaigning to raise awareness and advocate action within the community (Section 3.1.4)
4	*Unit A342* Citizenship, identity and community in the UK (Section 3.2.1)	**A341 Controlled Assessment**
5	*Unit A342* Fairness and justice in decision-making and the law (Section 3.2.2)	**A341 Controlled Assessment** A341 Controlled Assessment to OCR
6	*Unit A342* Fairness and justice in decision-making and the law (Section 3.2.2 continued)	**Opportunity to resit A342 Exam**

■ Model 2: Full Course for all, based on two themes: *Rights and Responsibilities* and *Identity, Democracy and Justice*

- This thematic approach integrates Short Course and Full Course content so as to improve coherence and save time. The two themes can be studied in any order but the A343 exam is not available until June 2011
- A two-year course starting in Year 9 or 10, based on two-hour lessons per week plus homework **OR** a three-year course starting in Year 9 based on a one-hour lesson per week plus homework
- Eleven terms of approximately six weeks each in the two-year option.

Terms	Year 9 or 10 Identity, Democracy and Justice	Year 10 or 11 Rights and Responsibilities
1	*Unit A342* Citizenship, identity and community in the UK (Section 3.2.1) *Unit A344* Citizenship, identity and community cohesion in the United Kingdom (Section 3.4.1) **A344 Controlled Assessment** Part 1 – Citizenship Enquiry (This assessment is first available in 2011)	*Unit A341* Rights and responsibilities to each other, within families and within the wider community (Section 3.1.1) *Unit A343* Rights and responsibilities at school/college and in the wider community (Section 3.3.1)
2	**A344 Controlled Assessment** Part 2 – Practical Citizenship Action	*Unit A341* Rights and responsibilities as citizens within the economy and welfare systems (Section 3.1.2) *Unit A343* Our rights and responsibilities as citizens within the economy and welfare systems (Section 3.3.2)
3	**A344 Controlled Assessment** Part 2 – Practical Citizenship Action	Opportunity to resit A342 exam *Unit A341* Rights and responsibilities as global citizens (Section 3.1.3) *Unit A343* Extending understanding of a global citizen's rights and responsibilities (Section 3.3.3) **A341 Controlled Assessment** *Unit A341* Campaigning to raise awareness and advocate action within the community (Section 3.1.4)
4	*Unit A342* Fairness and justice in decision-making and the law (Section 3.2.2) *Unit A342* The UK's relationships in Europe, including the EU, and relationships with the Commonwealth and the UN (Section 3.2.4)	**A341 Controlled Assessment**
5	*Unit A342* Democracy and voting (Section 3.2.3) *Unit A344* Democracy and voting (Section 3.4.3) A344 Controlled Assessment to OCR Exam preparation	**A341 Controlled Assessment** A341 Controlled Assessment to OCR Exam preparation
6	A342 Exam *Unit A344* Extending understanding of the legal and justice system (Section 3.4.2)	A343 Exam (This exam is first available in June 2011)

OCR Citizenship Studies Teacher's Resource Book for GCSE full and short course
© 2009 Hodder Education

■ Model 3: Full Course for all, but with an opt-out after the Short Course Assessments

- A two-year course starting in Year 9 or 10, based on two one-hour lessons per week plus homework **OR** a three-year course starting in Year 9 based on a one-hour lesson per week plus homework
- Eleven terms of approximately six weeks each in the two-year option.

Terms	Year 9 or 10	Year 10 or 11
1	*Unit A341* Rights and responsibilities to each other, within families and within the wider community (Section 3.1.1) *Unit A341* Rights and responsibilities as citizens within the economy and welfare systems (Section 3.1.2)	*Unit A344* Citizenship, identity and community cohesion in the UK (Section 3.4.1) **A344 Controlled Assessment** Part 1 – Citizenship Enquiry
2	*Unit A341* Rights and responsibilities as global citizens (Section 3.1.3) **A341 Controlled Assessment** *Unit A341* Campaigning to raise awareness and advocate action within the community (Section 3.1.4)	**A344 Controlled Assessment** Part 2 – Practical Citizenship Action
3	**A341 Controlled Assessment**	**A344 Controlled Assessment** Part 2 – Practical Citizenship Action **Opportunity to resit A342 exam**
4	*Unit A342* Citizenship, identity and community in the UK (Section 3.2.1) *Unit A342* Fairness and justice in decision-making and the law (Section 3.2.2)	*Unit A343* Rights and responsibilities at school/college and in the wider community (Section 3.3.1) *Unit A343* Our rights and responsibilities as citizens within the economy and welfare systems (Section 3.3.2)
5	*Unit A342* Democracy and voting (Section 3.2.3) *Unit A342* The UK's relationships in Europe, including the EU, and relationships with the Commonwealth and the UN (Section 3.2.4) A341 Controlled Assessment to OCR	*Unit A343* Extending understanding of a global citizen's rights and responsibilities (Section 3.3.3) Exam preparation A344 Controlled Assessment to OCR
6	**A342 Exam** *Unit A344* Extending understanding of the legal and justice system (Section 3.4.2) *Unit A344* Democracy and voting (Section 3.4.3)	**A343 Exam**

■ Model 4: Short Courses and Full Courses running in parallel (all students to follow one option)

- All students follow a minimum of the Short Course with a one-hour lesson per week (see Model 1 on page 13)
- Students can opt for a Full Course instead. They would form separate teaching groups from those following the Short Course and would be allocated teaching time of at least two hours per week.

■ Model 5: Short Course for all, with a Full Course extension option for a further year

- All students follow a minimum of the Short Course with a one-hour lesson per week over two years in Years 9 and 10 (see Model 1 on page 13)
- Students can opt to take the Full Course assessments in Year 11 with a one-hour lesson per week.

At the end of the Short Course in Year 10, students would opt for different alternatives in Year 11. These could be differentiated to meet individual students' ability and aspirations, as in the example below.

Years 9 and 10 (1 hour per week)	Year 11 (1 hour per week)
	Option 1 Full Course assessment for Citizenship
All students take Short Course Citizenship	**Option 2** Complementary Short Course GCSE, for example Religious Studies
	Option 3 Supported self-study to boost GCSE grades across the curriculum and to prepare students for college courses at 16+

Integrating Short Course and Full Course units

The two Full Course units broaden and deepen the content of the two Short Course units. This means that it is easy to bring together some of the content from the different units to create a more coherent learning experience for students. This is shown in Model 2 on page 14.

The sample scheme of work on pages 17–21 shows how matching sections from Units A341 and A343 on rights and responsibilities in the economy and welfare systems can be brought together in one coherent package of 12 lessons. Other sections from the Full Course can be integrated with the appropriate matching sections from the Short Course. (See section 1, page 3, to identify the links between content for the Short Course and the Full Course.)

Sample scheme of work

Full Course: Units A341 and A343 in combination			
SUGGESTED TEACHING TIME 12 hours plus homework		**TOPIC** Our rights and responsibilities in the economy and welfare systems (Sections 3.1.2 and 3.3.2 combined)	
TOPIC OUTLINE	**TEACHING AND HOMEWORK ACTIVITIES**	**RESOURCES**	**NOTES**
Lessons 1 and 2 Understand their responsibility for participation in the economy through employment and understand how, and for what purposes, taxes are raised (locally and nationally). (Content from *Unit A341 – Short Course*)	• Identify the needs of individuals and communities in the UK and link these needs to particular jobs and services. • Discuss which jobs and services provide a product or service that people pay for directly (e.g. engineer, surveyor, lorry driver) and which jobs provide a product or service for which there is no direct payment (e.g. teacher, police officer, soldier). • Students analyse wage slips to work out how taxation is used to provide services for which there is no or limited direct payment.	• A card set for each group of students showing basic (physiological) needs of the individual (food, water, clothing, shelter) as well as other categories of need (see notes). • A card set showing different occupations. • Wage slip showing deductions for tax, national insurance, pension contributions and student loan repayment. • *Young Citizen's Passport* – section on tax, page 68. • Student's Book, pages 88–89.	• Ensure that students understand the terms *economy* and *taxation*. • Card sets can be divided as follows, according to Maslow's hierarchy of needs: <u>Level 1</u> Physiological (food, water, shelter and clothing) <u>Level 2</u> Safety (freedom from disasters, wars, diseases and crime) <u>Level 3</u> Social needs (we need to feel that we belong to and are accepted by our community) <u>Level 4</u> Respect and control over our lives (this includes the right to take part in decision-making) <u>Level 5</u> The need to achieve our potential (this includes access to education as well as freedom from discrimination). • Introduce the idea that the economy is a series of interdependent relationships between people who, together, support each other's needs and where wealth is exchanged for goods and services.
Lessons 3 and 4 Understand the government's role in helping to manage the economy and the planning and regulation of public services. Evaluate and debate the different opinions on how far the state	• Identify the public services they and their family use each month as well as the ones they do not use currently. • Identify which services are provided by central government or local authorities and introduce the different forms of	• Use your local authority website for a list of services and a breakdown of the cost and proportion of overall expenditure taken up by each service. • The following website has a page about Your Council and Council Tax	• This lesson gives students the opportunity to design a survey on the use of public services by their family and friends. • More able students could prepare a debate on whether education or

SUGGESTED TEACHING TIME 12 hours plus homework	TOPIC Our rights and responsibilities in the economy and welfare systems (Sections 3.1.2 and 3.3.2 combined)		
TOPIC OUTLINE	**TEACHING AND HOMEWORK ACTIVITIES**	**RESOURCES**	**NOTES**
or individuals should take responsibility for the provision of income protection, health and education. (Content from *Unit A343 – Full Course*)	• taxation including council tax as a form of indirect taxation. • Analyse a list of the main areas of spending from their local authority and rank the services in order of importance for particular groups of people such as: young people, pensioners and parents with young children. Discuss which ones they would spend less or more money on. • Debate the advantages and disadvantages of paying for education directly. Should the way in which university education is funded with a mixture of government grants and student fees be introduced to secondary schools? Should parents be encouraged to set up their own schools or be given vouchers to use to buy their children's education?	• with links to local authority sites: www.direct.gov.uk • There are some good articles on the internet about Sweden's 'free school' movement. One of the most accessible is on the BBC website, *Swedish model of free schools*: http://news.bbc.co.uk • Student's Book, pages 46–47.	other services should be paid for directly by those who use them.
Lesson 5 Understand that employers and employees have rights and responsibilities that can compete and conflict, and that employees can be supported by trade unions. (Content from *Unit A341 – Short Course*) Understand the role of trade unions and employers' associations in supporting and representing their members. (Content from *Unit A343 – Full Course*)	• Analyse an employment contract to identify employee and employer rights and responsibilities. • Discuss rights that might conflict in certain situations, such as when an important order needs to be completed before the workplace shuts for the weekend. • Identify the main employment law provisions that are designed to protect employee rights and apply this knowledge through the use of case studies.	• Example of an employment contract. • *Young Citizen's Passport* – section on work and training, pages 36–52. • The BBC website has a clear, simple but detailed guide to employment law with useful examples: www.bbc.co.uk/consumer/guides_to/ • The National Youth Advice website has a clear and accessible section on employment rights and responsibilities including the national minimum wage: www.thesite.org • The TUC's *Worksmart* website gives a	• Students should understand the role of trade unions in the support for individual workplace rights as well as the collective negotiation of pay. • Different groups of students can research the role of trade unions or employers' associations and report back their findings.

Learning outcomes	Teaching and learning activities	Resources	Teacher notes
	• Research the role of trade unions and employers' associations.	• detailed coverage of employment rights and the benefits of trade union membership: www.worksmart.org.uk • The TUC also has a range of educational resources and a speaker service for schools: www.tuc.org.uk • The Federation of Small Businesses website gives an insight into the need for employers to be able to seek advice and support on rights and responsibilities: www.fsb.org.uk • Student's Book, page 78.	
Lessons 6 and 7 Understand that the rights of consumers and businesses can compete and conflict but that both have legal rights and responsibilities to each other when items are bought and sold, and that rights are supported and protected by statutory and non-statutory bodies. (Content from *Unit A341 – Short Course*)	• Identify the rights and responsibilities included in a contract to purchase a car, a holiday or a similar high-value item. Study the terms, conditions and regulations linked to a transport ticket or cinema ticket. • Identify basic consumer rights linked to the Sale of Goods Act 1979 and apply this knowledge to provide advice to consumers with particular problems. • Research and evaluate the services provided by the local authority and compare the support to consumers given by Citizens' Advice and the Consumers' Association.	• Examples of contracts for the purchase of goods or services. • *Young Citizen's Passport* – section on money (spending), pages 54–59. • The BBC website has a clear, simple but detailed guide to consumer law with useful examples: www.bbc.co.uk/consumer/guides_to/ • The Consumer Direct website has a very detailed guide to consumer rights in a wide variety of contexts: www.consumerdirect.gov.uk • The Consumers' Association *Which?* website enables students to find out about the purpose and value of an independent organisation representing consumers (use the *About Us* section): www.which.co.uk • Citizens' Advice website shows the value of a campaigning non-subscription charity for advice and support: www.citizensadvice.org.uk • Student's Book, pages 50–61.	• Make sure students are aware of consumers' responsibilities as well as their rights particularly with regard to proper payment for a product and service. • A comparison of the Consumers' Association and Citizens' Advice will be a useful exercise for able students. The Consumer's Association is a subscription-only service which concentrates on providing 'best buy' advice and legal support where necessary. Citizen's Advice offers free advice to everyone once they have a problem.

SUGGESTED TEACHING TIME 12 hours plus homework	TOPIC Our rights and responsibilities in the economy and welfare systems (Sections 3.1.2 and 3.3.2 combined)		
TOPIC OUTLINE	**TEACHING AND HOMEWORK ACTIVITIES**	**RESOURCES**	**NOTES**
Lessons 8 and 9 Understand that laws relating to employment and the production, taxation and sale of goods need to recognise the interests of employers, employees, buyers, sellers and the environmental impact of production. Understand how these interests can compete and conflict. (Content from *Unit A343 – Full Course*)	Evaluate the different viewpoints in favour and against adjusting taxation to discourage environmental damage/emissions/pollution. The debate on road pricing would be a good example. • Analyse and evaluate different viewpoints. • Discuss how differences of viewpoint are based on different interests. • Debate the issue using evidence – students could be allocated different roles.	A wide range of sources on road pricing is available on the internet. Start with the BBC website for the latest information. The Friends of the Earth site provides a good case in favour of road pricing while the Association of British Drivers has one of the strongest cases against.	Road pricing is one of several controversial issues that could form the basis of this lesson. Other areas could include: • increasing/extending the minimum wage • increasing fuel tax or tax on public utilities • extending rights to maternity or paternity leave.
Lessons 10 and 11 Understand that landlords and tenants have legal rights and responsibilities in relation to rents and deposits, health and safety and the condition of the property. Evaluate the extent to which rights are supported and protected by statutory and non-statutory bodies. (Content from *Unit A341 – Short Course*)	Design a simple leaflet for 18-year-olds thinking of renting their first flat, specifying their rights and responsibilities. • Evaluate the help and advice available for young people from the local authority and from one non-statutory organisation. • As an alternative to the second part of this task, challenge students to find the source of best advice on the internet and consider how easy such advice is to find.	• The BBC website has a clear, simple but detailed guide to renting with useful examples: www.bbc.co.uk/consumer/guides_to/ • *Young Citizen's Passport* – section on home, pages 80–86. • Evaluate the usefulness of your local authority website in providing advice to young people thinking of renting their first flat. • The Shelter website contains renting advice for young people: http://england.shelter.org.uk/get_advice/advice_topics/finding_a_place_to_live/renting_privately • Student Book, pages 126–129.	• You could use a visiting speaker from a local estate agent, letting agency or local authority to introduce the rights and responsibilities of landlords/tenants. • Clear, impartial advice on the internet tends to be swamped by the websites of commercial organisations. Showing students the location of useful advice sites is a valuable exercise in itself. • Students might also wish to discuss whether clearer advice on renting is needed on the National Youth Advice website: www.thesite.org/homelawandmoney/home/renting/findingaplace

OCR Citizenship Studies Teacher's Resource Book for GCSE full and short course
© 2009 Hodder Education

Lesson 12 Understand the importance of ethical behaviour and social responsibility in enterprise and business, including the moral and legal responsibilities businesses have towards each other and the wider community. (Content from *Unit A343 – Full course*)	• Research the purpose of laws on copyright and patents. • Identify the businesses that give financial or practical support to the school. What support have they given? What benefits do they gain from involvement with the school? • Consider the benefits to business that can come from involvement in community-based projects.	• The Intellectual Property Office runs a clear, interactive website that explains copyright and patents. It also includes an education section with excellent teaching ideas and resources: www.ipo.gov.uk/whatis.htm • The Business Link website gives a clear explanation of corporate social responsibility with examples: www.businesslink.gov.uk • The websites of many large businesses such as Tesco also include examples of corporate social responsibility.	Able students might set themselves the challenge of gaining business sponsorship/support for their *Practical Citizenship Action*. (Controlled Assessment for *Unit A344*)

Links with the school or college curriculum

There are many other parts of the school or college curriculum that can support students' understanding of the themes and issues they will encounter during citizenship lessons. While national curriculum citizenship cannot be taught adequately through the medium of other subjects' programmes of study, it will be very worthwhile for teachers to explore the links that exist between citizenship and the wider school or college curriculum.

Subject	Shared concepts or skills	Complementary content
Geography (National Curriculum – Key Stage 3)	• Interdependence • Sustainable development • Participation in informed and responsible action	• Interactions between people and their environments • Global links • European Union
History (National Curriculum – Key Stage 3)	• Interpretation and evaluation of evidence • Structured enquiry • Diversity • Identity	• The movement and settlement of diverse peoples to, from and within the British Isles including recent migration • Informed understanding of, and respect for, different identities • International institutions that resolve conflict and develop co-operation, including the European Union and the United Nations
Economic Wellbeing and Financial Capability (National Curriculum – Key Stage 4)	• Contact with people from business	• Rights and responsibilities at work
Personal Wellbeing (National Curriculum – Key Stage 4)	• Diversity • Critical reflection • Developing relationships and working with others • Negotiation • Working individually, together and in teams • Finding and evaluating information, advice and support from a variety of sources and being able to support others in doing so • Demonstrating respect for and acceptance of the differences between people	

Section 3: A whole school/college approach to Citizenship

This section introduces some factors that have an impact on the quality of citizenship education in your school or college. By workng with key colleagues you can help to build a whole-school/college approach to Citizenship education.

Introduction: shifting the culture, promoting community cohesion

As a Citizenship teacher you are in an excellent position to influence the whole culture of a school or college so that it becomes a more inclusive and democratic place of learning with strong links to the community. A formidable challenge perhaps, but the DCSF and OFSTED are on your side. The school or college's Leadership Team should also want you to play a major role in promoting community cohesion, which became an increasingly important area of focus in school inspections from September 2008 and now features prominently in the school or college's Self Evaluation Form (SEF).

What is community cohesion?

By community cohesion we mean working towards a society in which:

- there is a common vision and sense of belonging by all communities;
- the diversity of people's backgrounds and circumstances is appreciated and valued;
- similar life opportunities are available to all, and strong and positive relationships exist and continue to be developed in the workplace, in schools and in the wider community.

Guidance on the duty to promote community cohesion,
Department for Children, Schools and Families (DCSF), July 2007

The three dimensions of community cohesion

The chart below shows the three dimensions of community cohesion and highlights the areas where the school or college's Citizenship Team can make the most significant contributions.

Dimensions	Actions	Contribution from the school/college's Citizenship Team
Teaching, learning and curriculum	Students should • understand others and value diversity • understand shared values	*Unit A342* Identity, Democracy and Justice
	• understand human rights and apply these rights to different situations	*Unit A341* Rights and Responsibilities
	• develop the skills of participation and responsible action	Controlled Assessments – *Citizenship Campaign and Practical Citizenship Action*
Equity and excellence	Schools/colleges should • ensure equal opportunities for all to succeed at the highest level possible • remove barriers to access and participation in learning and wider activities • eliminate variations in outcomes for different groups	The Citizenship Controlled Assessment – *Citizenship Campaign* – can give some students the opportunity to research and promote equal opportunities in the school/college and local community

Dimensions	Actions	Contribution from the school/college's Citizenship Team
Engagement and extended services	Schools/colleges should • provide opportunities for young people and their families to interact with people from different backgrounds and build positive relationships • link with different schools, colleges and communities • provide extended services with opportunities for young people, families and the wider community to take part in activities and receive services which build positive interaction and achievement for all groups.	Citizenship Controlled Assessment *Practical Citizenship Action*

The four dimensions of 'community'

The Department for Communities, Schools and Families (DCSF) identifies four dimensions of community in its guidance on community cohesion. Citizenship Teams in schools and colleges should seek opportunities to support student understanding and engagement in all four dimensions.

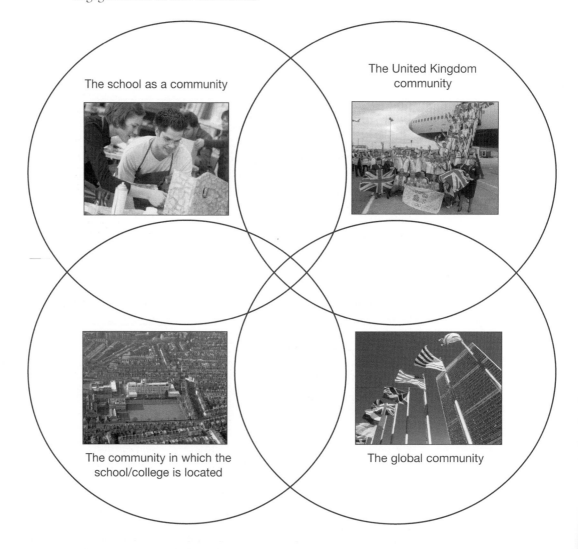

The school as a community

The United Kingdom community

The community in which the school/college is located

The global community

Where are we now? Developing the vision

A vision for the whole school/college is an essential prerequisite for promoting community cohesion and developing Citizenship education.

With a colleague, reflect on the quality of the vision for Citizenship in your school or college. How close are you to the vision for Citizenship identified by OFSTED in the first box below? How does your school or college rate on the 'Citizenship health check' in the second box below? What actions are needed to move closer to OFSTED's vision?

Creating a vision for Citizenship

To give Citizenship a presence in the school or college, effective Citizenship leaders:

- recognise that citizenship is a complex subject and needs well considered, whole-school/college planning
- seek to establish its status and visibility in the curriculum
- identify and promote examples of active citizenship in school and in the wider community
- encourage discussion and debate, including challenges to the status quo
- foster the characteristics of a democratic school/college.

From *Leading Citizenship in Schools*, OFSTED, Jan 2008

Citizenship health check – developing the vision

How far do the statements below apply to your school or college? Score each one as follows:

1 Agree strongly	4 Disagree
2 Agree	5 Disagree strongly
3 Neither agree nor disagree	

☐ Staff understand the implications of community cohesion for the school/college.

☐ The Leadership Team and Governors recognise the need for and promote whole-school/college planning of citizenship and community cohesion.

☐ Citizenship has high status amongst staff.

☐ Citizenship has high status amongst students.

☐ Students understand human rights and can apply their understanding in different contexts.

☐ Students understand others and value diversity.

☐ Students promote equal opportunities in the school/college and the wider community.

☐ Active citizenship by students in the school/college is well established.

☐ Active citizenship by students in the community is well established.

☐ The school has strong student-to-student links with schools/colleges and communities in other countries.

☐ Families are engaged in links with other groups or communities.

☐ Students have opportunities to develop citizenship skills through regular discussion and debate.

☐ Students and staff have opportunities to engage in decision-making within the school/college.

Where would we like to be and how will we get there?

Use the chart below to identify areas for development, actions that you may need to take and colleagues who may be able to help you.

- Highlight and rank in order of importance the health check statements on page 25 where your score is 4 or 5.
- Confirm who should be accountable for the development. (This is indicated on the chart already but you may wish to make amendments.)
- Identify the actions you should take to help address the issue. (An example has been done for you.)
- Identify colleagues who may be able to support you. (An example has been done for you.)

Change is more likely when you prioritise, take people with you and get senior staff on your side.

Areas for Development	Accountability			Actions	Allies
	Citizenship Team	Leadership Team	Governors		
Staff understand the implications of community cohesion for the school/college.		♦		*Example:* • Discuss and check understanding within your own team • Identify existing areas of strength and good practice within the school/college • Meet with potentially sympathetic pastoral middle leaders • Meet with a potentially sympathetic member of the Leadership Team • Offer to do a presentation to the Leadership Team • Offer to help plan and deliver staff training with key allies	*Example:* • Key members of Citizenship Team • Pastoral middle leaders • Members of Leadership Team responsible for Continuous Professional Development (CPD) and community development
Leadership Team and Governors recognise the need for and promote whole-school/college planning of citizenship and community cohesion.		♦	♦		
Citizenship has high status amongst the staff.	♦	♦			
Citizenship has high status amongst students.	♦				

OCR Citizenship Studies Teacher's Resource Book for GCSE full and short course
© 2009 Hodder Education

Statement			
Students understand human rights and can apply their understanding in different contexts.			◆
Students understand others and value diversity.		◆	◆
Students promote equal opportunities in the school/college and wider community.		◆	◆
Active citizenship by students in the school/college is well established.		◆	◆
Active citizenship by students in the community is well established.		◆	◆
The school/college has strong student-to-student links with schools, colleges and communities in other countries.	◆	◆	
Families are engaged in links with other groups or communities.	◆	◆	
Students have opportunities to develop citizenship skills through regular discussion and debate.		◆	◆
Students and staff have opportunities to engage in decision-making within the school/college.	◆	◆	

The school or college as a community

Action to develop the school or college as a cohesive, supportive community for all students is a prerequisite for effective community cohesion. The key to success is to engage all students in a systematic and progressive way.

The most effective strategies for engaging students recognise that many of them will have already held important positions of responsibility in their primary schools.

The case study below shows an example of a planned strategy for engaging students in their school community, based on an 11–16 school with 180 students in each year group. This should be in addition to ensuring that students rotate responsibilities in their tutor groups for such things as organising an end-of-term party, celebrating birthdays, maintaining the notice board and sending cards to students who are ill.

With all of the responsibilities below, it is important that students receive recognition in the form of special badges, certificates of achievement or letters home.

■ Case study: planned strategy for engaging students

Year 7 Citizenship focus: our tutor group and year group

With students joining the school from several primary schools, an important focus for Year 7 is building a tutor group and year group ethos. Use 'circle time' to include all students in discussions of bullying and behaviour. Stress the responsibility of each member of the group to support others.

Students should elect tutor group representatives for a Year Committee and other whole-school groups such as the Student Council or Eco Group.

The Year Committee could focus on charity fundraising and improving the school environment and could decide to adopt a charity or community project for action and support during the year.

The Year Group could organise a party for their grandparents during the year with every student playing an active part. In the summer term, students will enjoy the opportunity to visit their former primary school with school staff to assist in the induction of new pupils.

Year 8 Citizenship focus: our school community

Year 8 students can build on their charity fundraising and environmental improvements through their tutor groups and Year Committee.

The particular focus for Year 8 could be to become more involved in the life of the whole school and give young people an insight into how it works as a community.

To this end, every student could spend at least one day working with the school's Reception Office Team to meet and greet visitors, deal with the post and even update the school message boards and answer the phone. To make this a rewarding experience for all, students should receive simple training in the morning and a brief evaluation at the end of the day. A Teaching Assistant can support students with special needs if necessary. To be successful, the scheme should be explained to parents in advance.

Year 9 Citizenship focus: our wider community

In Year 9, every student could spend a morning assisting in a local nursery school or the reception class of a local primary school. Briefing should be provided on the needs of young children and the importance of the early education.

Year 9 students could also have planned visits to public services and businesses in the community. These could include the police station, the fire station and the local newspaper. Charity fundraising continues but may tend to focus on the needs of people outside the UK.

Towards the end of Year 9, students could be introduced to their future role as Year 10 Senior Partners (see below) and their responsibilities as senior members of the school (see below). This could be part of a special Key Stage 3 awards and graduation morning.

Year 10 Citizenship focus: supporting others

A Senior Partner or Junior Leader Scheme is a key feature of Year 10 for students in many schools and the aim should be for all students to join the scheme. Nevertheless the use of letters of application and interviews will raise the scheme's profile as well as focusing students on the responsibilities involved. Partners should be given training by students who took responsibility in the previous year and from pastoral staff attached to Year 7.

Senior Partners or Junior Leaders can support new Year 7 entrants to the school by helping them with problems, 'showing them the ropes' and assisting in Personal and Social Education lessons. The most successful schemes attach a group of trained Partners to each Year 7 tutor group where they can work with the tutor to plan activities. Senior Partners can also assist with helping to organise games in neighbouring primary schools at lunchtime.

Year 11 Citizenship focus: school leadership

All Year 11 students can apply for a variety of senior student or prefect positions in the school. These could include:
• school tours
• reception duties at lunchtime
• library
• ICT prefects
• transport prefects
• college shop
• student cloakroom
• supporters for adults with learning difficulties
• school year book
• school prom
• entertainments.

Appropriate training should be provided. Senior students from Year 11 could also organise the Student Council, attend meetings of the PTA and have places on the Board of Governors. Some could be involved in the interview process for new staff.

Decision-making in the school or college

Students learn important lessons about the process of decision-making, as well as a vital set of communication and social skills, when they are encouraged to evaluate their school or college and make recommendations for improvement. It is even more helpful to students' learning if they can be involved in implementing that change and in helping to inform policy within the school or college.

In many schools and colleges, School/College Councils are seen as a vital part of the mission to engage students. However, School/College Councils tend to involve relatively few students directly and so, by themselves, will have little impact on developing community cohesion within the school. School/College Councils that are ineffective – through lack of influence, uncertainty about parameters for decision-making and/or lack of interest by staff and Governors – can be counterproductive because student representatives will learn only cynicism about the political process. Thus, School/College Councils are something we all have a responsibility to get right.

Five key features of an effective School/College Council

- All students are involved in the process of decision-making
- The Council is student led
- The Council reflects a school ethos of engagement and openness
- Core issues are dealt with, such as student achievement, bullying and lesson quality
- The Council should be seen to make a difference.

School Councils – School Improvement, Professor Lynn Davies and Hiromi Yamashita, University of Birmingham, 2007

■ School/College Councils: ingredients for success

For a School/College Council to be a successful part of a democratic decision-making structure in a school, six key ingredients are required.

- Full and active support from the Headteacher and senior Leadership Team
- Integration of student participation into the decision-making structures of the school. This should cover all aspects of school life, including teaching and learning, not just the physical environment and organising events
- A structure that includes a full system of class councils and year/house councils – or some other structure that actively involves all students
- Regular and formalised meetings, timetabled and systematic ways for providing feedback, and the generation of sub-councils or sub-committees to involve as many students as possible
- A School Council link teacher who is sufficiently senior to be able to persuade and monitor form tutors to facilitate class discussions, and have School Council as a key (not minor) part of their job description
- Positive relationships between staff and pupils that are as adult in tone as possible, with equitable interactions, and sensible rules and sanctions.

From the School Councils UK website, www.schoolcouncils.org

The table below shows some of the structures and processes that encourage democratic decision-making and responsible action throughout a school or college.

Class or Tutor Group	Year or House Group	School/College
Regular discussion and feedback in class	Year Council with regular feedback in assemblies	School/College Council with executive and sub-committees. Regular feedback in assemblies
Elected School/College Council representative		
Elected Year Council representatives	Year Committee and sub-committees	Prefects
Class or tutor group captain	Year prefects	Sports captains
Posts of responsibility	Posts of responsibility	Posts of responsibility

OCR Citizenship Studies Teacher's Resource Book for GCSE full and short course
© 2009 Hodder Education

■ Benefits of an effective School/College Council

- Improvements in communication, advocacy, negotiation, decision-making and teamwork skills
- Development of knowledge and understanding in Citizenship
- More understanding and trust between all members of the school or college community
- Increased feelings of responsibility for students as they develop greater pride in themselves and their school or college
- Improved physical environment
- More effective and respected school or college policies.

■ School/College Council evaluation tool

Use the evaluation tool below as a basis for testing the effectiveness of your School/College or Student Council.

Statement A	Statement A applies strongly to our school/college	Statement A applies to our school/college	Undecided or don't know	Statement B applies to our school/college	Statement B applies strongly to our school/college	Statement B
Class representatives are elected democratically						Only some classes are represented and I'm not sure how they are chosen
It's easy to find out about the School/College Council through posters, a notice board or a web page						It's difficult to find out anything about the School/College Council
Representatives have a specific time when they report back to their class and staff encourage this						There is little or no reporting back
Students have the chance to discuss School/College Council issues and class or year group issues						There is little discussion of school/college, year group or class issues and no time set aside for this to happen
Council meetings are held regularly with the date, time and venue known around the school/college						Meetings don't happen very often and are sometimes cancelled. There are no notices of meetings visible in the school/college
Members of the Council receive training so they know what to do						There is no training. Students are expected to pick up skills from the meetings they attend

Statement A	Statement A applies strongly to our school/college	Statement A applies to our school/college	Undecided or don't know	Statement B applies to our school/college	Statement B applies strongly to our school/college	Statement B
The School/College Council has its own bank account and budget. Students can decide how to spend the money						There is no budget and few discussions about improvements students might make to the school/college
Staff listen to and take action on what the School/College Council recommends						Little happens as a result of the meetings
The School/College Council is important in giving students a voice						The School/College Council is a chance for staff to explain why things can't be done
The Council makes a real difference to the school/college						I can't think of anything the School/College Council has done

Promoting Student Voice

Article 12 of the *United Nations Convention on the Rights of the Child* says that children and young people have the '*right to express views freely in all matters affecting them*'. This includes views on their education and schooling.

OFSTED, during their inspections, will ask students about their views of the school. Students will also be asked how they are consulted and what action is taken as a result of the views they have expressed.

> When we come to inspect your school, we will ask the Headteacher to tell us how they collect your views and what they do with this information. We are most interested in how this makes things better, and so we ask them to tell us so that we can judge how well they are looking out for you.
>
> From the OFSTED children and young people's home page,
> www.ofsted.gov.uk/Ofsted-home/About-us/Children-and-young-people

Student Voice projects can emerge from concerns expressed in tutor groups, year or house committees, or the School/College Council. These concerns might include such issues as school or college safety, bullying, lunchtime queuing or transport to school/college.

However, in more developed projects, students are also encouraged to research and report back on more fundamental issues affecting teaching and learning such as:
• Why do girls achieve better than boys in History? What can be done to increase boys' achievements?
• Why don't girls choose Technology options at GCSE? What can be done to make Technology more attractive to girls?

- What feedback do students prefer from their teachers? Does this differ between students in Year 7 and Year 11?
- Is our system of rewards working? How can we make it more effective?

In order to be successful, such projects need a staff co-ordinator/coach who can guide students through the process of research and reporting back. It is also important that all staff are aware that the research is taking place, understand how the conclusions will be fed back and know that particular staff members will not be identified in the final report. Critically, students should know from the outset who will receive their report. In the most successful schemes, students will present their findings to senior staff and, perhaps, school or college governors.

Student Voice projects can easily be fitted into the requirements of the Citizenship Controlled Assessment – *Citizenship Campaign* – for Unit A341. For this to work, students should follow the process outlined in section 4 of this book and summarised below:
- **Research** issues, evidence and viewpoints
- **Plan** the campaign (appropriate presentations to students and to decision-makers in the school)
- **Engage** in the planned action (presentations and discussion)
- **Evaluate** the action.

Developing communication, community cohesion and campaigning: the use of assemblies

Assemblies are an important but often under-used resource for developing communication, encouraging community cohesion and campaigning.

Think about how you can influence and contribute to the assembly programme in order that it can be another valuable and stimulating Citizenship teaching and learning occasion.

Using assemblies to promote communcation and community cohesion

Developing communication	Encouraging community cohesion	Campaigning
Reporting back from Student Voice project teams and responses from senior staff	Celebration of British values, festivals and events	Reporting back from Student Voice project teams and responses from senior staff
Reporting back from Student Council and year committees	Celebration of diversity, religious/cultural festivals and community events	Presentations related to the *Campaign! Make an Impact* project* to illustrate campaigns from the past
Quick *hands up* surveys or the introduction of electronic questionnaires on particular issues. Feedback on survey results	Celebration of the skills and interests of students and staff, e.g. dance, music, hobbies	Presentations from student *Citizenship Campaign* groups – these could be to assemblies for younger age groups
Video of activities in link schools. Messages from students in link schools/colleges	Video of school/college projects to support others in the school/college and community – presentations by students	Election statements by students standing for school/college leadership or Student Council positions

*For more information on the Make an Impact project, due to be launched in spring 2009, refer to the British Library website www.bl.uk/learning

In addition there are particular days and weeks worth putting into the assembly programme because of their links to the content of the Citizenship specification. These include:

• Holocaust Memorial Day	27 January
• Commonwealth Day	10 March
• Red Nose Day	a Friday in March every two years

- St George's Day   23 April
- Europe Day   9 May
- United Nations Peace Day   24 October
- Remembrance Day   11 November
- BBC Children in Need   a Friday in November every year
- Anti-Bullying Week   Late November
- World Aids Day   1 December
- Human Rights Day   10 December.

School-to-school links: promoting community cohesion across the UK

There are considerable benefits to be gained from linking with a school or college located in a different community. There are some interesting case studies on the Teachernet website: http://www.teachernet.gov.uk/wholeschool/Communitycohesion/Community_cohesion_case_studies

Most of these case studies currently involve primary schools where students exchange messages and small gifts as well as sharing in a range of festivals and celebrations. Live video links and the use of the internet add relevance and immediacy to the exchanges. In Bradford, the local authority has promoted school-to-school links across the city to help break down some of the barriers that led to riots in the past.

Successful school-to-school links rely on:
- good staff links established initially with joint planning of a small number of manageable projects
- a staff co-ordinator with time to do the job and the support of their Headteacher and Leadership Team
- ensuring that parents understand the benefits of the proposed link
- taking things gently at first with exchanges of information between groups of students before the development of any student-to-student contacts
- careful monitoring of any student-to-student contacts according to well-understood protocols
- joint activities planned and prepared for well in advance.

International links

The DCSF International School Award provides a very useful template for anyone wishing to establish an international link that will engage students and make a real difference to their global understanding. Full details of the Award can be found on the British Council website: http://www.britishcouncil.org/learning-international-school-award.htm

The International School Award offers:
- a framework within which to form and develop international partnerships and achieve curriculum goals
- ideas for developing collaborative curriculum-based international work with partner schools
- recognition for teachers and their schools that instill a global dimension into the learning experience of all young people
- opportunities to raise the school's profile through local and national media coverage.

To achieve the Award, international links must have a substantial impact on students. The criteria for achieving the Award include:
- the majority of students affected by and involved in international work
- collaborative curriculum-based work, across a range of subjects, with several partner schools
- year-round international activity

- involvement of partner schools in the UK with the international links
- involvement of the wider community in the international links.

Links with outside agencies

Working with individuals and organisations from outside school may add to the quality of the teaching and learning of OCR GCSE Citizenship Studies. The table below lists a number of sources of help of this kind, and is arranged according the chapters in the Student's Book. The names of organisations or types of groups are highlighted in **bold**, and their main web addresses are given at the end of this section.

All schools have guidelines covering the legal and educational procedures associated with visiting speakers and visits out of school. Further information and guidance on both these aspects are available from the *Learning outside the classroom* website, http://www.lotc.org.uk.

Chapter and unit	Individual or organisation
Rules and laws	
It's the rule	Local **solicitors**, **police** officers and **magistrates** are able to clarify and enhance a number of the topics in this unit, particularly: the nature and extent of law; the idea of criminal responsibility; the treatment of young offenders; and the ways in which legal rights and responsibilities change with age.
The law machine	Further work on making and changing the law may be undertaken through a visit to the **Parliament** in Westminster (through **Parliament's Education Service**) or to the **National Assembly for Wales** in Cardiff. For a small number of students, a visit to the **European Parliament** in Brussels may also be a possibility. It may also be feasible to arrange a visit to school for your local **Member of Parliament** or **Assembly Member**. Further exploration about ideas of precedent and judge-made law may be undertaken during visits to the **Crown Court**, when it is sometimes possible to arrange for the judge to talk directly to students. You can find details of your local court from **Her Majesty's Court Service** (HMCS).
Human rights	
What are human rights?	The **Holocaust Centre** offers a range of facilities to explore the history of the holocaust, including the possibility of hearing the first-hand experiences of a holocaust survivor. The **Imperial War Museums** in London and Manchester both have facilities and exhibitions relating to work on the Holocaust, as does the **Jewish Museum** in London
Human rights law	**Solicitors**, **magistrates**, **judges** and **police** officers can all provide further information on the workings of the *Human Rights Act* within their own particular field. Questions of privacy and free speech may also be raised with journalists on visits to local, regional or national **media** (newspaper, radio or TV) offices.
International human rights	As well as producing information and teaching materials, **Amnesty International** runs its own programme of speakers for schools; links may also be formed through Amnesty's local group network.

Section 3: A whole school/college approach to Citizenship

Chapter and unit	Individual or organisation
Family and school	
Family	**Solicitors** specialising in family law are able to provide students with a more detailed understanding of how the law works in this area, particularly in the way in which courts are required to place the interests of the child above all other considerations.
	The Schools Department of the **NSPCC** (the National Society for the Prevention of Cruelty to Children) have fundraisers all over the country able to talk to students about the work of the NSPCC and to offer help organising sponsored events.
School	Links for further work on topics such as admissions, exclusions and faith schools are almost certainly available within your own school, college, or local authority. Governors, head teachers, principals and senior managers will have first-hand experience of dealing with these kinds of issues, and will be able to answer students' questions or explain some of the procedures involved in more detail. Local education officers may also be of assistance here.
	Local museums quite often have exhibitions of local schools in the nineteenth and early twentieth centuries, and the **British Schools Museum** at Hitchin in Hertfordshire tells the story of elementary education in Britain from 1810 until 1969.
	Schools Council UK can provide training in schools for staff and students.
Consumer law	
Consumer rights Consumer complaints	Further guidance on consumer law is available from a number of sources: local **trading standards departments**, the **Citizens Advice Bureau (CAB)**, and local **solicitors**.
	Some local **trading standards departments** and **CABs** are able to provide advisors to come into schools and to explain their role in more detail and to answer students' questions.
Employment	
Looking for work Fairness at work Working for a living Trade unions Losing your job	The **Trades Union Congress (TUC)** runs a schools programme with outside speakers able to talk about rights and work and the work of trade unions.
	Local contacts through the school or college governing body or work experience may provide links with people from local businesses who can speak to students and answer questions about some of the practicalities of running a business and employing people. The **Young Enterprise's** Company Programme offers students aged 15–19 the opportunity to set up and run their own company through the course of an academic year.
	There appears to be no single organisation (other than the **TUC**, see above) able to provide speakers in schools for general guidance on issues of equality at work. However, you may be able to develop links with local branches of pressure groups promoting the interests of people who may suffer discrimination at work on grounds of race, sex, age, sexuality, etc.

OCR Citizenship Studies Teacher's Resource Book for GCSE full and short course
© 2009 Hodder Education

Chapter and unit	Individual or organisation
	If time is available, you may wish to take a group of students to visit an employment tribunal. Obviously preparation and liaison are required, but watching a case can provide a useful insight into the workings of employment law.
	The **CAB** and local **solicitors** specialising in employment work may also be able to provide useful guidance.
Economy	
Managing the economy World trade Poverty	**MPs**, local business owners and local managers of large or multi-national companies may be able to give students a perspective on some of the issues that they face in the current economic climate.
	The charity **Oxfam** organises regional conferences and can arrange for speakers to come into school to talk about their campaigns concerning various aspects of world trade. Similarly, the **Fairtrade Foundation** runs conferences and offers schools guidance on promoting Fairtrade and becoming a Fairtrade School.
	People and Planet is a student-based group which, amongst many other things, will come to a school or college and run workshops for years 12 or 13 on Fairtrade or climate change.
Community	
Coming to Britain	Local community organisations may be able to provide speakers prepared to explain and discuss their reasons for coming to Britain and the experience of living here. Sometimes these people may be found within the school.
	Your local **STAR network** (Student Action for Refugees) may be able to provide someone to talk to students about the circumstances that refugees may have faced before coming to this country, and subsequently.
Identity	Community engagement is an important issue for all **local councils** in Britain today, and councils will an opportunity for an officer to come into school to discuss issues of community life within your area. Approaches may be made through local links, the council press office, or via 'democratic services' at your local district, city, borough or county council.
	Access to this is also available via local **police** contacts, through local PACT schemes (Partners and Communities Together).
Unequal Britain Older people	Although further information on issues covered in these sections is widely covered on the net, it seems to be difficult to find organisations with the capacity to send representatives into schools to talk in more detail about issues of inequality.
	A tangential approach to this is to ask questions about gender, race, disability, etc. to those who come into school, or whom you visit, in the context of other topics. For example, questions on these matters to police officers, employers, solicitors, etc. may shed some light on the extent of inequalities within certain professions, and on the measures that organisations are taking to address them.

Chapter and unit	Individual or organisation
Housing	**Solicitors**, **local council** officers and advice workers (from the council and the **CAB**) may be able to come into school to provide practical advice on some of the issues covered in the student materials. **Shelter Wales** has many links with schools and colleges in Wales, and also works with youth clubs and youth services.
Making a difference	
Voting and elections Party politics	**Local councillors**, **Assembly Members**, **Members of Parliament** and **Members of the European Parliament** can all provide useful guidance to students on voting and elections. Although almost all will represent an established political party, there is an informal agreement amongst the parties of non-partisanship in schools. Some schools, particularly at election time, may wish to invite representatives from all the parties standing locally to attend hustings. This is obviously not without complications, but guidance from the **Hansard Society**, an educational charity with a great deal of experience in this area, suggests that it is important for teachers to try to represent the full range of views being debated at the election. An alternative approach, which may be useful in mock elections, and again advocated by the Hansard Society, is to invite members of political parties into school to help students accurately represent the policies of the party when they themselves stand for election and present their views to other students. **Parliament's Education Service** offers a year-round programme of visits to Parliament for students involving interactive workshops, a tour of the Palace of Westminster and, for older students, a session with an MP or peer. The Service also offers workshops for teachers designed to increase teachers' confidence and familiarity with this area. It may also be possible to arrange a visit to Parliament through direct contact with your local MP.
Campaigning	A suitable representative from almost any pressure group could probably give students some idea of strengths and weaknesses of different forms of campaigning and ways of capturing public attention about a particular issue. The **Citizenship Foundation's** Giving Nation programme has considerable experience in supporting charity action in schools and colleges.
Government	
National government	As described above, students may gain greater understanding of this area through links with local **MPs** and **Parliament's Education Service**.
Devolution	The **National Assembly for Wales** offers educational visits to the Senedd and workshop activities as well as a service of peripatetic visits to schools and colleges throughout Wales.
Local government	Each year – normally in October – the Local Government Association organises a **Local Democracy Week** designed to connect young people with local politics and politicians.

OCR Citizenship Studies Teacher's Resource Book for GCSE full and short course
© 2009 Hodder Education

Chapter and unit	Individual or organisation
	Fruitful contacts may also be made, at any time of the year, with **local councillors**, and many **local councils** have well-established programmes that aim to develop young people's political engagement.
European government	Links with local **Members of the European Parliament** may be helpful here.
Media	
The power of the media	A useful way of developing students' understanding of the media is through visits to the local newspaper or television or radio station. It may also be possible to invite a local reporter (such as a crime correspondent) into school, who may be able to provide interesting insights into the reporting and presentation of news.
Environment	
Climate change Choices for the future	In some areas, **Friends of the Earth** local group members come into schools and colleges to talk about issues of climate change. You can find your local group via the **Friends of the Earth** website. **People and Planet** is a student-based group which, amongst many other things, will come to a school or college and run workshops for years 12 or 13 on climate change or Fairtrade. **Groundwork** might also run projects in the area that your students can get involved with.
Justice	
Civil law	Links with local **solicitors** can provide a very useful extension to students' understanding of this area. It is also possible to arrange visits to the local **county court** or to an **employment tribunal**. Prior liaison with the court or tribunal is essential.
Criminal law	Many schools have well-established links with local **police**, **magistrates** and **courts**, enabling students to visit a court or police station, speakers to come into school, or students to take part in mock trials. The **Galleries of Justice** in Nottingham also offer school visits and a wide range of law-related citizenship activities. The **Citizenship Foundation** runs two well-established mock trial programmes. The Bar National Mock Trial Competition is open to students in years 10–13. **Prison ME No-way** is an educational charity established by prison officers with the aim of turning young people away from crime. Amongst the programmes they offer is one giving students an insight into the life and routine of prison inmates.

Contact details

Organisation	Contact details
Assembly Member	AMs (and local councillors, MPs and MEPs) may be reached via www.writetothem.com
British Schools Museum	www.hitchinbritishschools.org.uk
Citizens Advice Bureau	To find your local bureau, see telephone book or www.citizensadvice.org.uk
Citizenship Foundation	www.citizenshipfoundation.org.uk
Crown Court	To find your local Crown Court, see www.hmcourts-service.gov.uk/infoabout/crown/index.htm
Employment tribunal	To find your nearest employment tribunal, see www.employmenttribunals.gov.uk
European Parliament	For details of the UK Office of the European Parliament, see www.europarl.org.uk
Fairtrade Foundation	www.fairtrade.org.uk
Galleries of Justice	www.galleriesofjustice.org.uk
Hansard Society	www.hansardsociety.org.uk
Her Majesty's Court Service (HMCS)	www.hmcourts-service.gov.uk/cms/index.htm
Holocaust Centre	www.hcentrenew.aegisdns.co.uk/index.php
Imperial War Museums	Imperial War Museum, London: www.iwm.org.uk Imperial War Museum North: http://north.iwm.org.uk
Jewish Museum	www.jewishmuseum.org.uk
Local council	Details of your local council may be found on the Directgov site www.direct.gov.uk
Local councillors	Local councillors (and AMs, MPs, and MEPs) may be reached via www.writetothem.com
Magistrates	Connections with magistrates may be made through the school's governing body or the Magistrates' Association's 'Magistrates in the Community Project': www.magistrates-association-temp.org.uk
Members of the European Parliament	MEPs (and local councillors, AMs and MPs) may be reached via www.writetothem.com
Member of Parliament	You may find the name of your local MP at http://findyourmp.parliament.uk and may email directly via www.writetothem.com
National Assembly for Wales	www.assemblywales.org
NSPCC	www.nspcc.org.uk
Oxfam	www.oxfam.org.uk
Parliament	www.parliament.uk
Parliament's Education Service	www.parliament.uk/education/index.htm
People and planet	http://peopleandplanet.org/

OCR Citizenship Studies Teacher's Resource Book for GCSE full and short course
© 2009 Hodder Education

Organisation	Contact details
Police	Many schools will have well-established links with the local **police**, and all constabularies have their own police–schools liaison schemes
Prison ME No-way	www.pmnw.co.uk
Schools Council UK	www.schoolcouncils.org
Shelter Wales	www.sheltercymru.org.uk
Solicitor	Contacts with local solicitors may be established through local connections, or perhaps the school governing body, through local Law Societies or, in some areas, through the Citizenship Foundation's Twinning Programme
Trades Union Congress (TUC)	www.tuc.org.uk – schools programme
Trading standards departments	You can find the address of your local trading standards office in the phone book, or via www.tradingstandards.gov.uk
Young Enterprise	www.young-enterprise.org.uk

Section 4: Success in the Short Course

This section provides advice on how to make a success of Units A341 *Rights and Responsibilities – Getting Started as an Active Citizen* and A342 *Identity, Democracy and Justice – Understanding our Role as Citizens.*

Unit A341 is assessed through a Controlled Assessment – *The Citizenship Campaign* – worth 60 per cent of the final mark for the Short Course or 30 per cent of the final mark for the Full Course. Unit A342 is assessed by a one-hour external examination worth 40 per cent of the final mark for the Short Course or 20 per cent of the final mark for the Full Course. The examination is available as a computer-based test or a paper-based exam.

Success in the Controlled Assessment (Unit A341)

■ The Citizenship Campaign

This unit is assessed by Controlled Assessment. Candidates have up to 37 hours to plan, manage and evaluate their Citizenship Campaign. The issue for the campaign can either be the OCR supplied issue (currently campaigning for a reduction in the voting age) or an issue of the candidate's own choice coming from one of the OCR approved themes:
• The legal rights or responsibilities of a young person
• Awareness of fundamental human rights
• Human rights in conflict
• Promoting greater student engagement in school or college
• Our rights and responsibilities in the economy
• Our rights and responsibilities as consumers
• Our rights and responsibilities in employment
• Our rights and responsibilities as tenants
• Our responsibilities for the earth's resources
• Our responsibilities as global citizens
• Our responsibilities to support the people of other nations.

Once a theme has been selected and an issue for the campaign decided, candidates must complete the candidate proposal form. Teachers need to sign this to confirm your approval of the campaign.

When researching, planning and managing the campaign, candidates need to work in groups. However, when writing their evaluations of the issues and evidence and of the campaign, they must work individually.

Evaluating the issues and evidence

Candidates have up to 10 hours to undertake research into the issue on which they have chosen to focus their campaign. After completing their research, they have up to three hours, under informal supervision, in which to write their evaluation. This can be three one-hour lessons rather than a block of three hours. Candidates cannot work on their evaluation outside this time.

On pages 44–47 are two examples of an evaluation of an issue with a commentary. The issue is a campaign to increase the amount of Fairtrade produce sold at school or college and bought by the local community. Different groups can focus on different aspects of the same issue.

Planning the campaign

When the evaluation of the issues is complete, candidates need to plan their campaigns. A planning sheet should be filled in and provided as evidence at the end of the campaign. Candidates have up to seven hours to plan their campaign.

OCR Citizenship Studies Teacher's Resource Book for GCSE full and short course
© 2009 Hodder Education

Managing the campaign

Candidates have up to 16 hours to manage their campaign. They need to provide evidence of what they actually did. This could take the form of:
- examples of posters, leaflets or other material, including websites linked to the campaign
- videos of activities, meetings, assemblies, lobbying or other responsible group action
- witness statements from those who have observed or been influenced by the campaign
- records of meetings or other communication with those in positions of power in the school, college or wider community about the campaign.

In this section, candidates will be assessed on their participation in the campaign rather than on their ability to provide a written description of everything they did.

Evaluating the campaign

Finally, students have to evaluate their Citizenship Campaign. (See the examples on pages 48–50.) They have a maximum of one hour under informal supervision to complete this work. Informal supervision (medium level of control) is defined by OCR as follows: questions/tasks are outlined, the use of resources is not tightly prescribed and assessable outcomes may be informed by group work. Supervision is confined to (i) ensuring that the contributions of individual candidates are recorded accurately, and (ii) ensuring that plagiarism does not take place. The supervision may provide limited guidance to candidates.

Evaluating the issues and evidence: example of a grade C response

We are going to do our campaign about fair trade. There is nowhere in our school where you can buy fair trade things. There is a Co-op in town that sells lots of fair trade food. The other small shops don't sell any fair trade food. We need to find out what people know about fair trade at the moment and then we can plan our campaign so that more people know about it and will buy the food.

We did a questionnaire to find out what people know about fair trade. We asked year 11 and year 7. Most had heard of fair trade but didn't really know why it was good to buy fair trade products. A lot of year 11s said it was too expensive and they preferred to buy the regular products. We thought it was good that most of the pupils knew about fair trade, as this would make our campaign easier.

I am in year 11 and don't have much money to spend on things so I can understand that other pupils might not want to buy fair trade if they think it is more expensive. Part of our campaign will need to look at prices and taste to show that they are very good products and worth the extra cost.

We asked the canteen staff why they don't sell fair trade food and they said no one had asked for it before. This would be a good place to campaign because we could try to get the canteen to sell the food so that pupils can easily buy it.

When you buy fair trade products more of the money goes to the farmer in Africa. That means that they can buy things for their own family and not be as poor or hungry. If we buy things that aren't fair trade then the farmers in Africa might get very little money and not be able to feed their own family.

I did some research on the Oxfam website. There was a coffee farmer called Lawrence Seguya on it. He was saying that he didn't pick his crop of coffee beans because the price he would get was so low that it wasn't worth it. Now he has no money to send his kids to school, or even to buy soap, or fuel to cook with. The famous-brand coffee companies are making a lot of money. Lawrence doesn't think this is right and nor do I.

Oxfam are campaigning to help farmers like Lawrence. I looked on the Traidcraft website and they said that it was very important to campaign to get the message across. Buying fair trade products is important but we have to show people in power that we think they should be helping farmers in Africa and other countries.

Governments in rich countries are giving their own farmers lots of money to help them and this means that farmers like Lawrence are suffering even more. On the Fairtrade Foundation website you can send a postcard to Gordon Brown. It says that we want the UK Government to fight for trade rules that directly address the needs of the poorest people in the world. This means stop spending lots of money looking after farmers in this country and doing more fair trade with countries in Africa.

We had to decide what we were going to try to do. We could have assemblies to tell all the pupils in the school about fair trade and try and encourage them to buy it. If we got pupils wanting to buy they would have to go to the Co-op in town and some people might not bother or they would have to tell their families to buy things when they went shopping. To get our families involved we could do a leaflet explaining about fair trade.

Our group decided that we needed to get the school canteen to start selling fair trade food. We could arrange to meet the manager of the Co-op to find out why she thinks it is important and then take our campaign to the canteen manager to get him to bring in fair trade food. Doing all of these things is a lot of work but it is important. If pupils at school want to buy fair trade but it is not available then our campaign might be pointless.

I really want to campaign for fair trade because I think that I can make a difference to farmers in Africa. If other pupils can be persuaded to buy fair trade food we can make a big change. The Fairtrade Foundation has information about becoming a Fairtrade school, this could be something we will look at if our campaign is successful.

Commentary

The candidate analyses the issue of fair trade and shows a good understanding. There is some evidence of the current position at their school and in the local area. There is reference to different groups. They have undertaken a lot of research into groups that are working for fair trade and they plan to use some of these resources to help their campaign.

Quotes from the farmer and Traidcraft add to the evidence for the campaign. They have used evidence to support their own viewpoint. The reasons for the campaign have been set out clearly. The candidate has lots of ideas about how to organise the campaign and understands the need to approach the issue from a range of angles.

Evaluating the issues and evidence: example of a grade A response

When we set up our group to campaign we asked people what issues they were interested in. Most people in our group felt strongly about fair trade so we decided to campaign on this issue. We started our research at the Fairtrade Foundation website where they have a questionnaire for schools to fill out.

The aim is to give a before and after picture of fair trade in our school. We thought it would make our campaign look more important if we used some resources with the fair trade logo on them.

There is currently nowhere in our school where we can buy fair trade products. In the staffroom the teachers drink fair trade tea and coffee. In our local town the Co-op sells a lot of fair trade food and they are well known for this. It might help our campaign if we went to speak to the manager to find out more.

When we asked pupils in our school about fair trade, 90 per cent had heard about it but only 20 per cent had tried any fair trade products. We felt that this could be because it is not available to buy in our school and children don't always go shopping in the Co-op. We asked why they didn't buy it and some pupils said they didn't think it would taste nice and they thought it was expensive.

If we could get the canteen to sell fair trade products we could do a taste test to prove it tastes good so as to encourage pupils to pay a bit extra to help less developed countries' farmers.

When we questioned the canteen manager about fair trade he knew about it but didn't know where he could buy it from. We would do some research for him before we went to see him with our campaign.

Fair trade is all about giving a fair deal to farmers in poorer countries. A greater proportion of the price you pay for a banana actually goes to the farmer.

On the Fairtrade Foundation website there are many case studies of farmers who are part of fair trade schemes. According to Herbert Babinyaga, a tea grower from Uganda, 'The Fairtrade premium helps pay for field extension officers who have given us advice on how to maintain the tea. This has improved the quality and we have also improved productivity. Fairtrade is good for the farmers as we have used the Fairtrade premium to build leaf collection sheds and improve roads and secondary schools.' This shows that fair trade is not just about giving one farmer a bit of extra money but allowing that money to go to the whole community so that everyone benefits.

The aims of our campaign will be to raise awareness of the issues as well as to get people buying more fair trade products. Traidcraft, on their website, say that it is very important to campaign so that people in power hear our message. Governments are subsidising their own farmers rather than supporting farmers in less economically developed countries.

I can understand that we want to look after our own industry but there are many farmers that we rely on in other countries who probably need our support more. We are demanding products all year round that can't be grown in this country, like bananas and pineapples, so if we want these products we have a responsibility to help farmers in those countries who are producing the products for us.

There are many groups already campaigning for fair trade. This helps our campaign as we will not be a lone voice. Also there are a range of resources and ideas for us to use. On the Fairtrade Foundation website we can send a postcard to Gordon Brown. It says that we want the UK Government to fight for trade rules that directly address the needs of the poorest people in the world. This agrees with my earlier comment about helping the banana growers.

We need to approach this campaign in a number of ways. There is no point in getting pupils interested in buying fair trade goods and there not being any for sale in school. We will contact the manager of the canteen to take our campaign to him. If we can show evidence that pupils will buy the food from our research he is more likely to be in favour of the idea. In order to take our campaign to pupils we will do assemblies and leaflets.

We want to do a taste test to show that the products taste as good if not better than some well known brands. We are planning to interview the manager of the Co-op to find out their view on fair trade. This might help us to persuade our school canteen manager as well.

I feel strongly about this issue because in this country most people are very lucky and get a lot of the things they want. We have free healthcare and education. Our roads and cars can be mended so that we can travel around in comfort. A lot of fair trade farmers join together as co-operatives so that the premium they earn through the fair trade system can go towards improving things for the community as a whole. That way everyone benefits.

If our campaign is successful we could take things further and try to become a Fairtrade school. This would be a good way to continue the work we have done and also to help more farmers to get a fair deal.

Commentary

The candidate has provided a thorough analysis of the issues surrounding fair trade. There is a detailed evaluation of the current position and the issue is widened as the candidate also mentions Government subsidies. They look at the ways in which different groups and individuals are affected; this is linked to evidence. Their own opinion is clearly expressed and backed up with evidence. Different options for campaigning are evaluated and appropriate recommendations are made. The candidate realises that the campaign needs to target the canteen as well as pupils in order to have any real impact.

Evaluating the campaign: example of a grade C response

I think that our campaign was successful. Before we started it, we asked other pupils about fair trade. At the end of our campaign we asked them again. Now everyone we asked has heard of fair trade and more of them are going to buy fair trade if it is on sale in the canteen. The plan worked well. Everybody in our group had a job to do throughout the campaign. We decided at the beginning who was good at what and gave people jobs based on what they were good at.

We did the assemblies to the other year groups and because we had planned everything out everybody was prepared and we were praised by teachers for a good assembly. The PowerPoint that we did had a good effect because we were able to show big pictures on the screen in the hall. The Fairtrade Foundation website was really useful for case studies and pictures of real people who are helped by us buying fair trade food. It was a good idea to talk to the manager of the Co-op because she gave us a lot of helpful information that we could tell the canteen manager. I think this helped to persuade the canteen manager to try to get fair trade food in the canteen.

It was difficult to find a time to meet the Co-op manager as she was very busy. Next time we should contact someone out of school at the beginning of our campaign so they had a lot of time to arrange to meet us. We couldn't meet the canteen manager till we'd been to the Co-op so this delayed things a bit.

What we want to do next is make sure that the canteen gets fair trade food in stock and then we said we'd help the canteen manager to advertise it. We need to do this quickly so that pupils don't forget about fair trade and as a school we can start helping farmers in Africa a lot more.

Commentary

The candidate has provided a limited reflection on the successes of the campaign. They have used some evidence from other pupils to back up their claims. They have reflected on the suitability of their plan in relation to the outcomes achieved. There is limited description of aspects of the campaign that went well and they know why they went well. Some difficulties have been described and they have considered how they could change things next time. There is a limited description of their next steps and how they could increase the impact of their campaign.

Evaluating the campaign: example of a grade A response

Our fair trade campaign has been really successful and has had a big impact on our school as a whole. Before we started our campaign 90 per cent of pupils had heard of fair trade but only 20 per cent had tried any products. When we asked pupils again at the end of our campaign 100 per cent had heard of fair trade and 50 per cent had tried at least one item of fair trade food. This is evidence of the success of our campaign. As part of our campaign we interviewed the manager of the Co-op to try to find out a bit more about fair trade and how we could sell it at school. She gave us a real insight into the difference the extra money from fair trade can make to farmers. I think this helped us to convince other pupils and them to tell their families. We have received a letter from the Co-op manager saying that they have seen an increase in sales of fair trade goods since our campaign at school. This shows that the message got home and makes me feel really proud of what we did.

We had planned our campaign very carefully, making sure that there were enough people involved at each stage so that if something went wrong we had another member of the group ready. We had planned when we wanted to do our assemblies but at the beginning we hadn't realised that the assembly rota is planned in advance so we couldn't just take the assemblies when we wanted to.

The school canteen now stocks fair trade fruit, fruit juices, cereal bars and dried fruit. I think that this is why 50 per cent of pupils have now tried the products. We knew before we started our campaign if we wanted people to take action and buy the products, they had to be for sale in the school canteen. I think that this was our biggest achievement. We were able to persuade the canteen manager with the help of information from the Fairtrade foundation website. We could find suppliers of fair trade goods in our area so that the canteen manager knew that it would not be difficult to make the switch. A lot of pupils thought fair trade wouldn't taste as nice. We organised a taste test to show them that this wasn't the case. Some pupils were amazed that they liked the fair trade food better and said they would get their families to buy them at the Co-op as well.

The main difficulty we had was trying to convince younger pupils to pay extra for fair trade goods. When we did the assemblies the feedback was positive in that they thought it was a good idea but didn't want to pay any extra. We persuaded them by saying how little the extra would be to them and what communities in less developed countries could do with that amount of money. They soon realised that they could make a big impact on a community. It was really useful to be able to use the Fairtrade foundation resources showing real people. This seemed to add weight to our arguments.

We completed the Fairtrade foundation questionnaire before starting our campaign. We now want to try to become a Fairtrade school and so we have arranged a meeting with the Head teacher to explain the process. I think if we could become a Fairtrade school it would mean that the issues would not be forgotten in our school.

Commentary

The candidate has provided a thorough evaluation of the successes of the campaign. They have linked this to evidence based on the perceptions of others. They have evaluated the suitability of their plan. The aspects of the campaign that went well have been evaluated. The candidate has a good understanding of why they were successful. They have looked at the difficulties and considered what they would change next time. The next steps have also been evaluated and they have considered how this might help to increase the impact of the campaign. This evaluation describes a well-thought-out campaign that was definitely successful.

OCR Citizenship Studies Teacher's Resource Book for GCSE full and short course
© 2009 Hodder Education

Success in the examination (Unit A342)

■ Introduction

This section analyses the format of the exam and offers advice on how to prepare students for success in Question 17 (worth 12 marks out of the 40 available for the paper). Also provided is a revision checklist and a glossary of key concepts for students' use to help them prepare for success in the exam.

The examination for Unit A342 can be taken in January and June each year.

Centres can opt for a computer-based test (CBT) rather than a paper-based exam. Both contain identical questions but the CBT has the following potential advantages for students and for schools:
- Many students will find the format less daunting and more motivating than the traditional paper-based exam.
- Students have fewer organisational problems and can navigate through the test easily.
- Handwriting is no barrier to achievement and it is easier to change or redraft answers than in a paper-based exam.
- There are controls on the amount of text students can input. This makes it more likely that the time spent on a question will match the number of marks on offer.
- The administrative burden on schools is reduced – no need to store or post exam papers.

■ The format and content of the exam

Whether teachers offer the CBT or the paper-based exam, the content of the exam is the same. This is shown in the table below. Students must answer all the questions.

Section	Question numbers	Question type	Focus	Example	Skills	Marks
A	1–5	Multiple choice (5 questions)	Whole of the Unit content	What is meant by the term European Union? (4 alternatives – students choose 1).	Understanding of key concepts and terminology	1 × 5
	6–10	Short answer (5 questions)	Whole of the Unit content	State **one** legal way in which a pressure group may try to influence the Government.	Understanding of key concepts and terminology	1 × 5
	11	Explanation	Whole of the Unit content	Explain why people's human rights are more likely to be protected in a democracy than in a dictatorship.	Understanding of key concepts and terminology	4
	12	Extracting information from a statistical diagram	Statistical diagram provided as a stimulus	Put a ring around the number of the statement (i, ii, iii or iv) that gives the best description of the differences in youth offending according to *Document 1*.	Analysis	1

Section	Question numbers	Question type	Focus	Example	Skills	Marks
	13	Interpretation of information from a statistical diagram	Statistical diagram provided as a stimulus	Put a ring around the number of the statement (i, ii, iii or iv) that gives the most suitable warning about our use of the statistics in *Document 1* to know about youth crime.	Interpretation	1
	14	Explanation	Statistical diagram and Unit content	Explain why crime threatens human rights.	Understanding of key concepts and terminology related to the statistical diagram	4
B	15–16	Short stimulus leading students to analyse a *case* and to offer advice (2 questions)	Unit content from Section 3.2.2 *Fairness and justice in decision-making and the law*	Your friend phones you. She has been arrested by the police for shoplifting and asks for your advice. (She received a police reprimand two months ago for a similar offence.) Evaluate the case and explain what is likely to happen.	Analysis and evaluation	4 × 2
C	17	Evaluation of a viewpoint	Whole of the Unit content	Evaluate the following viewpoint: 'There is little point in voting. There are better ways of making your voice heard in a democracy.'	Evaluation	12
Total marks						40

■ Success in Question 17

Question 17 asks students to evaluate a viewpoint related to the specification content. Worth 12 marks out of the 40 available for the paper, success in this question could make a very significant difference to the overall GCSE grade. Below are a sample question, a mark scheme and examples of candidates' responses for use with students.

To help your students achieve success, make sure that they:
- read the question carefully
- use the bullet points in the question to help them structure their answer
- challenge **or** support the viewpoint rather than 'sit on the fence'
- back up every **point** with **evidence** and **explain** how the point relates to the question (P.E.E.)
- recognise that not everyone will agree with their response and explain why
- include a reasoned conclusion in their answer.

Question 17

Evaluate the following viewpoint:

> 'There is little point in voting. There are better ways of making your voice heard in a democracy.'

In your answer, you should:

- explain how far you agree that 'there is little point in voting'
- evaluate the other ways of making your voice heard in a democracy
- use evidence or examples to support the points you make
- sum up your response to the viewpoint.

(12 marks)

Mark scheme for Question 17

Level 1 (1–3 marks)
You write a personal response to the statement in which you make some valid but limited points about the point of voting and/or show an understanding of the other ways to get your voice heard in a democracy (such as campaigning, joining a pressure group, forming a pressure group, lobbying, protesting, using the media).

Level 2 (4–6 marks)
Some evaluation of the statement based on some analysis of at least two pieces of valid evidence about the point of voting or the usefulness of alternative ways of promoting your views.

Level 3 (7–9 marks)
A sound personal response to the question supported by a sound analysis of at least two pieces of valid evidence that evaluates the importance of voting in relation to at least one other method of promoting your views. At this level, you should show an awareness that voting may appear more purposeful in some constituencies or types of election rather than others.

Level 4 (10–12 marks)
An informed personal response to the question based on a thorough analysis and evaluation of a range of evidence. At this level, your answer will contain specific examples of ways to promote your views. Each of these will be carefully evaluated so you can show which are likely to have the most impact.

How to decide a mark within a level
- Lowest mark in the level: meets most of the criteria for the level, but may have minor omissions from the level descriptor.
- Middle mark in the level: no doubt – meets the criteria for the level satisfactorily.
- Top mark in the level: a good response matching the criteria for the level well.

Evaluating student responses

Student A

People vote for a government. The government may do new things such as bring in new laws. These might affect people. A new law might increase the age for buying alcohol to 21. So there would be a point in voting if you didn't agree with this. You would vote for the person who didn't agree. This way you can help decide who forms the new government.

> A relevant **point** is made

> Some simple **evidence** is used to support the point

> A simple **evaluation** of the statement is given

> A simple **explanation** is given about why voting is important

You can also make your voice heard by supporting a pressure group such as Greenpeace. They want to protect the environment. You could also run your own campaign. In our school, we had a campaign against bullying. This helped people stand up against bullying and bullying went down. People took notice of what we were doing.

> A relevant **point** is made about another way of making your voice heard in a democracy

> Some **evidence** is used to support the point

> **Evidence** is given about how campaigns can get people's voices heard

The media can also help to make people's voices heard. You can get the local paper to tell your story if you have a problem. This might help to sort it out.

> A simple **point** is made with limited **evidence** about how the media can help get people's voices heard

I think there are many ways of making your voice heard in a democracy. Voting is just one. There is a point to voting, as you have no right to complain if you don't vote. If nobody voted, there would be no government.

> A simple **evaluation** of the point of voting

Student B

I disagree that there is little point in voting. There are major differences between the political parties on such issues as education, health, transport and whether or not our armed forces should be in Iraq. Voting is important because these matters affect the lives of everyone in the country. In some constituencies, such as Crawley in Sussex, there are sometimes only a few votes between the candidates. Here every vote really does count. Where there is proportional representation, such as in the European elections, every vote matters because MEPs are elected according to the proportion of votes given to each party.

A strong **point** is made in direct response to the question

Relevant **evidence** is used to support the point

A strong **explanation** is given to support the point. This is directly relevant to the question

The **point** is reinforced with further **evidence**

However, there can be as much as five years between elections for the UK Parliament. People who wish to get their voice heard between elections may wish to do so through membership of a pressure group. Pressure groups such as *Votes for 16* run campaigns and lobby politicians to get their message across. In 2008 they persuaded the Labour Party to reduce the voting age if they won the next election, showing just how effective pressure can be. Not all campaigns are successful straight away. The Countryside Alliance could not persuade the government to change its mind about the hunting ban.

An **explanation** is given about why people may need to get their voice heard in other ways

Specific and accurate **evidence** is used

An **evaluation** of the effectiveness of pressure groups is offered. This is supported by **evidence**

The news media help people to get their voice heard and sometimes even run campaigns of their own. In 2008, the Daily Telegraph ran a campaign to cut inheritance tax. This helped to persuade the government to do just that.

A further **point** is made about how the media can help get people's voices heard. This is supported with specific and accurate **evidence**

In a democracy, governments have to listen to pressure groups and the media. If governments do not listen, they won't win the next election. However, in the end, it's votes that matter. Elections decide the really big issues and the direction the country takes. This makes voting very important indeed. Of course, the way you vote can be affected by pressure group campaigns and also by the media.

An informed summary is written in which there is further **evaluation** of the statement in the question

Commentaries on the students' responses

■ Student A

This is a level 2 response. The candidate evaluates the statement clearly and simply. They include at least two pieces of valid evidence to support the points made. Other relevant methods of getting your voice heard are described to show reasonable understanding.

There is a simple final summary but this does not refer back to the question or sum up the candidate's viewpoint.

As this answer matches the level criteria well it would be given 6 marks.

A probable C grade.

■ Student B

This is a very good response given the age and experience of the candidate. It should be assessed as being level 4.

By expressing their viewpoint in the first sentence, the candidate finds it easy to write a convincing answer to the question and to stick to the point.

The candidate evaluates the statement thoroughly and uses a range of relevant evidence with confidence. Specific and relevant examples are given to support all the points made. The reasons why people use other methods of getting their voice heard are explained.

The final summary is carefully considered and well informed.

There is no reason why this answer should not be given full marks: 12/12.

A probable A★ grade.

OCR Citizenship Studies Teacher's Resource Book for GCSE full and short course
© 2009 Hodder Education

Revision checklist for Unit A342

Section and key statements Section 3.2.1 Citizenship, identity and community in the United Kingdom I can ...	No problem	Need more revision	Need to ask for help
Describe some of the cultural traditions that contribute to being British			
Describe the main values that contribute to being British			
Describe the nations of the United Kingdom (UK)			
Describe the regions in England or Wales			
Describe the main ethnic groups in the UK			
Describe the main religious groups in the UK			
Explain why people migrate from one place to another			
Explain why people seek asylum			
Explain why the UK is a country with wide cultural diversity			
Explain why people's sense of identity is often complex			
Describe how settlers and migrants contribute to the national economy			
Explain what is meant by the term community cohesion			

Section and key statements Section 3.2.2　Fairness and justice in decision-making and the law I can ...	No problem	Need more revision	Need to ask for help
Describe how the police, Crown Prosecution Service and criminal courts uphold the law and deal with witnesses, people who may have committed criminal offences and victims of criminal acts			
Explain why crime can threaten human rights			
Describe how the Universal Declaration of Human Rights, the Human Rights Act and International Humanitarian Law attempt to protect human rights in times of peace and war			
Describe how rights can compete and conflict			
Explain how the law can help where rights compete or conflict			
Describe the responsibilities a citizen has to obey the law and support the justice system			
Describe the rights a citizen has if stopped or arrested by the police			
Describe how a Bill passes through the UK Parliament to become an Act and new law			
Describe how legal advice and support may be obtained			

OCR Citizenship Studies Teacher's Resource Book for GCSE full and short course
© 2009 Hodder Education

Section and key statements Section 3.2.3 Democracy and voting I can ...	No problem	Need more revision	Need to ask for help
Participate in different democratic decision-making exercises that have an influence on school, college or community life			
Describe the development of, and struggle for, different kinds of rights and freedoms (speech, opinion, association and the right to vote) in the United Kingdom			
Understand the different operation of power and authority in democratic and non-democratic forms of government, historically and across the world today			
Explain the term *representative democracy*			
Compare the differences in power and authority in democratic and non-democratic forms of government			
Explain why non-democratic forms of government are likely to infringe human rights			
Evaluate Parliament's role in making the Government accountable			
Describe how citizens can play an active part in local and national elections			
Describe how citizens can influence decision-making through membership of political parties			
Describe how citizens can influence decision-making through membership of pressure groups or religious organisations			
Describe how the media influences public debate and decision-making			
Describe how citizens and politicians can make use of the media			
Evaluate how far citizens are able to hold decision-makers to account			
Explain why a free press is important in a democracy			

Section and key statements **Section 3.2.4 The United Kingdom's relationships in Europe, including the European Union (EU), and relationships with the Commonwealth and the United Nations (UN)** I can ...	No problem	Need more revision	Need to ask for help
Describe, in outline, the UK's economic relationships with other countries in Europe			
Describe, in outline, the UK's political and legal relationships with other countries in Europe			
Describe, in outline, the UK's cultural relationships with other countries in Europe			
Describe how European Union decisions have an impact upon citizens of the United Kingdom			
Evaluate the benefits and costs of the UK's membership of the European Union			
Describe the role of the British Commonwealth			
Describe the United Nations' role in helping to resolve international disagreements and conflict			
Explain why the UK is committed to adhere to the United Nations' agreements on human rights, international relations and the environment			
Evaluate the role and effectiveness of the United Nations in one international issue, emergency or dispute			

OCR Citizenship Studies Teacher's Resource Book for GCSE full and short course
© 2009 Hodder Education

Section 5: Success in the Full Course

This section provides advice on how to make a success of Units A343 *Rights and Responsibilities – Extending our Knowledge and Understanding* and A344 *Identity, Democracy and Justice – Leading the Way as an Active Citizen*.

Unit A343 is assessed by a one-hour external examination. This is worth 20 per cent of the final mark for the Full Course. Unit A344 is assessed through a Controlled Assessment. This is in two parts – *The Citizenship Enquiry* and *Practical Citizenship Action* – worth 30 per cent of the final mark for the Full Course.

Success in the Controlled Assessment (Unit A344)

The assessment for Unit A344 comes in two parts. First, candidates undertake a Citizenship Enquiry. OCR will issue a source book each year based on a topical theme or issue relating to the subject content for unit A344. Candidates have up to 10 hours to research the issues and make notes in their source book.

Once the research has been completed, candidates are then required to respond to one of two or three viewpoints on the issue. They have up to two hours under informal supervision to respond to the viewpoint. They can use their annotated copy of the source book and an additional four sources of information they have found to help them do this.

The exemplar answers on pages 62–64 are based on the issue used within the OCR specimen assessment materials: 'Should people have the right to wear religious symbols at school?' The sources quoted come from the OCR specimen source book.

The Citizenship Enquiry: example of a grade C response

I think that the law should be changed to prevent schools banning religious dress and symbols. I agree with one of the comments in source 4 that says that not allowing people to wear religious clothing in school is a form of discrimination.

I have done some of my own research and found a recent case on the BBC website. A 14-year-old Sikh girl from Wales was excluded from her school for refusing to take off her religious bangle. The girl took the school to court for discrimination and she won. The judge said the school was guilty of indirect discrimination under race relations and equality laws. This is evidence to back up my viewpoint.

In the European Convention on Human Rights it says that we have the right to religious freedom and can display our beliefs. Muslim girls have to show modesty and the way they do this is by covering their body. The faith commitments of Muslim pupils include all aspects of everyday life including school, according to source 6. If schools say they can't wear a hijab or a jilbab then the girls are having to go against a value in Islam. The Muslim Council of Britain says that girls should be allowed to cover their bodies at school.

On the other hand there are arguments against wearing religious dress. Source 2 shows that in France there is a ban on Muslim girls wearing headscarves. The French government have made this law so that all children at school will be equal. I don't think that this is fair as it is only affecting some students so it is discrimination. Lord Ahmed of Rotherham who is a Muslim says wearing veils is a 'barrier to integration' and has called for an end to their use.

At the moment there is no law about school uniform; it is up to the governors to decide what they want to do in their school. Some schools allow religious dress and others don't. This can cause problems. Source 2 shows Shabina did not win her right to wear a jilbab but one of my sources shows Sarika has won her right to wear the kara bangle. Everyone should be treated the same. It doesn't seem fair that one girl won her case and another didn't.

If the law was changed so that schools couldn't ban religious dress or symbols both girls would be allowed to show their religion. I think that the law should be changed so that schools can't ban religious dress or symbols then it would be up to the individuals if that is what they felt they should do for their religion.

Commentary

The candidate has used some Citizenship concepts and shown that they understand them. The text is legible and the meaning is communicated clearly for most of the answer. They have offered a personal response and included some explanation of the arguments for and against the case. Evidence has been drawn from the source book and there is reference to an additional source as well. The candidate begins to advocate their position. The answer is organised to add weight to their description.

The Citizenship Enquiry: example of a grade A response

I have been researching into the issue of allowing religious dress and symbols to be worn at school. This is a very emotive issue and has many arguments for and against changing the law. I believe that the law should be changed to prevent schools from banning religious dress or symbols.

Article 9 of the European Convention on Human Rights states that everyone has the right to display one's religion or belief. Therefore if schools are banning religious symbols they are acting against this right as a symbol is a way to display your religion.

In a recent case in Wales, Sakira won her right to be able to wear the Sikh bangle kara. The judge said that it was a form of indirect discrimination to say that religious symbols were not allowed at the school. Indirect discrimination is where a rule is set that only affects a particular group of people. In this case only religious pupils are affected by school rules on religious dress.

The Muslim Council of Britain explains in source 6 that schools should expect Muslim pupils to observe the principals of haya. This includes modesty and the way to show this particularly for girls is to cover their bodies with what is known as a hijab.

In France as it says in source 1 there has been a ban on Muslim girls wearing headscarves in state schools. The government brought in the ban so that everyone is seen as equal. Some people are reacting very strongly to this and two journalists were taken hostage by Iraqi militants who threatened to kill them if the ban wasn't scrapped. This does not really help the cause of these young Muslim girls in my opinion.

From my own research I found a source from Binnaz Toprak who is a political science professor at Bosporus University in Istanbul, Turkey, a secular country with a Muslim majority. She said 'I think they have got it right in France. Civil servants and schoolgirls should not wear the veil. Personally, I am against it, it is a symbol of the inferior status of women in Muslim countries.' The issue in Turkey at the moment is whether university students should be allowed to wear the hijab. Many students wear it for political reasons but others wear it for religious reasons.

A Muslim girl in source 2, Shabina, lost her case to be allowed to wear a jilbab in lessons. This goes to highlight that when there is no law it is left up to the judge at the time to make a decision and this does not seem a fair way to decide. If the law was changed at least every case would be treated the same.

The law as it stands in the UK is that, according to source 8, the governing body of each school has the right to decide for their own school. The DCSF says that if pupils look very different to their peers this can inhibit integration equality and cohesion. If pupils are to be allowed to wear the hijab then it can be in the colour of the rest of the school uniform so that the girl won't stand out.

At my school pupils are allowed to wear religious dress. There are only a small number of Muslim girls in my school and they are allowed to wear the hijab. They say they can express their true identity this way and feel more comfortable. There have not been any issues to do with health and safety.

I think that the law should be changed so that everyone is treated the same. It doesn't seem fair that someone who takes their case to court like Sakira wins and yet another student in a similar position, Shabina, loses. There would be greater respect for each other's religion, as there is in my school, if pupils were allowed to wear religious dress and symbols.

Commentary
There is a thorough use of appropriate and valid Citizenship concepts. The candidate understands the complexities of the issue and puts their case across clearly. They provide a thorough and reasoned evaluation of the arguments for and against to construct an informed personal response. Evidence is taken from the source book and their own research. The UK law is evaluated and there are some international comparisons. They provide an informed personal response about why they wish to change the law. Their view is supported with evidence.

OCR Citizenship Studies Teacher's Resource Book for GCSE full and short course
© 2009 Hodder Education

Practical Citizenship Action

Part two of the Controlled Assessment for Unit A344 is the Practical Citizenship Action. Candidates have to plan, take and evaluate Practical Citizenship Action to promote community cohesion, promote equal opportunity or discourage discrimination in their school or local community. They have to work in groups to plan and take the action but must work individually when evaluating the action.

OCR prescribes the following four contexts from which the candidate selects an issue and then develops the action:
• gender
• race, ethnicity and culture
• age
• disability.

For example, the group of students may have noticed that the school or college is culturally diverse but students find it very difficult to mix when they join in Year 7. This issue would come under the context of race, ethnicity and culture. A possible action to try to promote community cohesion would be to organise a special event for new students and their parents to celebrate cultural diversity in the school, college or wider community.

Students have to complete a candidate proposal form and the teacher is required to sign this to confirm approval of the action. The students then have up to six hours to plan their action. A planning sheet must be completed as evidence of this process.

Once planned, the action can take place. Students have up to 13 hours to manage and take the action. They are assessed for taking the action. Each candidate needs to provide evidence of their role in the action, which could be in the form of:
• examples of posters, leaflets or other material, including websites linked to the action
• videos of activities, meetings, assemblies, lobbying or other responsible group action
• witness statements from those who have observed or been influenced by the action.

In this section, candidates will be assessed on their participation in the Practical Citizenship Action rather than on their ability to provide a written description of everything they did.

Finally, students have to evaluate their Practical Citizenship Action. They have a maximum of one hour under informal supervision (see page 43) to complete this work.

The following examples on pages 66–67 show candidates' evaluation of their Practical Citizenship Action. Students organised an international evening to celebrate cultural diversity in their school or college.

··
Evaluation of a Practical Citizenship Action: example of a grade C response
··

We decided to organise an international evening at my school. The reason we did this was because we have a lot more pupils from different backgrounds coming to our school. When I started at the school the pupils and their families were mainly born in the local area. I think it is important to understand everybody's culture so that we can all get along at school. We started our action by doing a survey to see all the different countries pupils came from in our school. We were surprised that there were pupils from 16 different countries. The international evening gave pupils from each country a chance to do a display about their own country. Some pupils brought their parents in and they had cooked some traditional food for us to try. I think it was very successful because everyone enjoyed learning about the different cultures. Lots of people turned up to our event so they must have thought it was important to learn about different cultures as well.

We had planned everything really carefully to make sure that every country had a table to do a display. We thought it would have been really bad if we had missed a country out as those pupils from that country might have felt like we didn't care about them as much. We were able to do this and everyone said it was good to see so many different countries on display.

I think our advertising of the evening went well because there were so many people in the hall. This meant there was a real buzz about the place. Some of the countries played music as well which added to the atmosphere. We had looked into health and safety issues with the Site Supervisor and so no accidents happened.

Some countries only had one pupil who came from that country and they had a lot of work to do. If we were going to organise an event like this again someone from our group should offer to help out. It was important that they were able to show off their country.

To increase the impact of the activity we could put up permanent displays around the school showing all the different countries pupils come from. This will always remind us that people have different backgrounds.

Commentary

The candidate gives limited reasons for their choice of action and these are explained well. They reflect on the successes of the action and there is some link to the perceptions of others. They have commented on the suitability of the plan to achieve the outcomes. There is a limited description of the aspects of the activity that went well and of the difficulties encountered. The candidate has considered their next steps and ways in which the impact could be increased.

Evaluation of a Practical Citizenship Action: example of a grade A response

The cultural mix in my local area has changed a lot since I started at school. Most of the pupils were born in the local area and their families had lived there for many years. In the last couple of years there has been an increase in families from other countries coming to live in our area. There are a lot of job opportunities in the nearby town and this has encouraged people to move here. At school we have had a number of assemblies about anti-bullying as there seems to have been an increase in bullying as the number of pupils from different backgrounds has increased. I think this is a negative way of trying to deal with the issue. We need to understand everybody else so that we all get on together. We have therefore planned an international evening to celebrate the different countries represented in our school.

We needed to undertake some research to find out which countries pupils came from. We found out that 16 different countries were represented. Most were from the European Union as we might expect due to the freedom of EU citizens to live and work in other member countries. The international evening would give pupils from each country an opportunity to showcase their country. They could put up displays, do dances, play music, provide food or show photos of their country.

In order to check if our event was a success we interviewed some pupils from the different countries before and after the event. Our results showed that after the event pupils felt a better sense of belonging to the school community and that other pupils understood their culture better. The pupils who were originally from this area said they enjoyed the event because they got to understand other pupils' backgrounds better. The hall was very busy so people obviously thought it was an event worth supporting.

We were worried that other pupils might not take the event seriously as a chance to learn about different cultures so we made sure that we did lots of advertising. We went into the different tutor groups to tell each group personally about the event. I think planning it like this paid off as in the end the hall was very busy. As everyone had done so much work, it would have been a shame if people had not turned up. Our problem was actually that too many people turned up. The Site Supervisor had given us a talk on risk assessment and he had told us the maximum number of people allowed in the hall. It was difficult to keep track of numbers so that we didn't break health and safety law. If we did this type of event again we could use the gym as well because we now know that it would be very popular.

We can't leave this issue now that our international evening is over. We have asked for a slot on the assembly rota to be dedicated to different cultures. This will keep up the impact of our event. We also want to put together a booklet to give out to year 7s each year. This would have a page per country. Pupils from each country could contribute to it so we have a permanent document to use to introduce the new year 7s to the cultural diversity of our school. I think it was very important to celebrate the different cultures in our school as I feel that if we understand each other better we are more likely to all get on and work together at school.

Commentary

The reasons for selecting the particular action have been explained well. When evaluating the success of the action they have included evidence from some of the participants. The candidate has evaluated the suitability of their plan in relation to outcomes achieved. They have evaluated those aspects of the activity that went well and also the difficulties encountered. A thorough evaluation of the next steps and ways in which the impact could be increased has been included.

Success in the examination (Unit A343)

■ Introduction

This section analyses the format of the exam and offers advice on how to prepare students for success in Questions 6 and 9d (together worth 12 marks out of the 40 available for the paper). Also provided is a revision checklist and glossary of key concepts for students' use as they prepare for success in the exam.

The examination for Unit A343 is offered in June each year.

■ The format and content of the exam

The format and content of the exam are shown in the table below. Students have to answer all the questions.

Section	Question numbers	Question type	Focus	Example	Skills	Marks
A	1a–5b	Short answer (12 questions)	Whole of the Unit content	State **one** source of advice for people who want information about their rights.	Understanding of key concepts and terminology	1 × 12
	6	Explanation	Whole of the Unit content	Explain how employees benefit by being members of a trade union.	Understanding of key concepts and terminology	6
B	7a, b, c	Interpretation of information from a document through short answers (4 questions)	Document provided as a stimulus	State **one** piece of evidence from *Document 1* that shows that the BBC World Service does not always agree with the United Kingdom (UK) Government.	Interpretation	1 × 4
	8a, b	Interpretation of information from a document through short answers (3 questions)	Document provided as a stimulus	State **one** piece of evidence from *Document 2* that shows how fair trade can help people in a Less Economically Developed Country (LEDC).	Interpretation	1 × 3
	8c	Evaluation of a viewpoint	Document provided as a stimulus	Write a reasoned argument to **oppose** the viewpoint that 'donating money to Less Economically Developed Countries (LEDCs) is the best way for us to help them'.	Evaluation	6

OCR Citizenship Studies Teacher's Resource Book for GCSE full and short course
© 2009 Hodder Education

Section	Question numbers	Question type	Focus	Example	Skills	Marks
B ctd	9a, b, c	Interpretation of information from two documents through short answers (3 questions)	Two documents provided as a stimulus	State **one** person in *Document 4* who disagrees with the statement in *Document 3* that 'the real value of teachers' pay has gone down'.	Interpretation	1 × 3
	9d	Evaluation of a viewpoint	Two documents provided as a stimulus	Evaluate the viewpoint that teachers were right to strike in April 2008.	Evaluation	6
Total marks						40

■ Success in question 6

In the examination for Unit A343, Question 6 is an explanation question. The key feature of this question is that candidates can approach their answer in one of two ways. They can either explain one advantage in depth or at least two advantages in outline. This approach should help candidates with a broad knowledge as well as those with a deep knowledge.

Sample question

Explain how employees benefit by being members of a trade union.

In your answer you must:
- Explain one advantage in depth or at least two advantages in outline.
- Use examples to support your explanation.

(6 marks)

Example of a Grade C response

Employees are the workers in a business. They join a trade union so that their views can be taken to the managers of the business. If the employees want to have a pay rise then they would all tell the trade union and someone from the trade union would go to the managers and explain why the workers wanted a pay rise. The advantage to the employees is that the trade union has more power when they are speaking to the managers. They are speaking on behalf of all the employees. If each employee went to see the managers on their own this would not have as much power. Trade union representatives are trained to deal with managers so therefore they know how to speak to them to get the employees' voices heard. If an employee thought they were being discriminated against they could speak to the trade union in private and get advice about what should be done. The employee will then have someone on their side who knows the law when they go to see their manager about it. These are two good benefits to employees of being a member of a trade union.

Commentary

The candidate has offered a sound personal response to the question. They have covered two points in some detail. They clearly understand what is meant by employees and trade unions. They give examples to support their case and the explanation is sound. Text is legible and spelling, grammar and punctuation are mostly accurate. Meaning is communicated clearly.

Example of a Grade A response

Employees are often given the choice whether or not to join a trade union at their workplace. There are many advantages to the employees of doing this. The trade union will negotiate directly with the management on pay and conditions. The representative is specially trained in negotiation and will do his or her best to get the best deal for the employees. This collective bargaining gives the employees more power than each person going to the management individually and so they are more likely to get the outcome they wish for.

If an employee is being disciplined by their manager they can have a trade union representative with them. This is like someone who has been arrested having a solicitor with them when they are interviewed by the police. The trade union representative will know the law and the rules of the business to make sure the employee gets a fair hearing. The management might also be a bit scared of the representative and make sure that they conduct the disciplinary process correctly as they are being watched. These examples show some of the benefits of being a member of a trade union.

Commentary

The candidate offers an informed personal response to the question. In this example they develop two points in sufficient detail. They offer a convincing and relevant explanation with appropriate examples. They clearly understand the terms 'employees' and 'trade union'. Text is legible and spelling, grammar and punctuation are mostly accurate. Meaning is communicated clearly.

■ Success in question 9d

In question 9d, candidates are given two documents as stimulus material and then asked to evaluate a viewpoint. Questions 9a, b and c have already asked candidates to interpret information from these documents, so this question leads on from that.

• •

Sample question

• •

Study the two documents below and then answer the following question.

> Write a reasoned argument to oppose the viewpoint that 'donating money to Less Economically Developed Countries (LEDCs) is the best way for us to help them'.
>
> You must do the following in your answer:
> * Explain key terms such as Less Economically Developed Countries (LEDCs).
> * Explain other ways of helping LEDCs.
> * Use evidence to support your argument. **(6 marks)**

Document 1

Influencing and advocacy

Trade has the potential to lift millions of poor producers out of poverty, but only if current unfair trade practices and policies are changed. At Traidcraft we realise that, in order to maximise our impact, we need not just to grow our own work but also to influence others to change their own practices.

Our Policy Unit in London undertakes vital policy and advocacy work on key trade issues, both in the UK and in Europe. And in our overseas programmes a key focus is on building the capacity of poor producers to engage with decision makers, making sure their voices are heard and their needs taken into account.

Taken from www.traidcraft.co.uk

Document 2

Trade generates incredible wealth, and links the lives of everyone on the planet. Yet millions of people in poor countries are losing out. Why? Because the rules controlling trade heavily favour the rich nations that set the rules.

Something's very wrong with world trade. Oxfam's committed to putting it right. Why campaign on trade?

- Rich countries spend $1 billion a day subsidising their farmers. They produce too much, and the extra produce is dumped on developing countries at vastly reduced prices. This means poor farmers can't compete – or make a living.
- If Africa, Asia and Latin America increased their share of world exports by just one per cent, they would earn enough money to lift 128 million people out of poverty.

Instead of robbing half the world of a proper living, trade could help millions of poor farmers and workers in developing countries to beat poverty, and change their lives for good. But this will not happen unless countries change the way they trade. So we're campaigning hard to make sure they do.

Adapted from www.oxfam.org.uk

Example of a grade C response

Less economically developed countries are the poorer countries of the world like those in Asia and Africa. They do not make enough money for people to have everything that they want and quite often they have problems like droughts where the crops fail and they have even less to eat.

The UK is a more economically developed country and people in this country are not as poor as people in Africa. We can help people in Africa by donating money to charity. This can help people in these countries for a short time but if there is another drought then they are in the same situation again.

There are other ways that we can help them. We can buy fair trade goods as it says in the Oxfam source. This means that more of the money goes to the farmers in Africa so then they have money to buy things that their families need.

My school also buys goats that Oxfam send to Africa so we are helping the families with that as well. If we do these things we are trying to improve the situation for them for longer and if there is a drought again maybe they built a well with the money they got from fair trade which would help them to keep watering their crops. The Traidcraft source says we should campaign as well to help them.

I think that buying fair trade will help people in LEDCs to become richer and will help them for longer than if we just give them money.

Commentary

The candidate offers a sound personal response to the question. They use evidence to oppose the viewpoint that 'donating money to Less Economically Developed Countries (LEDCs) is the best way for us to help them'.

They clearly understand the term LEDCs and support their understanding with evidence. Text is legible and spelling, grammar and punctuation are mostly accurate. The meaning is communicated clearly.

··
Example of a grade A response
··

A less economically developed country has a low level of income and the people of the country are generally poor. LEDCs are found in Africa and Asia. Because they are poor they need our help to develop. The UK is a more economically developed country which means we are richer and can help out if LEDCs need our help.

Donating money could be just giving money to the LEDC. We don't know what happens to that money and in some countries where the Government is corrupt it might not actually get to the people who need it. The money might be used to buy food but once this food is eaten there is nothing left. It is a very short term way of helping. It is not wrong but not the best way to help.

Other ways that we can help can be seen in the two sources. The Traidcraft source says that it is important to campaign about these issues so that there is more awareness of the need for long term help. Oxfam says that we should trade with producers in these countries.

We can buy fair trade goods from our school canteen. I buy fair trade products; they are more expensive but I know that the extra I am paying is given directly to the producer so that they can use that money to feed their family and improve their business. Oxfam says that we spend $1 billion a day subsidising our farmers.

We should campaign to tell Governments that we want this money to be invested in improving trade with LEDCs. Trade will allow the countries to get richer and be able to look after themselves long term.

It is not wrong to donate money; sometimes if there is a natural disaster people need aid in the short term but by doing more long term projects that I have explained it can give these countries a better chance.

Commentary

The candidate offers an informed personal response to the question. They show understanding of different ways of helping LEDCs. Examples have been used to back up their points. They show that donating money has a role in helping LEDCs but that it is not necessarily the best way to help them.

Text is legible and spelling, grammar and punctuation are mostly accurate. Meaning is communicated clearly.

Revision checklist for Unit A343

Section and key statement **Section 3.3.1 Our rights and responsibilities at school/college and within the wider community** I can ...	No problem	Need more revision	Need to ask for help
Describe the moral rights of different groups of people in a school or college			
Describe the moral responsibilities of different groups of people in a school or college			
Describe the legal rights of different groups of people in a school or college			
Describe the legal responsibilities of different groups of people in a school or college			
Describe the informal ways in which legal rights and responsibilities are reinforced in schools			
Describe how the law reinforces and is designed to protect legal rights and responsibilities in schools			
Evaluate the support local authorities or government departments give to citizens who need information and advice about their rights			
Evaluate the support independent agencies such as Citizens' Advice give to citizens who need information and advice about their rights			
Describe how the Universal Declaration of Human Rights, the European Convention on Human Rights and the Human Rights Act seek to protect human rights			
Evaluate the effectiveness of the Universal Declaration of Human Rights by analysing examples of possible infringements of human rights in the UK and elsewhere			

OCR Citizenship Studies Teacher's Resource Book for GCSE full and short course
© 2009 Hodder Education

Section and key statement **Section 3.3.2 Our rights and responsibilities as citizens within the economy and welfare systems** **I can …**	No problem	Need more revision	Need to ask for help
Explain why the interests of employers and employees might conflict			
Describe how the law seeks to protect the interests of employers and employees			
Describe how the interests of employers may conflict with the need to protect the environment			
Describe how taxation and government regulation can be used to encourage environmentally responsible behaviour			
Describe how trade unions seek to support and represent their members			
Describe how employers' associations seek to support and represent their members			
Describe the ways in which the Government manages the economy			
Describe the services provided by the Government and local authorities			
Evaluate the different viewpoints on how far the state or individuals should take responsibility for the provision of income protection, health and education			
Explain why it is important for businesses to obey patent law or copyright law			
Explain why it is important for businesses to be socially responsible in supporting the wider community			

Section and key statement Section 3.3.3 Extending understanding of a global citizen's rights and responsibilities I can ...	No problem	Need more revision	Need to ask for help
Describe how sustainable development is promoted locally			
Describe how sustainable development is promoted nationally			
Describe how sustainable development is promoted globally			
Describe the barriers to sustainable development			
Describe the differences between fair and unfair trade			
Explain why pressure groups want to promote fair trade			
Describe how businesses can bring about change in trade			
Describe how governments can bring about change in trade			
Explain why More Economically Developed Countries (MEDCs) should give aid to Less Economically Developed Countries (LEDCs)			
Evaluate the different types of aid that may be offered to LEDCs			
Describe how the media can affect public opinion			
Describe how the media can help bring about change in democratic societies			
Describe how the media can help bring about change in non-democratic societies			
Evaluate one international citizenship issue related to trade or aid			

OCR Citizenship Studies Teacher's Resource Book for GCSE full and short course
© 2009 Hodder Education

Section 6: Answers to questions in the Student's Book

> **It's the rule**
> - Home time
> - Breaking the law
> - What is law?
> - Criminal responsibility
> - Legal rights and responsibilities
>
> **The law machine**
> - Law makers
> - Parliamentary process
> - Judge-made law
> - European law

It's the rule

The five topics in this unit are designed to help students understand more about the nature of law: its relationship with morality; the difference between criminal and civil law; and the circumstances in which people become legally responsible for their actions.

There is further coverage of some of these ideas in the chapter on **Justice** *pages 172–189.*

Home time, pages 6–7

This topic looks at the rule-laden nature of our behaviour and the relationship between law and morality.

> **OCR GCSE Citizenship Studies**
>
> **3.1.1** Understand the moral and legal rights and responsibilities that apply to our interactions with others.
> **3.2.2** Understand ways in which rights can compete and conflict and how the law is used to resolve these issues justly.
> **3.2.2** Understand the importance of law in maintaining order and resolving conflict and achieving just outcomes and understand that the law places a responsibility on all members of society to conform to a common code of behaviour, including obedience to civil and criminal law.
>
> **National Curriculum programme of study, key stage 4**
> **Key concepts** 1.1 b; 1.2 a, c
> **Range and content** 3 a, b

Q1 As stated later in the text, Lauren is behaving as a visitor or guest, and not as a close family member. Breaking rules in this way can be an effective means of identifying taken-for-granted rules and assumptions that underlie a lot of our daily life.

Q2 Students may disagree with a number of these statements on moral or religious grounds. There is an opportunity here to ask them to explain the reasoning behind their views and perhaps to identify the basis of their thinking.

Q3 The following statements have a basis in law: **age**, **faithful** and **support**, and (strictly speaking) **woman and man** – see below.

Age • Under the *Marriage Act 1949* and the *Matrimonial Causes Act 1973*, a marriage is void if either partner is under 16. The word 'void' means that, as far as the law is concerned, the marriage has never taken place.

Faithful • Married (but not unmarried) couples have a legal duty to remain faithful to their partner. However, adultery alone is not, strictly speaking, a ground for divorce. The person seeking the divorce must also convince the court that they find it intolerable to continue to live with their spouse.

Support • Married partners have a duty to support and behave reasonably towards one another. There is no similar legal requirement for unmarried couples.

Woman and man • Although civil partnerships are now permitted between members of the same sex, these do not, in law, constitute marriage. Marriage refers to a legal relationship between a man and a woman.

Q4 Issues, other than abortion and Sunday trading, that people may find morally wrong include gay and lesbian relationships, gambling, consumption of tobacco or alcohol, hunting, 'unnecessary' consumption of scarce resources, failure to recycle rubbish, suicide and certain aspects of treatment of people who are terminally ill.

This question may be used, by those students taking the OCR examination, as a starting point for a citizenship campaign.

Breaking the law, pages 8–9

In this topic, students assess a number of reasons that people give for breaking the law.

OCR GCSE Citizenship Studies

3.4.2 Evaluate the justifications people give for breaking the law, including to bring about change, and understand the reasons for upholding the rule of law.

National Curriculum programme of study, key stage 4
Key concepts 1.1 b
Range and content 3 a

Q1&Q2 Some responsibility for the loss will lie with the building society and those who programmed and installed the new computer system. However, prime responsibility arguably lies with those people who deliberately withdrew money from a cash machine either knowing, or later realising, that the money they were obtaining was not being debited from their account.

Q3 In these circumstances, some people may state that:
• it was the building society's fault for failing to check that the system was working properly
• they didn't realise they were committing an offence
• they deserve 'a bit of luck'
• taking money in this way is 'only human nature'
• the building society could probably afford, or wouldn't notice, the loss.

In court, defence counsel claimed that it was the failure of the system that led to the offences, and that the accused had faced a temptation that was impossible to resist. It was also stated that others who had benefited from the error had not been charged.

Q4 Members of the family who stole more than £134,000 were sentenced to between twelve and 15 months in prison. Other offenders also received prison sentences, community punishment orders (in one case for 180 hours) and fines. Some were also ordered to repay the amount taken. It was reported that the building society also received compensation for its losses from its insurers.

Q5 All of the examples are based on real cases, although only Molly, Ricky and Lee faced criminal charges:
• *Molly* was sentenced to prison a number of times and fined for criminal damage and aggravated trespass.
• *Ricky* and members of his family were found guilty of conspiracy to commit burglary and were each sentenced to between eight and eleven years in prison.

- *Lee* was stopped by the police, who checked on the police national computer to discover that he had only a provisional licence, which had expired some time ago. In court, magistrates issued Lee with a six-month driving ban, a £150 fine, with £35 costs, and required him to pay a further £15 surcharge for victims of crime.

What is law? Pages 10–11

In this topic, students look at the way in which laws apply to many aspects of everyday life, and at the distinction between civil and criminal law.

> **OCR GCSE Citizenship Studies**
>
> **3.2.2** Understand the different roles of the police ... criminal courts...
> **3.2.2** Understand the importance of law in maintaining order and resolving conflict and achieving just outcomes and understand that the law places a responsibility on all members of society to conform to a common code of behaviour, including obedience to civil and criminal law.
> **3.4.2** Understand the role of individuals, lawyers and courts in the civil legal and justice system.
>
> **National Curriculum programme of study, key stage 4**
> **Key concepts** 1.1 b
> **Range and content** 3 a, b

Q1 In the illustration of the woman at **home** the law:
- requires goods purchased for sale, e.g. kettles, lights, to be safe, as described and fit for purpose
- controls the quality of water and food that is purchased
- protects animals from cruelty and neglect
- controls the rent and ownership of property.

In **shops**, the law
- regulates the buying and selling of goods
- controls product safety, weights and measures, and trade descriptions
- controls the employment of staff
- controls the safety of customers, employees and anyone else who comes into the shop
- includes theft.

In **clubs/bars**, the law
- regulates the sale and consumption of alcohol
- controls disorderly behaviour
- regulates opening hours and the playing and performing of music
- controls the employment of staff.

Q2 Generally speaking, laws are created to protect rights and to achieve a level of fairness or justice. They are also used as a means of settling disputes:
- *Protecting individual rights*: for example, laws providing for individuals against theft or assault, and also against the abuse of state power, for example torture, invasion of privacy.
- *Safety*: for example, laws controlling health and safety at work, regulating traffic, the sale of goods.
- *Achieving fairness and justice*: for example, dealing with unfair discrimination, employment protection, the conduct of trials and sentencing procedures.
- *Settling disagreements*: for example, in relation to divorce, unfair dismissal, contract disputes.
- *Enforcing rules*: for example, setting out the powers and duties of the police and courts.

Q3 Anna's letter refers to the following law-related events:
- speeding conviction – criminal law
- parking fines – criminal law; however, they do not form part of a person's criminal record
- shoplifting – criminal law

- truancy – criminal law; technically, the offence is committed by the child's parents for failing to ensure that their child is in school
- injury at work – claims for compensation are made under civil law; however, employers may be prosecuted under criminal law for a serious breach of health and safety regulations
- divorce – civil law
- dispute with neighbour – civil law
- unfair dismissal – civil law
- criminal damage and theft – criminal law.

Criminal responsibility, pages 12–13

This topic asks whether there should be any changes in the age of criminal responsibility.

OCR GCSE Citizenship Studies

3.1.1 Understand the way in which moral and legal rights and responsibilities develop with maturity and age.

3.2.2 Understand the different roles of the … criminal courts…

3.2.2 Understand the importance of law in maintaining order and resolving conflict and achieving just outcomes.

National Curriculum programme of study, key stage 4
Key concepts 1.1 b; 1.2 a
Range and content 3 a, b

Q1 In law, a child under the age of ten is presumed to be incapable of committing a crime; therefore the little girl has not stolen the sweets.

Q2 She could have been charged with theft if she had taken the sweets and was aged 10 or over.

Q3 One of the issues underlying this question is how children who break the law should be treated, and by whom.

You may like to explore with students memories of their own perceptions of right and wrong and the degree to which children can understand or predict the likely consequences of their actions.

Further questions include whether children should be made aware of the consequences of their behaviour, to what degree the police or other authorities should become involved and whether the state should intervene in the way parents bring up their children.

This question may be used, by those students taking the OCR examination, as a starting point for a citizenship campaign.

Legal rights and responsibilities, pages 14–15

In this topic, students explore whether changes should be made in some of the other ages of legal rights and responsibilities.

OCR GCSE Citizenship Studies

3.1.1 Understand the way in which moral and legal rights and responsibilities develop with maturity and age.

National Curriculum programme of study, key stage 4
Key concepts 1.1 b; 1.2 a
Range and content 3 a

Q1 This question raises a number of options for discussion. Should greater legal constraints be placed on young or newly qualified drivers limiting, for example, the type of vehicle they can drive, whom they may carry as passengers, or the maximum speed at which they may travel?

Although the driver, in this case, was killed in the accident, should punishments for speeding be increased to discourage people from driving dangerously? Should greater efforts be made to monitor vehicle speeds through greater use of roadside cameras or in-car surveillance?

After the accident, the mother of two of the victims spoke publicly of the anger she felt when she saw young drivers 'taking risks and not realising what can happen next'. Students may like to debate whether more emphasis should be placed on driver education – particularly when someone is learning to drive.

Q2&Q3 If time is available, these questions could form the basis of a small piece of research linked to the requirement for OCR students to develop a *citizenship campaign*.

Students could begin their work by devising a simple questionnaire designed to test public legal understanding about the various ages of legal rights and responsibilities, and then move on to gauge public interest in whether any of these ages should be changed.

The first questionnaire can give rise to further work on the degree to which people know about and understand the law, perhaps followed by research and a campaign to address one particular area of uncertainty.

Alternatively, asking people's views on whether changes should be made to specific ages, for example criminal responsibility or voting, can also be used as the basis of further work assessing whether there is a need for changes to current practice.

This question may be used, by those students taking the OCR examination, as a starting point for a citizenship campaign.

The law machine

This unit outlines the way in which laws are made and changed – focusing in particular on statute, case and European law.

The chapter on Government, pages 148–159, provides further background information on the UK and European Parliament and on the legislative powers of the devolved governments in Northern Ireland, Scotland and Wales.

Law makers, pages 16–17

This topic sets out the three main ways in which the law in England and Wales is created and developed – through Parliament, by judges in court and through our links with Europe.

OCR GCSE Citizenship Studies

3.2.2 Know that international humanitarian law protects the human rights of individuals and communities in peace and conflict

3.2.2 Understand how a Bill passes through the UK Parliament to become an Act, which is then law

3.2.4 Know, in outline, about our economic, political, legal and cultural relationships with other countries in Europe. Evaluate the implications of the United Kingdom's membership of the European Union and that European Union decisions have an impact upon citizens in the UK

3.4.2 Understand, through the study of suitable examples, that the courts are charged with responsibility to interpret the law in reaching judgements and that this creates a precedent for future judgements and to judge-made case law.

National Curriculum programme of study, key stage 4
Key concepts 1.1 b, d; 1.2 a, c
Range and content 3 c, m

Parliamentary process, pages 18–19

An outline of the introduction and passage of a Bill through Parliament.

OCR GCSE Citizenship Studies

3.2.2 Understand how a Bill passes through the UK Parliament to become an Act, which is then law

National Curriculum programme of study, key stage 4
Key concepts 1.1 d; 1.2 b
Range and content 3 c

One way of getting students to work some of these details out for themselves is to reproduce the text on page 19, *First Reading, Second Reading, Committee Stage,* etc., as slips, and ask students to work out the order in which the various stages take place. A slightly more complicated is to separate the headings from the explanatory text. This requires students to link the process with the term and then to place them both in the appropriate order.

Judge-made law, pages 20–21

This section outlines how new law may be created by judges.

OCR GCSE Citizenship Studies

3.4.2 Understand through the study of suitable examples that the courts are charged with responsibility to interpret the law in reaching judgements and that this creates a precedent for future judgements and to judge-made case law.

National Curriculum programme of study, key stage 4
Key concepts 1.1 b; 1.2 b
Range and content 3 c

Q1 The practice of registering web addresses for profit may lead to extortion and misrepresentation.

Q2 Arguments in support of Marks & Spencer and the others involved include:
- companies should not be required to buy back a name that they themselves have established
- no one has the right to use these companies' names other than the companies themselves
- the public is likely to be misled and defrauded if companies other than Marks & Spencer, etc., use these names.

Arguments in support of the dealers' action include:
- registering the names provided a market opportunity, which they were the first to recognise
- by registering names and offering them as a package, they are offering the companies a genuinely useful service.

Q3 The main advantages of case law are:
- consistency – similar cases are dealt with in a similar way
- certainty – lawyers are better able to predict the outcome of a case in the light of a previous decision
- efficiency – there is a saving of time, as cases resting on similar facts do not have to be argued and can be settled without resort to the court
- flexibility and speed –judges can develop the law without waiting for Parliament to pass new legislation.

The main disadvantages of case law are:
- uncertainty – it is not always clear how well an existing case applies to a new situation
- other implications – the Court can only make its decision based on the facts before it, and this may not be a good way of exploring the wider implications of the decision

- too much power – developing the law through the decisions in Court raises the possibility of judges overstepping the mark and giving too much power to unelected officials.

Q4 Arguments in favour of having a more diverse judiciary include:
- judges with a wide range of views and experiences are likely to take more considered decisions in court
- a judiciary that reflects the wider society is more likely to retain public trust and confidence.

In the past, judges were selected for appointment by invitation. Today, the process is much more transparent. Those who want to be judges may apply for the post, as long as they have the required qualifications and experience.

However, as the student text suggests, changing the composition of the judiciary can be a slow process. Inevitably, many candidates come from senior levels in the legal profession, which is not marked by its diversity and it will clearly take further time for the younger more diverse members of the profession to gain the necessary level of experience.

European law, pages 22–23

This section outlines the nature of European law and how it is created.

OCR GCSE Citizenship Studies

3.2.4 Know, in outline, about our economic, political, legal and cultural relationships with other countries in Europe. Evaluate the implications of the United Kingdom's membership of the European Union and that European Union decisions have an impact upon citizens of the UK.

National Curriculum programme of study, key stage 4
Key concepts 1.1 c
Range and content 3 c, m

Q1 Students may suggest that EU law has brought the following benefits to the UK:
- opportunities and standards of protection for British individuals and businesses similar to most other European countries (this prevents one country from paying significantly lower wages than another, and in doing so giving businesses in that country a strong economic advantage)
- standardisation of labour and consumer laws which help the free movement of labour and goods, benefiting UK exporters and making European goods more widely available to UK customers
- beneficial effects on the environment with its requirement for the UK to raise its standards of environmental protection.

The drawbacks may include:
- some loss of UK sovereignty
- the potential for the creation of laws that are unsuitable for the circumstances in Britain
- a 'democratic deficit' caused by the apparent remoteness of EU law-making machinery, the failure of the public to understand how the EU works, and the lack of parliamentary involvement in the legislative process.

Q2 European Union law is superior to national law and national constitutions. However, the EU's law-making powers do not cover all areas of life. They are generally confined to employment, trade, industry, fishing, agriculture, immigration and rights of travel. Other areas, such as education, health, crime and family matters are not affected by EU law. For example, changes to the law concerning divorce, school-leaving age, abortion, the age of consent and the age of criminal responsibility are not likely to be affected by Britain's EU membership.

Human rights

> **What are human rights?**
> • The abuse of power
>
> **Human rights law**
> • Protecting human rights
> • The European Convention on Human Rights
> • Rights and freedoms in Britain
> • Held in detention
>
> **International Human Rights**
> • The United Nations

What are human rights?

The abuse of power, pages 24–25

This topic tries to explain the nature of human rights – that is, rights possessed by all citizens that should not be withheld or removed by government or those with official authority, unless for a reason that can be properly justified.

There is further coverage of human rights issues in the chapter on Government, pages 148–159.

> **OCR GCSE Citizenship Studies**
>
> **3.1.1** Understand the range and importance of fundamental human rights and their impact on national and international law. Identify and debate cases where different human rights may be in conflict.
> **3.3.1** Analyse the ... European Convention on Human Rights
>
> **National Curriculum programme of study, key stage 4**
> **Key concepts** 1.1 b, c; 1.2 a, b, c
> **Range and content** 3 a, f

Q1 Students' answers may include the following comments:

28 February – an emergency decree allowing any suspicious person to be arrested ... may be seen as an effective way of dealing with troublemakers and those wishing to delay or hamper Hitler's plans for development. However, a measure of this kind raises the question of how the authorities defined a troublemaker – and creates the possibility of large numbers of people being denied their liberty for spurious reasons, without any attention to the due process of law.

24 March – all powers to create new laws pass to the leader ... has the benefit of ensuring that policies are put into practice more quickly than they would be under conditions of normal parliamentary debate. However, it also means that proposals for new laws cannot be challenged, amended or overturned, increasing the likelihood of unfair and unjust law.

2 May – restrictions on workers' rights and the arrest of union leaders ... may be seen as an aid to production by removing restrictions on working hours and conditions. It might also give rise to lower labour costs, making the nation's industry more internationally competitive. The cost of these measures, however, may be injustice for workers and union leaders alike, and a decline in living standards and the quality of people's lives.

10 May – the establishment of a ministry of propaganda and the destruction of certain literary works ... by restricting and shaping the flow of information to the public, a ministry of this kind may serve to encourage citizens to work harder and make greater efforts in what is perceived to be the national interest.

However, a ministry of propaganda is likely to restrict debate on important public issues, and to result in significant public misinformation. In some circumstances, the propaganda machine may turn against certain social, national, religious or ethnic groups, resulting in persecution and serious loss of life.

OCR Citizenship Studies Teacher's Resource Book for GCSE full and short course
© 2009 Hodder Education

The destruction of items of literature which fail to reflect a leader's priorities may result in the loss of important parts of the country's cultural history and lead to significant restrictions being placed on the country's current writers and artists.

22 June – outlawing all political opposition … again this is a means designed to maximise a leader's control over the nation; increasing the likelihood (at least in the short run) that his or her policies will go forward unopposed. It also sets the standard for debate and discussion amongst the wider population, indicating that criticism and opposition will not be tolerated.

Again these measures are likely to result in considerable suppression by the state, probably leading to the removal of many legal and moral rights, including rights to freedom of speech, assembly and privacy. Other rights may be restricted or removed in the exercise of these powers, for example the right to a fair trial.

Q2&Q3 Under this legislation, Jewish people were denied the right to be treated in the same way as other German citizens. They were prevented from:
• playing any part in either the German justice or political systems
• working in their chosen profession
• reading or contributing to newspapers written for the Jewish community
• having a friend or partner of their choice
• travelling abroad where and when they wish
• attending school or university
• having access to justice.

These measures reduced the influence of Jewish people in society, damaged the quality of their lives and gave rise to further discrimination and abuse against them.

Q4 The text refers to a number of basic human rights and freedoms, namely:
• the right to life
• freedom from slavery
• the right to liberty
• the right to a fair trial
• the right to respect for their private life
• freedom of thought, conscience and religion
• freedom of expression
• freedom of assembly
• the right to marry
• the right to education
• the right to free and fair elections
• freedom from unfair discrimination.

Q5 It is helpful for students to see human rights in terms of the difference in power between the citizen and the state. In all cases, the machinery of the state is more powerful than the individual, and the idea of human rights provides a much-needed protection against the abuse of such power.

Without constitutional rights of this kind, and the means through which they can be protected, citizens face the possibility of considerable injustice at the hand of the state.

Human rights law

The four topics in this unit outline the nature of human rights law in Britain and its links to the European Convention on Human Rights.

Protecting human rights, pages 26–27

This topic outlines the background to the European Convention on Human Rights and introduces students to the idea that, although some human rights may be regarded as absolute, most human rights are restricted in some way. The topic also indicates how rights may compete in certain circumstances, raising the question of which rights should prevail.

OCR GCSE Citizenship Studies

3.1.1 Understand the range and importance of fundamental human rights and their impact on national and international law. Identify and debate cases where different human rights may be in conflict.

3.2.2 Understand ways in which rights can compete and conflict and how the law is used to resolve these issues justly.

3.3.1 Analyse the … European Convention on Human Rights. With reference to these documents, analyse possible infringements of human rights in the UK and elsewhere.

National Curriculum programme of study, key stage 4
Key concepts 1.1 b, c, d; 1.2 a, b, c
Range and content 3 a, f, m

Q1 Students' suggestions might include the following circumstances:

• *right to respect for a person's private and family life (Article 8)*: the state may interfere with a person's privacy to protect the public interest, for example for reasons of national security or public safety, where there is authority in law to do so. A person may legitimately lose their right to privacy when the police enter a building to make an arrest in connection with a serious offence or to search the premises. Normally the police need a search warrant to be able to do this, but there are some circumstances in which they can act simply on the permission of a senior officer of the rank of superintendent or above. The police, and other officials, may also intercept communications, but again normally need a warrant to do so. However, a warrant is not needed to tap into telephone conversations in a prison or a young offenders' institution.

• *freedom of thought, conscience, and religion (Article 9)*: there are no restrictions on thought, but limits may be placed on the exercise of one's views or beliefs if they are likely to have a negative impact on others. In 2007, a High Court Judge accepted a school's decision not to allow a 12-year-old girl to wear a full-face veil in class. The school had said that the ban was in place for a number reasons, including security, uniform policy and the difficulties the full-face veil imposed for teachers relating and communicating with pupils. It also added that the girl had been offered a place at another school where the niqab was permitted. The judge decided that, in the circumstances, the school's decision not to allow the girl into school wearing the niqab was reasonable and proportionate.

• *freedom of expression (Article 10)*: under some circumstances, the state is permitted to limit people's freedom to say or write what they wish. Laws on censorship and blasphemy are examples of this, along with those making it an offence to stir up racial hatred or to distribute threatening and abusive material.

• *freedom of assembly or association (Article 11)*: almost everyone is free to join a political party, to stand for election or to take an active part in politics. Not all these freedoms, however, are available to people who work for the police and certain sections of the civil service and local government. Certain organisations are banned under the *Terrorism Act 2000*, and public meetings, marches and demonstrations may all be banned if they are likely to cause a breach of the peace, block roads or paths, or prevent the police from carrying out their duties.

Q2 A case based on this issue came to court during 2002–3. During the general election of 2001, the ProLife Alliance Party fielded enough candidates to entitle it to make one party political broadcast in Wales. Shortly before the election, the party submitted a tape of its proposed broadcast to the BBC, ITV, and Channels Four and Five. All the broadcasters were unhappy with the many graphic images contained in the film, and refused to screen the programme. Their objections related only to the images of still and aborted fetuses, and not to the proposed soundtrack.

The ProLife Alliance Party attempted to have this decision overruled by judicial review, but were refused permission to proceed with the challenge. The case then moved to the Appeal Court, which allowed the judicial review to take place and proceeded to hear the case, deciding that the broadcasters' decision to refuse to transmit the programme was unlawful. The case moved on to the House of Lords for final consideration. Here it was decided, by four judges in favour and one against that, as long as broadcasters are required

---

not to transmit offensive material, the cumulative effects of the large number of images contained in the broadcast went beyond what is acceptable, and that it made no difference that this amounted to political censorship.

The European Convention on Human Rights, pages 28–29

This topic provides a simplified summary of the European Convention on Human Rights.

> **OCR GCSE Citizenship Studies**
>
> **3.1.1** Understand the range and importance of fundamental human rights and their impact on national and international law.
> **3.2.2** Know that International Humanitarian Law protects the human rights of individuals and communities in peace and conflict. Understand that individuals, organisations and governments have responsibility to ensure that rights are balanced, are supported and protected
> **3.3.1** Analyse the …European Convention on Human Rights and the Human Rights Act.
>
> **National Curriculum programme of study, key stage 4**
> **Key concepts** 1.1 b; 1.2 b
> **Range and content** 3 a, 3 m

Rights and freedoms in Britain, pages 30–31

This topic gives a brief overview of the development of certain rights in Britain, and outlines the background to and workings of the Human Rights Act. In the final section, students are asked to address some of the criticisms that are made of the Act, and to discuss whether it should be changed in any way.

> **OCR GCSE Citizenship Studies**
>
> **3.1.1** Understand the range and importance of fundamental human rights and their impact on national and international law. Identify and debate cases where human rights may be in conflict.
> **3.2.1** Understand the … value system that contributes to being British.
> **3.2.2** Understand that individuals, organisations and governments have responsibility to ensure that rights are balanced, supported and protected.
> **3.2.3** Understand the development of, and struggle for, different kinds of rights and freedoms … in the UK as part of securing a representative democracy.
>
> **National Curriculum programme of study, key stage 4**
> **Key concepts** 1.1 b, d; 1.2 b
> **Range and content** 3 a, c, f

Q1 To a large degree, the answer to this question is determined by students' understanding of and personal views on the strengths and weaknesses of the *Human Rights Act*. Prior to answering this question, you may find it helpful to take the three views given in the question, and ask students in pairs or small groups to put together statements in support of just one of these. Compare and discuss these statements as a whole class, before asking students to give their own individual reasoned response to the question.

Held in detention, pages 32–33

This topic is designed to develop discussion on ideas surrounding the powers and limitations that should be placed on the state concerning the detention of political suspects.

> **OCR GCSE Citizenship Studies**
>
> **3.1.1** Understand the range and importance of fundamental human rights and their impact on national and international law. Identify and debate cases where human rights may be in conflict.
> **3.2.2** Understand that individuals, organisations and governments have responsibility to ensure that rights are balanced, supported and protected.
>
> **National Curriculum programme of study, key stage 4**
> **Key concepts** 1.1 b, d; 1.2 b
> **Range and content** 3 a

Q1

a) The note is an order from the Home Secretary in 1940 ordering the detention of Jack Perlzweig, also known as Robert Liversidge.

b) The date of the note, 26 May 1940, suggests that it may be associated with the wartime conditions that then prevailed in Britain. In 1939, a week before the outbreak of war, Parliament had passed the *Emergency Powers (Defence) Act*. As the student text describes, a number of amendments were made soon afterwards giving the Home Secretary the power to detain anyone indefinitely merely by claiming that they were 'of hostile origins or associations'. It is reported that about 1800 people were detained in this way.

c) Students may point out a number of missing elements. There is no indication of:
- any evidence of what Jack Perlzweig has actually done, nor of the charges that he faces, other than being someone of 'hostile associations'
- how long Jack Perlzweig may be held in custody, nor when or whether he will face trial.

Both these points undermine Jack Perlzweig's rights to be informed of the reason for his arrest and to have a fair and public hearing, within a reasonable period of time.

Q2 In answering this question, students are likely to balance the Government's duty to protect the nation, particularly in time of war, with the right of individuals to retain their freedom and liberty need until there is evidence that they have broken the law.

Q3 You may find it helpful to organise the following activity prior to students answering this question:
- Type out and print on cards or slips of paper all the arguments listed on page 33 of the student material both In favour and Against the Government extending the period over which a suspect can be held. You may wish to amend these and add further arguments of your own.
- Give students, working in twos or threes, a complete set of cards or slips and ask them to a) divide them into points for and against raising the limits, and b) extract those arguments they find particularly strong (or weak).
- After the discussions and explanations following each of these activities, students may find it easier to outline their overall point of view.

International human rights

The United Nations, pages 34–35

This topic outlines some basic aspects of the human rights' work of the United Nations.

OCR GCSE Citizenship Studies

3.2.2 Know that international humanitarian law protects the human rights of individuals and communities in peace and conflict. Understand that individuals, organisations and governments have responsibility to ensure that rights are balanced, supported and protected.

3.2.4 Understand the United Nations' role in helping to resolve international disagreements and conflict. Understand that the United Kingdom, as a member country, is committed to adhere to the United Nations' agreements on human rights …

National Curriculum programme of study, key stage 4
Key concepts 1.1 b; 1.2 a; 1.3 c
Range and content 3 a, e, m

Q1 As the question indicates, each of the alternatives has a number of drawbacks.

The former Human Rights Commission was modelled on method B, with each member state voting for the country of its choice. This sometimes resulted in deals being struck in secret and in the election to the Commission of countries such as Zimbabwe, whom many felt had a very poor human rights record.

The membership of the current Human Rights Council is elected following method B. Although this seems to be an improvement on the previous body, criticisms remain that its membership still includes countries with poor human rights records.

Q2 In answer to this question, some students may argue in favour of countries trying to influence others by making trade agreements or development aid conditional on the maintenance or improvement of human rights. In the 1990s, President Clinton insisted that America's trading links with China were linked to specific improvements in human rights in that country.

Some students, however, may point out that those countries that are encouraging or requiring improvements in the human rights records of other nations may not be without fault themselves, a criticism that was particularly levelled against the United States under the presidency of George W. Bush.

Q3 There are possibly two points in favour of this argument. Giving a relatively low priority to human rights may help a country to develop more quickly by:
• focusing more of its resources on economic development, and
• removing various constraints that might hold back or slow down economic development.

On the other hand, a failure to uphold human rights is, arguably, morally and legally wrong, and may hold back the development of the country. It is widely acknowledged, for example, that improvements in the rights of women not only contribute to the lives of individuals, but also produce a more educated population and one that is much more able to contribute to the economic development of the country as a whole.

Family and school

> **Family**
> • Changing times
> • Parents' rights and responsibilities
> • Parents' rights and wrongs
>
> **School**
> • A right to education?
> • A matter of faith
> • School choice
> • Student voice

Family

This unit looks at the changing nature of the family and examines a number of issues surrounding parenting.

Changing times, pages 36–37

This topic looks at the way families have changed over the past 25 years and the diversity of family patterns.

> **OCR GCSE Citizenship Studies**
>
> **3.1.1** Understand the moral and legal rights and responsibilities that apply to our interactions with others and know that members of families have responsibilities (moral and legal) as well as rights
> **3.2.1** Understand that the United Kingdom is a country with wide cultural diversity where people's sense of identity is often complex.
>
> **National Curriculum programme of study, key stage 4**
> **Key concepts** 1.2 a; 1.3 a
> **Range and content** 3 a, l

Q1 Some of the advantages that students could identify are:
• the high level of support that may be available to members of a large family, particularly in times of difficulty
• greater levels of security both for children who are living at home and away from home.

Disadvantages may include:
• the financial and practical difficulties imposed by a large family
• children in large families may not receive as much parental guidance and support as those in smaller families
• some may argue that children who live at home into middle age are not as independent as those who leave at 18 or 19 years of age.

Q2 Students may suggest that marriage is no longer vital in a relationship and that living together is sufficient – perhaps a reflection of the decline in support for traditional religion.

Arguably many people also choose to remain independent to enable them to develop their career, or perhaps because they do not want to become completely tied to one person. This life choice, particularly for women, has become more accepted in recent years.

Q3 Students should observe that:
• the percentage of couples who marry has decreased, and
• the proportion of lone parent families and couples choosing to cohabit has increased.

Q4 Positive consequences may include:
• greater choices and possibilities on the way to structure a family

- less pressure on couples to remain in a marriage where they are unhappy
- the opportunity for couples to cohabit at first, rather than marry, to help them decide the long-term future of their relationship.

Negative consequences may include:
- in some circumstances single parent families or cohabiting couples may offer less stability for their children
- unmarried couples may be less inclined than married couples to try to overcome difficulties in their relationship
- unmarried partners generally have less legal and financial security than their married counterparts.

Q5 Family responsibilities, roles and patterns of behaviour may vary with regard to:
- looking after the house and garden (cooking, cleaning, washing, etc.)
- childcare
- disciplining children
- going to work
- financial responsibilities
- decision-making
- the kinds and levels of activities done together: eating together, talking, going out together
- discussions, arguments, dealing with difficulties
- keeping in touch with other family members.

Q6 Using the tax and benefit system to encourage parents to get married and stay together may provide greater stability for children, and help to ensure that people are more careful about entering into a relationship and having children.

However, some may argue that this intervention is ineffective because it fails to address the direct causes of family break-up. People may also argue that it is not a government's role to intervene in personal relationships or the way people choose to live their lives, and that people should not be forced to marry or to stay together if their relationship isn't working.

Parents' rights and responsibilities, pages 38–39

This topic looks at the rights and responsibilities of parents bringing up children.

OCR GCSE Citizenship Studies

3.1.1 Understand the moral and legal rights and responsibilities that apply to our interactions with others and know that members of families have responsibilities (moral and legal) as well as rights
3.1.4 Research and present a convincing argument in the context of our rights and responsibilities …

National Curriculum programme of study, key stage 4
Key concepts 1.2 a, b
Range and content 3 a

Q1 Ideas might include:
- escorting the young people to and from school and throughout their day
- making greater efforts to understand why the child is failing to attend school
- introducing truancy patrols in areas where children who are not attending school are known to go
- greater punishments for the parents of children who fail to attend school
- making more effort to help young people understand the importance of going to school
- changing the curriculum to make school more relevant for young people.

Q2 Some of the reasons that the law tries to keep parents and children together are:
- to maintain children's family and social ties
- reduce instability and maintain continuity for children.

Some of the difficulties with this are:
- children may be left in a home environment that is physically and/or emotionally damaging
- it can be hard to monitor what is happening in a child's home and to ensure that they are being cared for appropriately.

Q3 The key questions for magistrates are:
- the interests of the child, which should take priority
- the child's wishes, needs, age and background
- the capability of the child's parents and how much help they have already been given to improve things
- the degree to which the child is at risk of abuse or neglect
- the likely effect on the child of a change of circumstances.

Parents' rights and wrongs, pages 40–41

This topic looks at the subject of smacking children from legal and moral perspectives

---

OCR GCSE Citizenship Studies

3.1.1 Understand the moral and legal rights and responsibilities that apply to our interactions with others and know that members of families have responsibilities (moral and legal) as well as rights

3.1.4 Research and present a convincing argument in the context of our rights and responsibilities …

National Curriculum programme of study, key stage 4
Key concepts 1.2 a, b;
Range and content 3 a, f

Q1 Ideas could include:
- someone could speak to the child's mother, to offer help or to try to defuse the situation
- intervene and remove the child from the situation (but likely to be difficult and cause further conflict)
- ask the restaurant manager or other staff to do something
- call the police
- do nothing.

Q2 The key pieces of evidence that students could comment on are as follows:
- the statement from the witness saying that the mother hit the child with great force
- the statement from the manager who said that he called the police because the blow was so severe
- the mother's statement claiming that she loved her daughter and would never do anything to harm her.

The evidence indicates that the mother used unreasonable force, given that someone felt that the police should be called. Hitting her daughter around the face and twice on the bottom is rather forceful. However, some might argue that the mother's actions were done in the heat of the moment as her daughter was misbehaving and accept that this was a mistake.

In this case, the mother was found guilty of assault. In court, the judge said that parents must not be allowed to get into a culture of smacking children too hard, adding 'this lady needs help and support and a little bit of punishment that does not separate her from her children'.

Q3 Some students might argue that smacking is a decision for parents, and that the incident was none of the manager's business. As for the mother, she had had only acted in the heat of the moment when her daughter misbehaved.

Others might argue that the restaurant manager was right to call the police because the mother reacted so forcibly.

OCR Citizenship Studies Teacher's Resource Book for GCSE full and short course
© 2009 Hodder Education

Section 6: Answers to questions in the Student's Book

Q4 The text provides students with the key arguments for and against smacking. You may find it helpful to copy the points onto cards, asking students to sort and rank them according to how convincing they find each one.

Q5 This question may be used, by those students taking the OCR examination, as a starting point for a citizenship campaign.

School

The topics in this unit cover a number of issues: dealing in school with disruptive children, faith schools, parental choice and school democracy.

A right to education? Pages 42–43

This topic asks how schools should deal with disruptive students, in the light of the local authority's duty to provide all children in the area with an appropriate education.

OCR GCSE Citizenship Studies

3.2.2 Understand the ways in which rights can compete and conflict and how the law is used to resolve these issues justly

3.3.1 Know that members of the school/college community have responsibilities (moral and legal) as well as rights; understand the formal (legal) and informal means through which rights and responsibilities can be balanced, supported and safeguarded in schools

National Curriculum programme of study, key stage 4
Key concepts 1.1 b; 1.2 a, b, c
Range and content 3 a

Q1 The impact of Chris's behaviour on other students includes:
- less work can be completed in class
- students probably get less help and support from their teachers than they would otherwise
- this can be frustrating for them
- they may worry that they are not making as much progress as they should
- they may find Chris's behaviour upsetting
- their own behaviour may deteriorate as a result of their lack of achievement in class.

Q2 Action that the school could take includes:
- putting Chris on report
- providing Chris with support in class
- working with Chris's parents to try to improve his behaviour
- providing Chris with specialist support, such as anger management
- asking other students to 'buddy' Chris and help support him.

Q3 Arguably, the school has a legal and moral duty to help Chris. It has a statutory duty to provide him with an education, but also a moral duty to help him – perhaps because the reasons for his bad behaviour are beyond his control and he is unable to help himself. The school may be able to offer greater help and support with this than his parents.

Some students may argue that the school should not help Chris because he appears unwilling to help himself, and he is not the school's direct responsibility. In this case, you might like to ask them who they think should help him and why.

Q4&Q5 Some of the benefits and drawbacks of each option are as follows:

a) Fixed-term exclusion
- serves as a punishment for the student's behaviour
- gives the student time to reflect on their behaviour in school
- gives the school time to put a plan into place to help improve the student's behaviour.

However:
- the student may not see the exclusion as punishment, and might enjoy being away from school
- parents, particularly if they work, might not be able to monitor their child's behaviour during the day

- the punishment doesn't address the cause, but merely removes the student for a short time.

b) Permanent exclusion
- is almost the ultimate punishment for poor behaviour
- may give the student access to more specialist help.

However:
- it may take some time to find alternative education provision
- exclusion can have a negative impact on the student's self-esteem and perception of society and the education system
- it may fail to address the underlying problems.

c) School transfer
- may give Chris access to more specialised help and support
- will not cause a break in his education
- may allow him to start afresh, without other students expecting him to misbehave.

But:
- Chris may resent being pushed out of his old school
- he may miss his friends, and find it hard to settle
- it may just transfer the problem from one school to another.

d) Making arrangements for Chris to stay at his present school
- will not disrupt his schooling
- will avoid possible feelings of rejection, and make Chris respond positively.

However:
- the school might not be able to offer as much specialist help as in other settings
- his previous behaviour may mean that teachers and others are less keen to work with him
- he may feel that he has been let off and fail to make efforts to improve.

Q6 Students' ideas for avoiding permanent exclusion might include:
- having a strict and clear system for discipline that every teacher must follow
- putting all students on report if their behaviour is unsatisfactory
- rewarding students who exhibit good behaviour
- internally excluding pupils who misbehave, and having a special area where they can work
- providing more learning support in class.

Ideas for supporting excluded students could include:
- making sure they understand why they were excluded
- helping them get back into school
- helping them with other problems that might have contributed to their behaviour in school.

A matter of faith, pages 44–45

This topic looks at the role of religion in school, focusing in particular on faith schools.

OCR GCSE Citizenship Studies

3.2.1 Explore the diverse ... religious groups and communities in the United Kingdom and understand the different forces that bring about change in communities over time; understand ... the need for mutual respect and understanding ...

3.3.2 Evaluate and debate the different opinions on how far the state or individuals should take responsibility for the provision of ... education.

3.4.1 Understand the conditions which may lead to strain and conflict between communities in the UK

National Curriculum programme of study, key stage 4
Key concepts 1.2 b: 1.3 b
Range and content 3 l

Q1 Arguments in favour of setting up the school include:
- it enables Hindu families to carry on their traditions at home and at school
- the school meets the needs of many members of the local community
- children at the school are taught the National Curriculum and learn about their own religion.

Critics may argue:
- that having schools linked to a particular faith segregates the community
- that children will not get a balanced education because the focus of the school will inevitably be on Hindu beliefs
- that religion should be taught and practised at home – not at school.

Q2 Some of the arguments in favour of refusing a child entry to a school on the basis of religion (or the lack of it) are:
- the ethos of the school may be unsuitable for the child
- certain parts of the school's curriculum will be irrelevant to the child
- the place at school would be better used by giving it to someone from a family who were practising members of the religion.

Some of the arguments against could be:
- being refused entry may mean that the child has to travel a long way to an alternative school
- discriminating on the basis of religion is and not permitted in other areas of life
- restricting admission to children of a certain religious background is divisive.

Q3 Arguments in favour of forcing faith schools to take children from other/non-religious backgrounds include:
- it may help to prevent segregation within a community
- it may more accurately reflect the cultural and social mix of the area
- allowing children to attend their local school avoids the problem of some having to travel long distances for their education.

Arguments against compulsion include:
- that many faith schools would find it difficult to keep their religious character if most of the pupils were from outside the faith
- if most places went to local children, others who would genuinely welcome and benefit from a faith-based education, but lived outside the area, would be prevented from attending.

Q4 Students could consider many of the views expressed in questions 1 to 3 in answer to this. For alternative policies, they might suggest that schools should not be based around one particular faith, but should instead educate young people about all faiths, or perhaps that faith education is not the school's job.

School choice, pages 46–47

This topic raises the issue of parental choice in education, and asks whether this, or other approaches, should determine which school a young person attends.

OCR GCSE Citizenship Studies

3.3.1 Understand the formal (legal) and informal means through which rights and responsibilities can be balanced, supported and safeguarded in schools

3.3.2 Understand the Government's role in ... the planning and regulation of public services. Evaluate and debate the different opinions on how far the state or individuals should take responsibility for the provision of ... education

National Curriculum programme of study, key stage 4
Key concepts 1.1 b, d; 1.2 a, b
Range and content 3 a

Q1 Students may suggest that Mr and Mrs Watson should make their decision on the basis of:

- what they believe is in Priya's best interests, selecting the school that they feel would best meet her needs
- Priya's own views and wishes
- the school offering the best facilities
- what they can afford (or not afford to do)
- how Priya and the rest of her family would be able to handle a long journey to and from school.

Q2 Students might identify the independent school option as being unobtainable given Mr and Mrs Watson's income. They might also decide that the grammar school and Catholic school are too far away to be viable options. Some students might not agree with having to take an entrance examination for the grammar school and discount this. They may feel that examinations put pressure on children and that they could feel like a failure if they do not pass. It may be interesting to explore here students' perspectives on key factors in school choice, for example, location, facilities, retaining contact with friends etc.

Q3 Students' responses may include the following points:

a) 'All parents have a right to choose where their children are educated.'

For: parents have the right to decide what kind of education is best for their children; giving parents a choice makes schools more competitive and improves the overall standard of education

Against: wider choice can lead to less cohesive communities, as young people end up attending schools far away from home; it is very difficult to judge a school, sometimes parents make judgments on very minor factors; parents and children will not always get their first choice, which can lead to disappointment; choice tends to favour children from a wealthier background, whose parents are more likely to have the resources to obtain a place for their child in the school of their choice.

b) 'The more choice you give, the more you raise expectations, and the more you are disappointed.'

For: many parents and children will not obtain their first choice of school, some schools will be heavily over-subscribed and disappointment is inevitable; placing a child in school becomes increasingly random and uncertain, neither of these benefit the children, school or parents.

Against: the need to compete for students encourages schools to try to continually improve their standards and facilities; in a competitive environment, parents gain more information about the schools that their child might attend.

c) 'Choice doesn't help me decide where my children go to school; public transport is poor where I live, and I can't drive. Choice benefits children from wealthier families.'

For: wealthier families are more likely to have the resources and knowledge to be able to research schools more fully and make an informed choice; wealthier families are more likely to be able to pay the extra travel costs involved in sending a child to school outside the immediate local area.

Against: even though this may be the case, parents should still be given the opportunity for their child to attend the school of their choice; many parents are very resourceful and will find ways to overcome the extra expense that may be involved.

Q4 All of the key arguments for and against these options are covered in the answers to questions 1–3.

Student voice, pages 48–49

This topic considers the role of schools councils and the importance of student voice.

OCR GCSE Citizenship Studies

3.1.1 Engage in responsible action to develop the school community, including understanding the benefits of an active School Council or Student Council

3.2.3 Engage in different democratic decision-making exercises that have an influence on school or community life.

3.3.1 Know that members of the school/college community have responsibilities (moral and legal) as well as rights. Understand the formal (legal) and informal means through which rights and responsibilities can be balanced, supported and safeguarded in schools.

National Curriculum programme of study, key stage 4
Key concepts 1.1 a, b; 1.2 b, c
Range and content 3 d, h

Q1 Some advantages that students might identify include:
- it ensures that every student has the chance to express their views to the head teacher
- some students may feel more confident to voice opinions away from their peers
- an informal system could be more productive than the student council, which may not meet very frequently and is limited by time in what it can discuss.

Potential disadvantages include:
- views raised by individual students may not be representative of the student body as a whole
- some students may not feel comfortable speaking directly to the head
- there is no formal system to record or take forward students' ideas.

Q2 Some of the contrasts and comparisons that could be made are:
- both schools are of a similar size
- the schools differ in the way in which members of the councils are selected
- there is a big difference in the size of the main school councils; in one school there are six representatives, and in the other, there are 60
- one school has several adults on their main school council (the head, staff, a governor and a parent), the other has two teachers
- both school councils seem to discuss a variety of issues, but some of those discussed by council in Havenden seem to bee of more strategic importance.

Q3 The student is critical of the school council because she feels that it is only able to impact on minor issues within the school. She believes that students should also have a say on those policies affecting students' education.

Improvements could be made by:
- widening the scope of the school council to include policy decisions
- ensuring that staff and students understand the role of the school council, and developing a constitution
- giving students a wider role in the operational elements of the school, for example by electing student governors or involving them in appointing senior members of staff.

Q4 Students may suggest that a school council should not:
- discuss student exclusion, because of its legal aspects and the need for confidentiality
- discuss child protection issues, which are also sensitive and confidential
- be involved in major financial and strategic decisions, where responsibility ultimately lies with the head teacher and governing body.

Q5 Students may identify that school councils are not always representative because only a small proportion may attend meetings and may not necessarily voice the views of those whom they represent. This could be addressed by:
- rotating student membership of students, although this may lead to a lack of continuity
- instigating a system to ensure that, prior to meetings, council members gather the views of the group they represent
- publishing the agenda and minutes of meeting to give all students an opportunity to comment and contribute
- having comments box that any student can contribute to, anonymously.

Q6 Students might identify issues such as:
- subject options
- the teaching of specific topics/subject areas
- facilities and equipment
- travel to and from school
- behaviour policies
- school uniform
- assemblies/form time.

This question may be used, by those students taking the OCR examination, as a starting point for a citizenship campaign.

Consumer Law

Consumer rights
- Contract
- When things go wrong
- Borrowing money
- Selling old as new
- Dangerous goods

Consumer complaints
- Taking action
- Problem solving – a guide

Consumer rights

The topics in this unit are designed to give students an understanding of their legal rights as consumers.

Contract, pages 50–51

This topic outlines the nature of the contract that consumers and retailers enter into when buying and selling goods or services.

OCR GCSE Citizenship Studies

3.1.2 Understand that the rights of consumers and businesses can compete and conflict but that both have legal rights and responsibilities towards each other when items are bought and sold, and that rights are supported and protected by statutory and non-statutory bodies.

3.3.2 Understand that the laws relating to … the sale of goods need to recognise the interests of … buyers, sellers …

National Curriculum programme of study, key stage 4
Key concepts 1.2 a, c
Range and content 3 a, k

Q1 Picture A
The coffee is cold: if the coffee is served to the customer cold (or not as hot as it should be) the café owner has almost certainly broken the contract made with her. An implied term of a contract of this kind is that the coffee supplied should be hot. If it is not, the contract has been broken.

The failure of the café to provide the customer with coffee that is hot also breaks one of the provisions of the *Sale of Goods Act 1979* (outlined in the student textbook, page 61). Cold coffee, in this context, is clearly not of *satisfactory quality*. The customer is entitled to her money back.

The customer would rather have tea: the contract has been broken by the customer.

Picture B
The customer buys the PC, but later decides she can't afford it: there is little the customer can do if, having already purchased and paid for the PC, she realises that the cost is beyond her means. The contract has been completed, with the shop supplying the PC and the customer paying the agreed price.

If the customer agreed to pay for the computer in a series of instalments and fails to make payments in accordance with the agreement, she will have broken her contract. In these circumstances, the shop will almost certainly be entitled to damages to compensate them and possibly the return of the computer itself – depending on the exact terms of the agreement.

Some credit agreements may be cancelled within a five-day cooling off period but, generally speaking, only if they were signed somewhere other than the trader's or creditor's business premises, for example in the customer's home.

The customer has to wait much longer than expected for the computer to be delivered: if the customer specified a time limit when placing her order, to which the shop agreed, the contract has been broken. The delay in delivery means that a specific term of the contract has not been met. The customer is entitled to compensation for any loss suffered as a result.

If a delivery time is not specified at the time of purchase, the retailer is expected to deliver the goods in a 'reasonable time'. Exactly what this is depends on the circumstances of the case – perhaps the goods need to be sent from abroad, or specially manufactured. However, if the delivery time became unreasonably long, the customer would be entitled to terminate the contract and withdraw from the sale – and ask for the return of any money that she had paid. It is in this kind of circumstance, however, that either side may seek legal advice and representation or eventual recourse to the law, perhaps through the small claims procedure (see page 60 of the student textbook).

Picture C

The customer wishes to change the carton of orange juice for a cheaper brand: if the customer changes her mind *before* paying for the juice, there is no contract, and she still has the right to change the carton for a cheaper brand. If the juice has already been paid for, the shop is under no obligation to change the goods – although the shop may agree to do this as a gesture of goodwill.

The drinking chocolate is wrongly priced: once again the first question is whether the customer and shop have already entered into a contract. There is no contract until the customer pays for the drinking chocolate and the cashier is entitled to ask for a further £2. The customer must decide whether to pay the additional sum or to refuse to buy the chocolate.

However, if the customer has already paid for the item, a contract has been formed. This means that the shop cannot change the price. The customer need not pay the additional two pounds.

Q2 The disappointments faced by Elaine and Gary include:
the unexpected charges of a number of the facilities at the resort, which the couple had expected to be free
- the need to travel outside the resort in order to learn how to scuba dive
- the absence of certain facilities, such as archery and proper training machines
- unexpected limitations on the availability of free alcoholic drinks
- the high additional costs of the holiday.

Q3 Responsibility for the failure of the holiday to live up to expectations lies with either or both the tour operator and the hotel manager.

If, as the hotel manager stated, the travel company continued to offer the holiday in its brochure, despite knowing that some of these arrangements had been withdrawn earlier in the year, then responsibility for the disappointment lies with the tour operator.

As well as failing to meet its obligations under civil law, the tour operator may also have committed a criminal offence under the *Trade Descriptions Act 1968* by deliberately describing the facilities available in an inaccurate and misleading way.

However, it is also possible that the hotel was simply failing to offer the facilities that it had agreed with the operator to provide and that the manager was lying. In this case, the hotel would also be responsible for the honeymooners' disappointment. In practice many tour operators will accept responsibility in these circumstances and in turn claim against the hotel.

Q4 In their letter to the tour operator, Elaine and Gary could:
- point out the way in which the holiday was advertised, enclosing a copy of the relevant section of the tour operator's brochure – since goods and services must be 'as described' (*Sale of Goods Act 1979* and the *Supply of Goods and Services Act 1982*)
- explain how the holiday they experienced differed from the one described in the brochure, outlining, for example, the lack of archery and scuba diving facilities, and the

limited choice of free drinks. They should also include a copy of the list of free services and facilities which they were provided with on arrival, to demonstrate how this differs from the advertisement in the brochure
- outline the damage that they have suffered for which they wish to claim compensation from the tour operator. This will amount to the difference between the value of the holiday they actually received, and the one that they paid for. In this case, it appears that this difference will be at least £600, since Gary states that 'The fortnight's holiday cost £3,000 – and I reckon that we had to pay another £600 just to do the things that we had planned.'

Our legal system does not allow a person, under these circumstances, to make a claim for disappointment. However Gary and Elaine may wish to stress how much their holiday fell short of their expectations in the hope of obtaining a goodwill payment from the tour operator for this inconvenience.

In law, Gary and Elaine are entitled to compensation for breach of contract by the tour operator. Strictly this means working out the cost of the holiday that they actually had, and compensating them for the extra paid.

In this particular case, Elaine and Gary complained to the tour operator as soon as they got home, and were offered £100, first in holiday vouchers, and then in cash. It was at this stage that they sought advice from their local trading standards office, where they were advised to take their case to the local small claims court. The tour operator then raised their offer to £545, which Gary and Elaine rejected, eventually settling out of court for £1,000.

In a separate action, the local trading standards office brought its own case against the tour operator, which was heard at the local magistrates' court. The company pleaded guilty to giving misleading and inaccurate information in their brochure and were fined £2,000.

When things go wrong, pages 52–53

This topic looks at consumer rights from a historical perspective and introduces students to the Sale of Goods Act 1979.

OCR GCSE Citizenship Studies

3.1.2 Understand that the rights of consumers and businesses … are supported and protected by statutory and non-statutory bodies.

3.3.2 Understand that laws relating to … the production … and sale of goods need to recognise the interests of … buyers, sellers… Understand how these interests can compete and conflict.

National Curriculum programme of study, key stage 4
Key concepts 1.2 a, b
Range and content 3 a, k

Q1

Peter: the retailer from whom Peter bought the CD has failed, under the *Sale of Goods Act 1979,* to sell goods 'as described'.

Peter should immediately return the CD he was sent in error. He is entitled to receive either the item he actually ordered or a full refund. However, if he uses the CD, or fails to return it within a reasonable time, he may be treated in law to have accepted the goods and it will be much more difficult for him to claim a refund or exchange.

Chris: if Chris received the wrong item after showing his watch to the retailer and asking for a battery to fit it, he has the right to return the battery and claim a refund or exchange it for a battery of the right size.

If, however, he simply bought the wrong size battery in error, Chris has no right to ask for a refund or an exchange. The shop may be willing to swap the item for him as a gesture of goodwill, but is not required to do so by law. Once again he should return the item as soon as possible.

Lena: the television bought by Lena is not of 'satisfactory quality', as required by the *Sale of Goods Act 1979*. She is entitled to return the set and claim a refund.

Goods sold by businesses to consumers should be free from defects, such as scratches to the casing. Again she should return the item as soon as possible.

Jasmine: the instructions for the assembly of the unit form part of the goods sold to Jasmine and are subject to the *Sale of Goods Act 1979* – which means that they should be 'fit for their intended purpose'.

If the instructions are difficult to follow they are not suitable for their intended purpose of enabling the customer to assemble the furniture in question, and Jasmine has a right to return the unit on this basis.

Jasmine's difficulty in putting the unit together also suggests that it is not easy to assemble, as stated on the packaging. Jasmine may therefore be entitled to return the unit on the basis that it is not 'as described' on the box. Once again she should return the item as soon as possible.

Vicky: unfortunately for Vicky, she has no claim against her colleague over the unsatisfactory quality of the car under the *Sale of Goods Act 1979*. Goods bought privately are not subject to the requirement that they are of 'satisfactory quality'.

However, under the *Sale of Goods Act 1979* second-hand items sold privately must be 'as described'. Therefore, if Vicky's colleague told her that the car was particularly roadworthy, had no major faults, and had been tested by a reliable garage to ensure this, she may have a claim against him under this provision.

She may also be able to claim for misrepresentation, provided that it can be shown that her colleague made a false statement that led her to buy the car, which he either knew was false or had reasonable grounds to believe was not true.

Borrowing money, pages 54–55

This topic introduces the concepts of credit and debt and considers the benefits and problems associated with borrowing money.

OCR GCSE Citizenship Studies

3.1.1 Understand the moral and legal rights and responsibilities that apply to our interactions with others …

3.1.2 Understand that the rights of consumers and businesses … are supported and protected by statutory and non-statutory bodies.

3.3.2 Understand that laws relating to … the production … and sale of goods need to recognise the interests of … buyers, sellers… Understand how these interests can compete and conflict.

National Curriculum programme of study, key stage 4
1. Key concepts 1.2 b
3. Range and content 3 a, k

Q1 The advice students may give may include the following:
- to seek guidance and advice from organisations such as the Citizens Advice Bureau
- to stop using her credit cards and try to pay off the amount owing as quickly as she can
- to explain her position to the bank and credit card companies
- to look for further ways of saving money and reducing her debts, possibly including the sale of her car
- check to see if she is paying excessively high rates of interest on her existing loans and whether cheaper loans are available
- to look for ways of increasing her income, for example by looking for a better-paid job, taking a second job, or (if permitted) by taking in an extra person to share her flat.

Q2 Nikki has prime responsibility for her debts, because of her failure to manage her money as carefully as she should. Students might also identify the companies that gave her the credit and store cards as having some responsibility as they should have been aware of the debts she already had when undertaking credit checks. This particularly applies if credit and store card companies had written to Nikki offering her credit.

Q3 Students may suggest that the benefits of the widespread availability of credit provide:
- opportunities for people to pay for expensive items (over a period of time), giving them access to goods and services that they would not otherwise be able to afford
- greater choice and lower interest rates as credit companies compete for custom. (Teachers may like to question and examine this point in more detail with students.)

Some of the drawbacks include:
- the widespread availability of credit may result in some people borrowing more than they can afford to pay back, and result in unmanageable debts
- excessive debt can give rise to a number of personal and social problems, placing particular stress on family and social relationships
- easy credit may encourage some people to be frivolous with their spending – buying things they neither need nor can afford

Q4 Suggestions here may include:
- lower limits on the amount of credit a person can have, particularly for those on a low income
- better school and public education on budgeting and personal finance, warning people of the consequences of debt and to help them manage their money properly
- greater regulation of the financial services industry to limit the ways in which companies can offer credit, such as through mass mailings and phone calls

Selling old as new, pages 56–57

In this topic, students are introduced to the problem of false descriptions of goods by traders, and the consequences of selling dangerous goods

---

OCR GCSE Citizenship Studies

3.1.1 Understand the moral and legal rights and responsibilities that apply to our interactions with others …

3.1.2 Understand that the rights of consumers and businesses … are supported and protected by statutory and non-statutory bodies.

3.2.2 Know how legal advice and support may be obtained

3.3.2 Understand that laws relating to … the production … and sale of goods need to recognise the interests of … buyers, sellers… Understand how these interests can compete and conflict.

National Curriculum programme of study, key stage 4
Key concepts 1.1 b
Range and content 3 a, k

Q1 A lawyer's answer to the question is that falsely describing something for sale is a crime because it was made a crime under the *Trade Descriptions Act 1968*. But why exactly is it a crime?

For many years, dishonest trading has been regarded by society as an issue of such significance that the state itself should intervene to deal with the matter; and it is intervention by the state that gives actions the status of a crime. In this case, local trading standards officers have the power to prosecute a dishonest trader in a criminal court, possibly resulting in a fine or even imprisonment.

This is in contrast to a civil matter, in which the state does not directly become involved. Instead it is up to the individual to take their own case to court, if no other solution can be found, where a judge will decide on the merits of the case.

Q2
- Item *A* is relevant since it suggests that the slides were not unsafe – many are in use and (presumably) no other accidents have occurred.
- Items *B* and *F* could be used as evidence that the slide was defective, since the company has now modified the design.

- Item *C* provides important evidence, because it has been given by an expert. An expert's opinion on technical matters carries more weight in court than the evidence of an ordinary witness.
- Item *D* would probably not be regarded as significant. Generally it supports the point made in *A* above.
- Statement *E* is relevant, as the company will use this to argue that Chloe's mother was responsible for the accident by allowing her three-year-old-child to play on the slide unsupervised.
- Statement *G* is not, in itself, evidence that the slide was or was not unsafe.
- Item *H*, like *A*, indicates that the slide is safe, but also suggests it requires supervision.

Q5 In court the company from whom Chloe's mother had bought the slide was found guilty of selling an unsafe toy. The company was fined £4,000 and ordered to pay £1,123 costs.

Consumer complaints

This unit outlines what consumers can do if they have a complaint about a good or service they have been sold.

Taking action, pages 58–59

This topic looks at what consumers should do if something they purchase is faulty.

OCR GCSE Citizenship Studies

3.1.1 Understand the moral and legal rights and responsibilities that apply to our interactions with others …

3.1.2 Understand that the rights of consumers and businesses … are supported and protected by statutory and non-statutory bodies.

3.3.2 Understand that laws relating to … the production … and sale of goods need to recognise the interests of … buyers, sellers… Understand how these interests can compete and conflict.

National Curriculum programme of study, key stage 4
Key concepts 1.2 a
Range and content 3 a, k

Q1 Difficulties faced by Mrs O'Dell might include:
- the time, the cost and the inconvenience of calling the manufacturer to arrange repairs
- the cost and inconvenience of having to find some other way of getting her washing done
- the losses associated with taking time off work to wait for the engineer to call.

Q2 The main difficulty seems to be the time, effort and frustration involved in trying to get the manufacturer to deal with the problem properly.

Q3 Commenting on this case, a lawyer said that, although the manufacturer complied with Mrs O'Dell's requests (albeit slowly), it does seems that the machine is defective, since the replacement parts did not solve the problem.

The lawyer felt that Mrs O'Dell should ask for the machine to be replaced either by the shop from which she bought it or by the manufacturer. If they are unwilling to do this, Mrs O'Dell should return the machine and ask for a full refund.

Strictly speaking Mrs O'Dell's contract is with the firm who sold her the machine, which has a responsibility under the *Sale of Goods Act 1979* that the goods sold are of a reasonable quality and fit for the purpose for which they were sold. It is reasonable to expect a washing machine to work for more than six months before breaking down (assuming that Mrs O'Dell used it in the correct manner).

If Mrs O'Dell is unable to obtain a replacement or refund, she may bring court proceedings against the store where she purchased the washer. Advice and help in doing this is available from a solicitor or her local Citizens Advice Bureau.

In fact, on hearing from the engineer that there would be a further delay, Mrs O'Dell decided to take matters into her own hands. She blocked the engineer's van in her drive and locked him in the house, explaining that he was allowed one phone call and one drink, but would not be released until her machine had been repaired or replaced. Resisting the efforts of the police to break the deadlock, Mrs O'Dell held out for three hours – until the makers promised to replace her machine.

By taking this action, Mrs O'Dell was in fact breaking the law herself, as the engineer could easily have chosen to bring an action against Mrs O'Dell for unlawful detention.

Q4 The legal position is as follows:

Louisa reported the matter to her local trading standards department who, after investigating her claim, decided to prosecute the supermarket from which she had bought the bread pudding.

Two other serious complaints had also been made about products made in this particular company's in-store bakery, and the supermarket chain was fined a total of £40,000.

Louisa also had a civil remedy available to her and was able to claim a refund of the cost of the bread pudding. Her son did not, in this case, suffer any injury and was therefore not eligible for compensation.

Adam has a claim against the seller since the package that he bought is not as the sales assistant described *(Sale of Goods Act 1979)*. Given the sum of money involved, Adam may well feel it is worth taking his case to the small claims court. He should contact a local solicitor, the Citizens Advice Bureau or his local county court in order to launch a claim.

Should the case go to court, Adam will need to provide evidence of the sales assistant's claims about the speed of the printer – although he could additionally argue that, by today's standards, a package that takes a minute to print a normal page of text is not of satisfactory quality – again as laid down in the *Sale of Goods Act 1979*.

Clive may have rights under the *Sale of Goods Act 1979*, which requires goods sold to be of a satisfactory quality. However, it applies only to goods sold in the course of the seller's business. If the seller was running a car sales business, the Act applies and Clive has a claim against the seller. Even if the seller was not selling in the course of business it is possible that Clive would have an alternative claim since the seller may have made a misrepresentation under the *Misrepresentation Act 1967*.

In both cases the question will be whether the term used to describe the car, '*a good runner*', is a really factual statement about the vehicle, or just exaggerated sales talk with no clear meaning.

If Clive bought the car from a dealer he has a good case under the *Sale of Goods Act 1979*. However, if it was a private sale he would have to rely on misrepresentation and is less likely to succeed, since he would have to prove that the seller's description of the car as '*a good runner*' was an intentional attempt to mislead.

Yvonne believes that she entered into a contract with the shop to buy a bath at a price of £340. However, she could find the shop claiming that this price was just a quote and not a firm offer to supply the bath at the agreed price. If the figure of £340 was merely a quotation, Yvonne would have no legal redress. Under these circumstances receipts or a copy of a sale agreement provide important evidence in support of Yvonne's case.

The Citizens Advice Bureau, a Law Centre or solicitor would help Yvonne decide whether or not she has a case in law and, if she does, will help her pursue her claim in the small claims division of the local county court.

Sairah can ask the store to repair or replace the television, but, as she bought it more than six months ago, the store can ask her to prove that it was faulty at the time of purchase. If the television had broken down within six months, the store would have to accept that they were faulty at the time of purchase. You can ask a shop to repair or replace an item for up to six years after purchase if it is reasonable to expect it to have lasted that long.

If the store cannot repair or replace the item, fails to do this within a reasonable period of time or if the repair would cause significant inconvenience, Sairah can ask for some or all of her money back. It is likely that she would only get some of her money back as the television worked for some time before the fault occurred.

Lenny will find that the shop is not required to take the disk drive back. As far as they are concerned, Lenny has simply changed his mind about the purchase because he has seen it for less, elsewhere.

Many shops do offer to refund the difference if a consumer finds the same item for less elsewhere within a certain time period. But they are not legally obliged to do this.

Problem-solving – a guide, pages 60–61

This topic outlines the main areas of law covering everyday purchases, and indicates where people might be able to get help in the event of a consumer dispute.

OCR GCSE Citizenship Studies

3.1.2 Understand that the rights of consumers and businesses … are supported and protected by statutory and non-statutory bodies.
3.2.2 Know how legal advice and support may be obtained.
3.3.1 Evaluate the additional formal and independent support available to individuals requiring information and advice, including that available from Government departments, agencies and official regulators, Citizens advice, consumer protection or rights organisations and solicitors.

National Curriculum programme of study, key stage 4
Key concepts 1.2 a
Range and content 3 a, k

Employment

> **Looking for work**
> - Equal opportunities
> - Race discrimination
>
> **Fairness at work**
> - Religious discrimination
> - Sexuality and age discrimination
> - Disability discrimination
>
> **Working for a living**
> - In work
> - A working life
>
> **Trade unions**
> - Trade unions
> - Employers' organisations
> - Working hours
>
> **Losing your job**
> - Fired!
> - Claiming unfair dismissal
> - The employment tribunal

Looking for work

The two units in the chapter focus primarily on sex and race discrimination at work.

Equal opportunities (Car crazy), pages 62–63

This two-part topic examines sex discrimination and stereotypes in employment.

> **OCR GCSE Citizenship Studies**
>
> **3.1.1** Understand the moral and legal rights and responsibilities that apply to our interactions with others …
> **3.1.2** Understand that employers and employees have rights and responsibilities that compete and conflict and that employees can be supported by trade unions.
> **3.2.2** Understand the importance of the law in maintaining order, resolving conflict and achieving just outcomes …
> **3.3.2** Understand that laws relating to employment … need to recognise the interests of employers, employees … Understand how these interests can compete and conflict.
> **3.4.1** Evaluate the effectiveness of the law in discouraging unfair discrimination.
>
> **National Curriculum programme of study, key stage 4**
> **Key concepts** 1.1 b; 1.2 a, c
> **Range and content** 3 a, b, k

Q1 Questions that Karen was asked that might not have been asked of a man going for the same job include:
- Did she mind getting her hands dirty?
- Did she think she would 'fit in'?

Q2 A tribunal decided that Karen had been unlawfully discriminated against. Despite Karen being the best qualified of the candidates, and with relevant work experience, the apprenticeships were given to two boys.

Q3 Karen was awarded £24,000 in compensation for loss of earnings and injury to her feelings.

In cases where employers are found to have broken the *Sex Discrimination Act 1975*, employment tribunals may:
- order compensation for a victim's financial loss, injury to feelings, or injury to health

- award exemplary damages, that is, award additional money to punish the employer (only awarded in serious or repeat cases)
- recommend further action that the employer might take, for example to display an apology to the complainant on the staff notice board.

Q4 Answers here are likely to suggest that this is largely a result of the effects of stereotypes in the workplace and in society more generally – that is, women and men being selected for particular jobs, and aspiring for particular careers in line with traditional female/male stereotypes.

Q5 The dominance of certain genders in particular careers is not necessarily a bad thing. Men and women may be better suited to certain types of job, and society doesn't necessarily push them into this.

However, students might suggest that stereotypes could prevent young people from pursuing careers that are not 'usual' for their gender. It may also lead to people being taunted if they choose to follow a non-stereotypical career path, both by their peers and in the work place.

Q6 Although the question is asking students to think about male and female capabilities in general, it may be helpful here to know that the law does allow sex discrimination in employment in certain circumstances. For example, a male actor may be chosen for a male role in a play, and a female police officer may be selected to counsel female victims of crime. In addition, the European courts have ruled that it is not illegal to specify that only women can apply for a job as a midwife.

Equal opportunities (Train departure), pages 64–65

This topic introduces the idea of direct and indirect discrimination and outlines some of the issues relating to equal pay for men and women

---

OCR GCSE Citizenship Studies

3.1.1 Understand the moral and legal rights and responsibilities that apply to our interactions with others …

3.1.2 Understand that employers and employees have rights and responsibilities that compete and conflict and that employees can be supported by trade unions.

3.2.2 Understand the importance of the law in maintaining order, resolving conflict and achieving just outcomes …

3.3.2 Understand that laws relating to employment … need to recognise the interests of employers, employees … Understand how these interests can compete and conflict.

3.4.1 Evaluate the effectiveness of the law in discouraging unfair discrimination.

National Curriculum programme of study, key stage 4
Key concepts 1.1 b; 1.2 a, c
Range and content 3 a, b, e, k

Q1 Answers are as follows:
- *Judy:* direct discrimination
- *Neil:* direct discrimination
- *Linda:* indirect discrimination, and also direct age discrimination
- *Nathan:* direct discrimination
- *Rhianna:* direct discrimination.

Q2 Students may explain the continuing pay gap because:
- women are more likely to take a career break after having a baby, and so take longer to progress to higher paid positions
- women are more likely to work part-time (and earn less) to enable them to spend more time with their children
- traditional female employment, for example nursing or administrative work, is often less well paid.

Q3 This question could be tackled by dividing the class into groups that represent for and against each scenario. The groups can then decide on their key arguments from what they have learnt and, if there is time, additional research and present their findings. The group can then vote on which they think is the best option.

Race discrimination, pages 66–67

This topic unit outlines how race discrimination at work may be dealt with in law.

OCR GCSE Citizenship Studies

3.1.1 Understand the moral and legal rights and responsibilities that apply to our interactions with others …

3.1.2 Understand that employers and employees have rights and responsibilities that compete and conflict and that employees can be supported by trade unions.

3.2.1 Understand the interdependence of individuals, groups and communities, the need for mutual respect and understanding …

3.2.2 Understand the importance of the law in maintaining order, resolving conflict and achieving just outcomes …

3.3.2 Understand that laws relating to employment … need to recognise the interests of employers, employees … Understand how these interests can compete and conflict.

3.4.1 Evaluate the effectiveness of the law in discouraging unfair discrimination.

3.4.2 Understand the role of individuals, lawyers and courts in the civil legal and justice system.

National Curriculum programme of study, key stage 4
Key concepts 1.1 b; 1.2 a, c
Range and content 3 a, b, e, k

Q1 The key points of evidence in this case are:

- that Suzanne was rejected for the job when she was interviewed, despite holding all the necessary qualifications
- Mr Wheeler's reaction when Suzanne attended a second interview
- Mr Wheeler's comment to Deborah.

Q2 The employment tribunal decided that the colour of Suzanne's skin was an important factor in Mr Wheeler's decision to reject her application. She was awarded (in 1980) £75 for injury to feelings and loss of opportunity.

Mr Wheeler appealed against this decision, but this was dismissed by the Employment Appeal Tribunal. The Tribunal decided that Mr Wheeler had acted in breach of the *Race Relations Act* because he had treated Ms Jones less favourably than the other applicants (for example Ms Cook) on the grounds of the colour of her skin.

Q3 Mr Wheeler's prejudice was possibly based on the view that non-white applicants were intrinsically less suited to the work (and less capable) than others.

Q4 Some of the key arguments in favour of such legislation might include:
- it prevents unfair treatment on the basis of race, and reduces the likelihood of significant numbers of people being treated unfairly
- it gives people an opportunity to act on unfair treatment.

Fairness at work

The three topics in this unit deal with different types of discrimination in the workplace.

Religious discrimination, pages 68–69

This topic outlines the law protecting people from religious discrimination at work, and asks students to consider whether the law should be extended further.

OCR GCSE Citizenship Studies

3.1.1 Understand the moral and legal rights and responsibilities that apply to our interactions with others …

3.1.2 Understand that employers and employees have rights and responsibilities that compete and conflict and that employees can be supported by trade unions.

3.2.2 Understand the importance of the law in maintaining order, resolving conflict and achieving just outcomes …

3.3.2 Understand that laws relating to employment … need to recognise the interests of employers, employees … Understand how these interests can compete and conflict.

3.4.1 Evaluate the effectiveness of the law in discouraging unfair discrimination.

National Curriculum programme of study, key stage 4
Key concepts 1.1 b, c; 1.2 a, c; 1.3 a, b
Range and content 3 a, b, e, k, l

Q1

a) Sarah took her case to an employment tribunal where she claimed religious discrimination and constructive dismissal as a victim (constructive dismissal refers to a situation in which an employee is forced to resign because of their employer's behaviour).

After listening to the evidence from both sides, the tribunal decided that being a Christian was not a genuine occupational requirement for many of the charity's employees – including Sarah. The tribunal unanimously agreed that Sarah had suffered unlawful discrimination and had been constructively dismissed.

b) Aisha took her case to an employment tribunal, reportedly claiming direct discrimination and compensation to the value of £15,000 for injury to her feelings. The tribunal rejected the claim of direct discrimination, but did find that Aisha had been indirectly discriminated against. She received £4,000 compensation for injury to feelings.

Commenting about this case in the press, a number of articles argued that (i) this case was more about our litigious society than religious discrimination, (ii) cases of this kind are particularly damaging to small businesses, (iii) that the case might not have come to the tribunal had the owner of the salon made up an excuse, and not given the real reason, for deciding not to employ Aisha.

Q2 Students may argue that significant days for religions other than Christianity should be recognised as public holidays to ensure that everyone is treated equally. They may add that this may also help to inform people about other religions and their festivals.

However, they may also state that if all major religious celebrations became public holidays, many employers and businesses would face extra costs. The effect of this could be reduced if holiday time was given only to those who were regular practitioners, but regulating this could be very difficult. Arguably, a measure of this kind would also be unfair to atheists and others who do not belong to religion.

Students may like to consider the case for replacing religious with national holidays, as a fairer solution.

This question may be used, by those students taking the OCR examination, as a starting point for a citizenship campaign.

Sexuality and age discrimination, pages 70–71

This topic outlines the law relating discrimination at work on grounds of sexuality and age, and asks students to consider the need for further changes in the law.

Section 6: Answers to questions in the Student's Book

> **OCR GCSE Citizenship Studies**
>
> **3.1.1** Understand the moral and legal rights and responsibilities that apply to our interactions with others …
>
> **3.1.2** Understand that employers and employees have rights and responsibilities that compete and conflict and that employees can be supported by trade unions.
>
> **3.2.2** Understand the importance of the law in maintaining order, resolving conflict and achieving just outcomes …
>
> **3.3.2** Understand that laws relating to employment … need to recognise the interests of employers, employees … Understand how these interests can compete and conflict.
>
> **3.4.1** Evaluate the effectiveness of the law in discouraging unfair discrimination.
>
> **National Curriculum programme of study, key stage 4**
> **Key concepts** 1.1 b, c; 1.2 a, c;
> **Range and content** 3 a, b, f, k,

Q1 None of the advertisements obviously break the age discrimination regulations because they do not require applicants to be of a particular age. However, the wording of some may, arguably, indicate discriminatory intent:

- *James Gilinski*: the term 'youthful enthusiasm' could be interpreted as being discriminatory as it might discourage older people from applying. However, the company could argue that a person does not need to be young to have 'youthful enthusiasm' and the expression merely refers to the high level of keenness and enthusiasm that the company is looking for in the successful applicant.
- *Chapelgate Insurance*: The word 'mature' in the advertisement could be taken to refer to an older person or to someone with a competent and well-balanced outlook. The fact that this post advertised for someone with experience indicates that the company may be looking for a slightly older person. This may indicate unlawful discrimination, unless the company can establish that relatively long term experience is required for the role.
- *Phone-atics plc*: The phrase 'only the fit need apply' may be interpreted as discriminatory, as older people are, in general, more likely to have health problems than younger people. The need to 'keep up with the pace of modern technology' may also be seen as discriminatory, unless familiarity with modern developments in telecommunications is an essential occupational requirement.
- *Fanlight Construction*: This advertisement also specifically asks for experience, which an older person is more likely to have than someone younger. However, in a similar case, a construction company was able to establish that experience of putting up and taking down scaffolding was a genuine occupational requirement, and that competence in carrying out and supervising this only came about with a number of years of experience.

In 2007, an Industrial Tribunal in Northern Ireland heard the case of a man, aged 59, who had unsuccessfully applied for a post as a sales representative. The advertisement for the job had asked for someone with at least five years experience and 'youthful enthusiasm', and during his interview the applicant was asked several times about his age, and whether he still had the necessary drive and enthusiasm. The Tribunal decided that the applicant had suffered unlawful discrimination and the wording of the advertisement served to confirm to the panel that the company had been intent on discriminating against older applicants.

Q2 Some of the arguments in favour of dispensing with a compulsory retirement age are that:

- it enables people to work for as long as they wish, and are able
- it allows them to maintain a higher standard of living than they would be able to on a state pension
- older people can often help younger people in the early stages of their career.

Some of the arguments against this are:

- fewer jobs will be available for young people, particularly in an ageing population
- removing the retirement age may pressurise some older people to remain in work against their wishes.

This question may be used, by those students taking the OCR examination, as a starting point for a citizenship campaign.

Disability discrimination, pages 72–73

This topic looks outlines the law covering disability discrimination in the workplace, which students apply to a number of case studies. Further coverage of disability discrimination is given in the chapter on **Community***, pages 120–121.*

> **OCR GCSE Citizenship Studies**
>
> **3.1.1** Understand the moral and legal rights and responsibilities that apply to our interactions with others …
> **3.1.2** Understand that employers and employees have rights and responsibilities that compete and conflict and that employees can be supported by trade unions.
> **3.2.2** Understand the importance of the law in maintaining order, resolving conflict and achieving just outcomes …
> **3.3.2** Understand that laws relating to employment … need to recognise the interests of employers, employees … Understand how these interests can compete and conflict.
> **3.4.1** Evaluate the effectiveness of the law in discouraging unfair discrimination.
>
> **National Curriculum programme of study, key stage 4**
> **Key concepts** 1.1 b; 1.2 a, c;
> **Range and content** 3 a, b, f, k,

Each of the examples given in the opening part of this section could be challenged as being contrary to the *Disability Discrimination Act 1995* (the *DDA*).

Under the *DDA* newly licensed taxis in most areas have to be fully accessible to disabled travellers. Therefore wheelchair users should be allowed access to taxis that are built to accommodate wheelchairs and refusing to do so is generally unlawful. Minicabs and private hire cars are generally unaffected by the *DDA*.

However, under a much older piece of legislation, the *Town Police Clauses Act 1847,* drivers of taxis and private hire cars may be *prosecuted* for unreasonably refusing to take a disabled passenger.

Under the *DDA* the wine bar is acting unlawfully in asking James to stay away because of his disability.

Q1 The legal position in each case is as follows:
- *Will:* Although the firm to which Will is applying is small and employs only six people, it is still subject to the *DDA*. If it turns down Will's application, it needs to be able to demonstrate that it has done all it can to make reasonable adjustments to accommodate someone in Will's position. If it has not done this, it could find itself subject to action under the *DDA*.
- *Melissa:* If Melissa has been refused an interview simply because of the way in which her appearance has been affected by her restricted growth, the shop is almost certainly discriminating against her unlawfully. Melissa has clearly been treated less favourably than someone without a disability, and in order to justify such treatment, the shop would need to show that its reason is both material to the circumstances of the case and substantial. The shop *may* have had grounds for turning Melissa down if it felt that her restricted growth prevented her from coping with the physical demands of the job (for example lifting dresses on and off racks) and that it was not possible for the shop to make reasonable adjustments to enable Melissa to carry out these tasks.
- *Paul* has a progressive disability, which has an adverse effect, often very small, on his normal day-to-day activities. By his dismissal, he appears to have been treated less favourably than someone without this. Paul has a strong case, under the *DDA*, as it will be hard for his employers to say that they had a substantial reason for dismissing him. First, there is no reason to suppose that Paul's condition would become known to the customers. Secondly, it seems unlikely, even if the customers did hear of Paul's condition, that a large number would be put off shopping in the store because of it. Thirdly, even if some customers were deterred (in the mistaken belief that his condition

is infectious in these circumstances) this is probably not a substantial enough reason for Paul to be sacked.

- *David:* David's learning difficulties may well mean that he is classified as disabled for the purposes of the DDA. In this case it appears that the store treated him less favourably than other applicants by not calling him for interview. The store must show that it has a substantial reason for doing this, which is likely to be very difficult, as David's learning difficulties may well have little or no effect on his ability to collect the trolleys.

Q2 This statement was made by one of the directors of the Disability Rights Commission (now the Equality and Human Rights Commission). It may be used to challenge students to consider how people with a disability can be given access to a wide range of work, often with relatively little adaptation or support.

Working for a living

This unit follows the story of a young man with a part-time job, with further details of the rights and responsibilities or employers and employees.

In work, pages 74–75

This topic covers the terms and conditions of employment.

OCR GCSE Citizenship Studies

3.1.2 Understand that employers and employees have rights and responsibilities that compete and conflict and that employees can be supported by trade unions.

3.2.2 Understand the importance of the law in maintaining order, resolving conflict and achieving just outcomes, and understand that the law places a responsibility on all members of society to conform to a common code of behaviour, including obedience to … civil law

3.3.2 Understand that laws relating to employment … need to recognise the interests of employers, employees … Understand how these interests can compete and conflict.

National Curriculum programme of study, key stage 4
Key concepts 1.1 b, 1.2 a, b
Range and content 3 a, k

Q1 Anit's list might include:
- the days and hours that he will be expected to work
- the amount of money he will be paid
- the type of job that he is being employed to do, and what his main tasks will be
- training possibilities
- his holiday entitlement
- whether he will be required to wear a uniform, and if so who pays for it
- whether there is to be a trial period
- his notice period
- to whom he will report.

Q2 Although Anit's basic questions about the job such as his hours, his pay and expectations of appearance are answered, he has not found out anything about the terms and conditions of his contract, such as his notice period.

Q3 A written contract or a statement of terms and conditions (which is not a contract but provides evidence of terms and conditions) clarifies what both employer and employee can expect from their relationship. A written statement of terms helps both Anit and Mr Bonner in the event of a disagreement over either person's rights or duties.

A working life, pages 76–77

This topic looks at a number of problems at work that employees might face.

OCR GCSE Citizenship Studies

3.1.2 Understand that employers and employees have rights and responsibilities that compete and conflict and that employees can be supported by trade unions.

3.2.2 Understand the importance of the law in maintaining order, resolving conflict and achieving just outcomes, and understand that the law places a responsibility on all members of society to conform to a common code of behaviour, including obedience to ... civil law

3.3.2 Understand that laws relating to employment ... need to recognise the interests of employers, employees ... Understand how these interests can compete and conflict.

National Curriculum programme of study, key stage 4
Key concepts 1.1 b, 1.2 a, b
Range and content 3 a, k

Q1 Anit's legal position is as follows:
- *Pay:* Anit is 17 years old and therefore entitled to receive the national minimum wage. He should raise the matter with his employer and ask to receive the correct amount of money. If his employer fails to pay this, Anit should seek advice.
- An employer who fails to pay the appropriate minimum wage commits a criminal offence. An employee can take his or her employer to a tribunal to insist on the minimum being paid.
- *Mistake:* an employer may only make a deduction of this nature if the employee has agreed it in writing beforehand. Anit has not agreed to this, and should tell Mr Bonner that he does not agree to the deductions that he is proposing. If Mr Bonner still deducts the money this will be unlawful and Anit can either apply to an employment tribunal (within three months) or to the court (generally within six years) to get his money back.
- Even if an employee in the retail trade does agree to deductions from his or her pay for shortfalls, these deductions must not normally exceed 10 per cent of his or her gross pay.

Q2 Young workers tend to get paid less than older ones because they generally have less experience. Older workers may also have some additional responsibilities which mean that they are entitled to be paid more.

Some employment contracts provide workers who stay longer with a higher rate of pay or benefits, linked to their years of service. Subject to certain requirements, this is generally not unlawful.

Q3 Some of the consequences of a flat minimum wage of £6 for all ages might be:
- greater wage equality and clarity
- higher business costs, perhaps making some businesses unviable
- its contribution to broader wage inflation as other wages rise to compensate for the change.

Q4 Anit's legal position is as follows:
- *Fall*: Anit's legal position will depend on whether Mr Bonner has acted negligently and whether he has complied with a range of different legal requirements relating to health and safety. Practically, Anit should ask Mr Bonner to pay him for his absence. Mr Bonner would be ill-advised not to do this as Anit potentially has a range of legal remedies that he could use against Mr Bonner (the main ones are likely to be: negligence, breach of contract and breach of statutory duty, that is, failing to follow laws passed by Parliament).
- *Abuse*: the abuse Anit received may well amount to race discrimination under the *Race Relations Act 1976* (page 67 of the student textbook). The fact that the abuse came from customers, rather than from fellow employees, does not stop it from being potentially unlawful. Anit should point out to Mr Bonner that such abuse is not acceptable. At the very least, Mr Bonner should ask abusive customers to stop their abuse or to leave. If the abuse continues, Anit may be entitled to resign because of it and claim damages from Mr Bonner.

- Anit is also entitled to be treated no less favourably by Mr Bonner because he has complained of racial abuse.

Q5 The basis of Anit's contract is what was agreed orally between Mr Bonner and Anit when Anit accepted the job. Additionally, as discussed above, Anit's contract has implied terms in relation to things such as health and safety and deduction of wages.

Q6 Anit's legal position is as follows:
- *The wrong shoes*: when Mr Bonner offered Anit his job he told him that he would be required to wear a uniform, including black shoes. The fact that Anit was not wearing the correct shoes is probably a breach of contract. As such, Mr Bonner would be entitled to send Anit home to change and not pay him for his absence.
- *No work*: when Mr Bonner offered Anit his job he told him he would normally be required to work for four hours on a Saturday and Sunday. This is a term of his contract that should be respected by Mr Bonner and, strictly speaking, by not paying Anit, Mr Bonner is probably in breach of contract. More practically, however, if Anit wishes to stay in this job, he may well be best advised to try and discuss the issue of hours with Mr Bonner and work out in advance when he is likely to be required.
- *Jobs*: when Anit was offered the job, he was told that his duties included 'making sure that the restaurant itself was clean and tidy'. Whether or not the men's toilets are included in this is far from certain, and Mr Bonner may be in breach of contract by asking Anit to clean the toilets. Although Anit may have a legal claim against Mr Bonner, he would probably be best advised to try and reach some kind of understanding with Mr Bonner, rather than pursuing his claim. This situation illustrates the benefits of putting the job description in writing.
- *Hours*: when Anit was offered his job by Mr Bonner, Mr Bonner implied that there could be some flexibility required as to hours (he would 'normally work ...'). As such, Anit may well not have a claim against Mr Bonner for requiring him to work a little later, as long as Mr Bonner pays him for his time. This is something that Anit may be best advised to try and come to some kind of agreement about with Mr Bonner.
- *Holiday*: it is generally unlawful to treat a part-time employee less favourably than a full-time employee. Refusing to pay Anit for his holiday entitlement because of his part-time status is unlawful, and Anit could take action against Mr Bonner in the employment tribunal. Employees working five days a week are now (2009) entitled to 28 days' paid holiday, or an appropriate percentage of this if they work part-time.

Trade unions

This unit provides a basic outline of the role of trade unions and employer associations, and examines conflicting views on implementing the European Working Directive.

Trade unions/Employers' organisations/Working hours, pages 78–79

OCR GCSE Citizenship Studies

3.1.2 Understand that employers and employees have rights and responsibilities that compete and conflict and that employees can be supported by trade unions.

3.2.4 Evaluate the implications of the United Kingdom's membership of the European Union and that European Union decisions have an impact upon citizens of the United Kingdom

3.3.2 Understand the role of trade unions and employers' associations in supporting and representing their members. Understand that laws relating to employment ... need to recognise the interests of employers, employees ... Understand how these interests can compete and conflict.

National Curriculum programme of study, key stage 4
Key concepts 1.1 b, 1.2 a, b
Range and content 3 a, j, k, m

Q1 Some of the consequences of employees working long hours include:
- more work may be undertaken and completed
- UK businesses become more competitive than those in countries where shorter hours are worked

- greater possibility of an accident through tiredness
- other effects of excessively long working hours, such as stress and strain, leading to illness.

Q2 The Trades Union Congress (TUC) is running a campaign to reduce working hours and improve the work–life balance, and suggests the following options:
- increase the number of part-time work opportunities
- voluntarily reduce hours for a set period of time
- introduce more job-sharing, with two people sharing the same job
- allow parents with children at school to restrict their working hours to term-times
- give people time-off in lieu, instead of overtime pay
- allow more people to work from home, where possible
- compress the working week, allowing people to do five days' work in four and have a longer weekend
- develop a system of 'banking' extra hours, allowing overtime to be accumulated and saved, enabling employees to take extended holidays or a sabbatical break.

See the TUC website for further details.

Q3 This question could be used as the basis of a class debate on working hours, or could form the basis of an examination-style essay question.

This question may be used, by those students taking the OCR examination, as a starting point for a citizenship campaign.

Losing your job

This unit outlines basic aspects of the law surrounding dismissal from work

Fired! pages 80–81

This topic outlines the circumstances in which an employee may face instant dismissal.

OCR GCSE Citizenship Studies

3.1.1 Understand the moral and legal rights and responsibilities that apply to our interactions with others

3.1.2 Understand that employers and employees have rights and responsibilities that compete and conflict and that employees can be supported by trade unions.

3.2.2 Understand ways in which rights can compete and conflict and how the law is used to resolve these issues justly

3.3.2 Understand that laws relating to employment … need to recognise the interests of employers, employees … Understand how these interests can compete and conflict.

National Curriculum programme of study, key stage 4
Key concepts 1.1 b; 1.2 a, c
Range and content 3 a, k

Q1 Dorothy was entitled to one weeks' notice as she had been in her job for more than one month but less than two years.

Q2 Kassie was entitled to five weeks' notice as she had been in her job for five years. The fact that she worked part-time is irrelevant to her notice entitlement.

Q3 Bruno was told to leave work immediately probably because his boss felt that Bruno would again arrive at work drunk during his notice period. This could damage the business or put Bruno himself and/or other employees at risk.

Q4 At the employment tribunal, Claire said that she had largely used her lunch breaks for arranging her holiday and that the amount of work time spent on this had been minimal. She also claimed that her boss had known what she was doing and had not objected.

However, the tribunal decided that, although her personal use of the company's computer made her guilty of misconduct, she should not have been instantly dismissed, and she was awarded a month's pay in lieu of the period of notice to which she was entitled.

Claiming unfair dismissal, pages 82–83

This topic examines the circumstances in which dismissal from work is regarded in law as fair and unfair.

OCR GCSE Citizenship Studies

3.1.1 Understand the moral and legal rights and responsibilities that apply to our interactions with others

3.1.2 Understand that employers and employees have rights and responsibilities that compete and conflict

3.2.2 Understand ways in which rights can compete and conflict and how the law is used to resolve these issues justly

3.3.2 Understand that laws relating to employment … need to recognise the interests of employers, employees … Understand how these interests can compete and conflict.

3.4.2 Understand the role of individuals, lawyers and courts in the civil legal and justice system

National Curriculum programme of study, key stage 4
Key concepts 1.1 b; 1.2 a, c
Range and content 3 a, k

Q1 The outcome of each case was as follows:

- *Colette* was, in law, fairly dismissed. She could not claim unfair dismissal, as she had been working for her employer for less than a year.
- *Martine* could not claim for unfair dismissal. Lying about a recent criminal conviction, especially when it relates to dishonesty, generally constitutes gross misconduct.
- *John* took his case to an employment tribunal, which decided that he had been unfairly dismissed on the grounds that his employer had failed to consider whether there was any other work he might be able to do instead. The tribunal said that a large organisation such as the ambulance service could almost certainly have provided John with alternative work that did not involve heavy lifting.
- *Evan* took his case to an employment tribunal, under the *Employment Relations Act 1999*. This allows time off to care for dependants from the first day of employment, rather than the normal 12-month qualifying period for unfair dismissal. The tribunal decided that Evan had been unfairly dismissed and he was awarded £2,000 in compensation.
- *Dean* was found to have been sacked unfairly. The tribunal decided that the immediate employment of someone else indicated that the low level of trading profits was not the real reason for Dean's dismissal. If it had been (and his employer had followed the appropriate procedures) his dismissal would not have been unfair.
- *Natasha* does not have a claim for unfair dismissal, as she had been employed for less than a year. However, the supermarket should give her notice or pay in lieu as a few mistakes do not justify dismissal without notice.

The employment tribunal, pages 84–85

This topic looks at what happens at an employment tribunal.

OCR GCSE Citizenship Studies

3.1.1 Understand the moral and legal rights and responsibilities that apply to our interactions with others

3.1.2 Understand that employers and employees have rights and responsibilities that compete and conflict and that employees can be supported by trade unions.

3.2.2 Understand ways in which rights can compete and conflict and how the law is used to resolve these issues justly

3.3.2 Understand that laws relating to employment … need to recognise the interests of employers, employees … Understand how these interests can compete and conflict. Understand the role of trade unions … in supporting and representing their members.

3.4.2 Understand the role of individuals, lawyers and courts in the civil legal and justice system

National Curriculum programme of study, key stage 4
Key concepts 1.1 b; 1.2 a, c
Range and content 3 a, k

Q1 Kirsty is not, under normal circumstances, able to claim unfair dismissal, because she had worked for her employer for less than 12 months.

However, like *Evan* (page 82), she was able to bring her claim under the *Employment Relations Act 1999,* which states that employees have a right to time off work to care for dependants and that this applies from the moment at which a person is employed.

The employment tribunal ruled that Kirsty was unfairly dismissed because she had lost her job for taking up her right to have time off to look after her son.

Kirsty found a new job a day after Mr Collier had dismissed her. Because her losses were therefore very small, Kirsty was awarded just one day's pay in compensation for her dismissal.

Q2 Students should note that the main reason why many people do not take action is because they do not know how to go about it or are unaware that their employer may have acted unlawfully. In addition, some people are reluctant to take action because they do not wish to get a reputation as a troublemaker or through a concern over high costs.

Arguably, a failure of people to obtain their rights in law is an indictment of the justice system, and increases the likelihood of further mistreatment of staff.

OCR Citizenship Studies Teacher's Resource Book for GCSE full and short course
© 2009 Hodder Education

Economy

> **Managing the economy**
> - All change
> - Taxation
>
> **World trade**
> - Globalisation
> - Anti-globalisation
> - A fair price to pay?
> - Ironing out the highs and lows
>
> **Poverty**
> - Foreign aid

Managing the economy

The two topics in this unit are designed to give some indication of the part that governments may play in managing the economy.

All change, pages 86–87

This topic introduces students to the cyclical nature of economic growth and provides an overview of the economic downturn that began in 2007. Following on from this, students are asked to consider what should be a government's priorities during times of recession.

> **OCR GCSE Citizenship Studies**
>
> **3.1.3** Understand the interdependence of individuals, groups and communities …
> **3.3.2** Understand the Government's role in helping to manage the economy … Evaluate and debate the different opinions on how far the state or individuals should take responsibility for the provision of income protection, health and education.
>
> **National Curriculum programme of study, key stage 4**
> **Key concepts** 1.1 b, d; 1.2 a; 1.3 c
> **Range and content** 3 j, m, n

Q1 By *intervening* to protect the banking system the Government was, arguably:
- protecting the accounts and savings of millions of people using banking services
- ensuring the continued supply of credit to many businesses (although limitations were placed on this subsequently)
- preventing wide scale unemployment in the financial services industry
- ensuring that normal conditions of purchase, sale and trade were maintained; something that would have become impossible without a banking system
- preventing widespread social disorder and hardship, which was likely to follow a collapse of the banks.

Shortly after the crisis, the Chancellor of the Exchequer told the BBC, 'If we had not intervened … the banking system would have gone down, taking millions of families, millions of businesses with it. No responsible government could have done that.'

Amongst the arguments in favour of non-intervention are:
- the high cost of the Government's bail-out of the banks raises public debt and will hamper the country for many years to come; it will result in higher taxes and fewer public services
- it is a mistake for governments to support weak businesses; those banks that made serious commercial mistakes should face closure or being taken over by other more profitable organisations
- after many years of success, and arguably excessive profits, the banking industry did not deserve to be bailed out by the tax payer
- companies making serious commercial errors should be punished and not helped.

Q2 In an interview on the *Today* programme in January 2009, the Prime Minister, Gordon Brown, outlined the Government's three-part strategy to deal with the recession. He explained that the Government would: a) provide a banking system that offered safety and security to businesses and the public alike; b) give people practical help to weather the recession, for example by raising the pension and child benefit, by lowering tax allowances, and by instigating a public works programme that is 'investing in the future'; and c) try to restore business confidence and get lending moving again for mortgage holders and businesses.

Taxation, pages 88–89

This topic provides a broad outline of the nature and purposes of taxation in Britain, and asks students to consider the arguments surrounding the question of whether tax rates should rise or fall.

OCR GCSE Citizenship Studies

3.1.2 … Understand how, and for what purposes, taxes are raised (locally and nationally)

3.3.2 Understand that laws relating to … the taxation … of goods need to recognise the interests of … buyers, sellers … Understand how these interests can compete and conflict. Understand the Government's role in helping to manage the economy … Evaluate and debate the different opinions on how far the state or individuals should take responsibility for the provision of income protection, health and education.

National Curriculum programme of study, key stage 4
Key concepts 1.1 a; 1.2 a, b
Range and content 3 c, j

Q1 In the discussion following the announcement of Lewis Hamilton's decision, those supporting the racing driver maintained that he had every right to protect his personal interests and move to Switzerland, or some other country, where tax rates were significantly lower. In an interview at the time, Lewis Hamilton's father stated, 'It could be a very short career, and you have to take care of what you have got.'

Lewis Hamilton is not alone in motor racing for taking such action. Britons Jenson Button, David Coulthard and Sir Jackie Stewart have all moved overseas for tax purposes.

Critics tended to argue that, as a famous British sportsman, Lewis Hamilton had a duty to remain in Britain, particularly in view of the official recognition he had been given through the award of an MBE. They also said that tax avoidance was morally wrong, and that, even if they have to pay the higher rate of taxation in the UK, high earners are still likely to have more than enough money to live on.

Q2
Statement A
For: it's fairer; people have a greater incentive to work

Against: lower tax rates may limit government income; they do little to combat inequality

Statement B
For: the wealthy have a greater capacity (and therefore a greater duty) to contribute to the public good; lower tax rates for the poor help them to live – and to save; higher tax rates for the rich help to reduce inequality and social exclusion

Against: most rich people work hard for their money, often harder than poorer people, and should not be penalised for that extra effort; high tax rates discourage people from working harder; high tax rates may drive rich and successful people away from Britain to countries where they can retain more of their income; a lot of wealthy people use fewer public services than the bulk of the population (they have their children privately educated and pay for private healthcare instead of using the NHS), so why should they pay more tax?

Statement C
For: people have a right to retain all that they have earned

Against: without taxing income and profit, it would be impossible to offer services required by the whole community, eg law enforcement, roads, defence, health care, education etc, unless some other way of government was used. The provision of these services privately or independently would result in a very fragmented society

Statement D
For: this would have the merit of being simple and transparent, and give people a much clearer idea of how the tax system works; it would not penalise those who earn more money, although in real terms, they would always more money in tax than the less well-off

Against: it would do little to reduce inequality; it would particularly hit the very poor, who may not be able to survive on an income that is reduced even further through taxation.

World trade

The four topics in this unit look at two of the current debates surrounding world trade: globalisation and fair trade.

Globalisation, pages 90–91

This topic provides some indication of the extent of globalisation today, and encourages students to think about some of the implications of the development of multinational companies.

> **OCR GCSE Citizenship Studies**
>
> **3.1.3** Understand the interdependence of individuals, groups and communities …
> **3.3.2** Understand the importance of ethical behaviour and social responsibility in business, including the moral and legal responsibilities businesses have towards each other and the wider community
> **3.3.3** Evaluate the key points of one international citizenship issue related to trade or aid
>
> **National Curriculum programme of study, key stage 4**
> **Key concepts** 1.1 b; 1.2 b; 1.3 c
> **Range and content** 3 d, n

Q1 In addition to the benefits listed in the question, the scheme may provide shoppers with better quality goods. It may also act as a catalyst for further development (such as improved transport links) and provide new skills and training for the existing workforce.

However, lower prices and more attractive facilities may drive some local traders out of business, perhaps resulting (in the long run) in less choice for the consumer. Again in the longer term, if shopping becomes more centralised, people may have to travel further for essential supplies and, as a result, some sectors of society may become more isolated. If the supermarkets develop a dominant position they may also exert a downward influence on suppliers' prices in the area.

Q2 Students may suggest that the supermarkets be required to help by:
- contributing to the development of the local infrastructure, perhaps with support for improvements to schools, medical care, water and sewage facilities, local transport or other amenities
- providing education and training for employees that is transferable to other employment settings
- undertaking to ensure that a certain percentage of the labour force is drawn from the local area
- assisting with conservation and environmental improvements
- undertaking to stock a minimum percentage of products grown or manufactured locally.

Anti-globalisation, pages 92–93

This topic looks briefly at the cases for and against globalisation and asks whether anti-globalisation protests are acceptable and appropriate.

> **OCR GCSE Citizenship Studies**
>
> **3.1.3** Understand the interdependence of individuals, groups and communities …
> **3.3.2** Understand that the laws relating to employment and the production, taxation and sale of goods need to recognise the interests of employers, employees, buyers, sellers and the environmental impact of production. Understand how these interests may compete and conflict. Understand the importance of ethical behaviour and social responsibility in business, including the moral and legal responsibilities businesses have towards each other and the wider community
> **3.3.3** Understand the differences between fair and unfair trade … Evaluate the key points of one international citizenship issue related to trade or aid
>
> **National Curriculum programme of study, key stage 4**
> **Key concepts** 1.1 b; 1.2 b; 1.3 c
> **Range and content** 3 d, n

Q1 Other forms of protest or lobbying include
- writing to local AMs, MPs, and MEPs over a particular issue
- lobbying individual companies where malpractice is believed to have occurred
- contacting the press or other media
- deciding (and encouraging others) not to purchase products or services from companies that are not working in the wider social interest.

This part of the topic also provides an opportunity to discuss methods used by the police, both in Britain and overseas, in dealing with mass anti-globalisation protests.

Q2 Although this question comes at the end of the topic, it may be effective, with some groups, to begin the session with a kind of word-association exercise around the meaning of globalisation. Questions to the group may include
- With what do you associate globalisation?
- What pictures or images come to mind?
- What are these based upon?
- What kinds of things are said about globalisation?

Write students' responses on the board and ask them to clarify or exemplify where appropriate. Now look at the words and notes you have made of their responses. Ask the group if they can identify any patterns, or perhaps sort the responses into groups. Use this approach to draw out and build up a picture of the meaning of globalisation and its strengths and weaknesses, using the text to reinforce or extend these ideas. The students' thoughts and contributions that you have already collected may be used as the basis for answering this question.

A fair price to pay? Pages 94–95

This topic provides some indication of the extent of globalisation today, and encourages students to think about some of the implications of the development of multinational companies.

> **OCR GCSE Citizenship Studies**
>
> **3.1.3** Understand the interdependence of individuals, groups and communities, and assess critically the impact of their own actions on communities and the wider world now and in the future. Make recommendations to others for action and change.
> **3.3.3** Understand the differences between fair and unfair trade and the role of traders' organisations, pressure groups and governments in bringing about change.
>
> **National Curriculum programme of study, key stage 4**
> **Key concepts** 1.1 b; 1.2 b; 1.3 c
> **Range and content** 3 d, h, k, n

Q1 Companies who move their production facilities overseas may benefit from lower labour costs, and possibly higher quality and production rates, making their products more competitive.

Benefits will also be felt by shareholders, local overseas' workers, and by local companies supplying the new factories. Consumers may also benefit from lower prices.

Workers in former production plants may lose their jobs or have fewer employment possibilities, and a similar impact may be felt by former local suppliers.

Q2 Although manufacturing facilities may be moved overseas, the research and design surrounding many products often continues in the 'home' country, and allows the product to retain its key traditional characteristics.

It may also be worth asking here about how much importance students attach to a product's country of origin. Some may argue that this is of little importance, and that they place much greater emphasis, in deciding what to buy, on the perceived value of the brand. Arguably the country of origin becomes less important with global brands manufactured and developed in many countries throughout the world.

Q3 The manufacture of a pair of jeans involves:
• planting and growing the cotton; treating it with pesticides; picking, processing and weaving the cotton; dyeing and finishing the fabric, and transporting it to a factory
• designing the jeans; cutting the material according to the pattern; sewing the pieces together, with zips, buttons, etc.
• finishing and inspecting the garments; bagging, placing in large cartons, transporting to a port and shipping to the UK
• delivering them to the British store, where they are displayed and sold.

Q4 This question revolves around two issues; the responsibility of consumers not to buy products that have been 'unethically' produced and whether boycotting 'unethically' produced goods has any impact on employment or purchasing practices of major companies.

You may like to ask students how much responsibility we have for the goods that we buy. Do the less well-off have less responsibility, in this regard, than the wealthy? Is it fair to buy something that has almost certainly been produced by a labour force that has suffered or been ill-treated in some way? How realistic is this viewpoint? Should individuals take action on this, or is it something that should be left to governments?

This question may be used, by those students taking the OCR examination, as a starting point for a citizenship campaign.

Ironing out the highs and lows, pages 96–97

This topic introduces and outlines the notion of fair trade, asking whether consumers have any responsibility towards the individuals and communities supplying the products and raw materials that they buy.

OCR GCSE Citizenship Studies

3.1.3 Understand the interdependence of individuals, groups and communities, and assess critically the impact of their own actions on communities and the wider world now and in the future. Make recommendations to others for action and change.

3.3.3 Understand the differences between fair and unfair trade and the role of traders' organisations, pressure groups and governments in bringing about change. Evaluate the key points of one international citizenship issue related to trade or aid

National Curriculum programme of study, key stage 4
Key concepts 1.1 b; 1.2 b; 1.3 c
Range and content 3 d, h, k, n

Q1 Sudden shifts upwards in commodity prices are likely to benefit some producers and processors or manufacturers, but possibly damage others. If the increase is sustained the benefits are likely to be maintained, as long as the price does not become too high to discourage demand.

The losers in this situation are likely to be consumers and manufacturers who are unable to pass on the increased price. An example of this is the sudden increase in the price of crude oil, leading to greater manufacturing and transport costs in a wide range of industries.

As the text indicates, sharp increases in the price of primary commodities may lead to a rush to exploit the crop or mineral etc., leading to environmental damage and social disturbance.

Sudden falls in commodity prices can have a particularly damaging on producers. Farmers who have spent time and money all year on planting, tending, spraying their crops, etc., face huge losses if the price suddenly falls once all this work has been done. Forward planning and consistency of supply become highly problematic.

Q2&Q3 There are opportunities, in answering both these questions, for students to undertake further research into the arguments surrounding Fairtrade goods, and to assess both the claims and the criticisms of the movement.

Schools, local authorities and other public bodies sometimes actively promote Fairtrade. You may like to ask students if this is appropriate for public organisations to align themselves with political movements of this kind.

This question may be used, by those students taking the OCR examination, as a starting point for a citizenship campaign.

Poverty

The topic in this unit raises a number of questions about the provision of development aid – and, in particular, whether it generally benefits those countries that receive it and whether it is appropriate for aid to be supplied subject to conditions.

Foreign aid, pages 98–99

> **OCR GCSE Citizenship Studies**
>
> **3.1.3** Understand the interdependence of individuals, groups and communities, and assess critically the impact of their own actions on communities and the wider world now and in the future. Make recommendations to others for action and change.
>
> **3.3.3** Understand the differences between fair and unfair trade and the role of traders' organisations, pressure groups and governments in bringing about change. Evaluate the different types of aid that may be offered to Less Economically Developed Countries (LEDCs) and the relative merits of these for people in the donor and recipient countries. Evaluate the key points of one international citizenship issue related to trade or aid
>
> **National Curriculum programme of study, key stage 4**
> **Key concepts** 1.1 b; 1.2 b; 1.3 c
> **Range and content** 3 d, n

Q1 Students' answers may include the following points:
- widespread loss of life, short- and long-term injury
- loss of family, friends and community
- shock and trauma resulting from these losses
- loss of property and valuables
- loss of work and income
- major medium- and long-term social and economic disruption.

Q2 Arguably, all nations have a duty to offer help and support to countries affected by such widespread tragedies.

Q3 The following points may be helpful with the discussion:
- historically aid has almost always been given with 'strings attached', although, since the early 1980s, conditions have tended to become more specific and formal
- it is not unreasonable for governments and NGOs to expect that money given is spent as efficiently and effectively as possible
- studies have shown that conditionality generally does not work, in the sense that recipient countries who are resistant to the terms and conditions do not have the

resources or the will to implement the changes or practices required – and tend not to do so. However, those who agree with the donor's policies make stronger efforts and are more likely to comply

- more recently (from 2005 onwards) attempts have been made, led by Britain, to give recipient countries more control over their plans for poverty reduction.

It may be helpful, at some stage, to point out to students that strategies for reducing poverty are hugely problematic. There is no guarantee that the policies promoted by donor agencies are the right ones. The International Monetary Fund has said that knowledge and understanding of the links between policies and growth remain uncertain; there is no guarantee that certain policies will work, particularly when other extraneous factors may intervene.

Q4 Prior to this exercise, you may like to ask students for arguments in support of giving aid, and – together with those listed in the student text – present these on cards or slips. With students in pairs or small groups, ask them to discuss and try to agree and rank the statements in order of importance. Back as a whole, discuss their choices, focusing in particular on those reasons they felt to be the strongest.

Community

Coming to Britain	Older people
• Migration	• The future is grey
• Seeking asylum	• An age-old problem
Identity	**Housing**
• Parallel lives	• A place of your own
• Being British	• Dealing with problems
Unequal Britain	
• Racism	
• Sexual equality	
• Challenging disability	

Coming to Britain

The two topics in this unit examine the background and impact of people who have come to the UK seeking economic benefit or political asylum.

Migration, pages 100–101

This topic provides a brief history of migration to the UK, indicating some of the main reasons why people seek to migrate.

OCR GCSE Citizenship Studies

3.2.1 Explore the diverse national, regional, ethnic and religious groups and communities in the United Kingdom and understand the different forces that bring about change in communities over time. Understand that the United Kingdom is a country with wide cultural diversity where people's sense of identity is often complex.

3.2.4 Know, in outline, about our economic, political, legal and cultural relationships with other countries in Europe. Evaluate the implications of the United Kingdom's membership of the European Union and that European Union decisions have an impact upon citizens of the United Kingdom. Understand that the British Commonwealth is a family of nations and has an important role in promoting cultural understanding and the exchange of ideas

National Curriculum programme of study, key stage 4
Key concepts 1.1 c; 1.3 b, c, d
Range and content 3 l, m

Q1 As you discuss their answers, you may like to introduce to students a piece of research on emigration conducted in 2006 by IPPR. This study found that the main reasons for people leaving the UK were as follows:

- *Family ties* – people moving to be with a partner or returning to their country of origin after spending many years in the UK.
- *Lifestyle* – working-age families and retirees who were attracted by the prospects abroad of a better quality of life, a better climate, better value for money and better recreational options.
- *Overseas adventure* – primarily young adults spending a short period abroad looking to gain new experiences and skills, some of which may help them with their career when they return.
- *Work* – workers, usually skilled, lured by career opportunities abroad.

A summary of the research is available from
http://ippr.typepad.com/brits_abroad/files/brits_abroad_final_exec_summary_pdf.pdf

Q2 Students' suggestions here are likely to include: isolation through lack of friends and contacts, unfamiliarity with the culture and official procedures, language difficulties, financial difficulties, and prejudice and ostracism by host community.

Q3 Here students may suggest that, as adults, they have primary responsibility for their own well-being. Additionally, they may feel that some responsibility is borne also by the community and administration in the area in which they settle.

Migration, pages 102–103

This topic focuses largely on the issue of economic migration to Britain, and encourages students to think about and outline what policies they feel the Government should currently adopt.

OCR GCSE Citizenship Studies

3.2.1 Explore the diverse national, regional, ethnic and religious groups and communities in the United Kingdom and understand the different forces that bring about change in communities over time. Understand that the United Kingdom is a country with wide cultural diversity where people's sense of identity is often complex.

3.2.4 Know, in outline, about our economic, political, legal and cultural relationships with other countries in Europe. Evaluate the implications of the United Kingdom's membership of the European Union and that European Union decisions have an impact upon citizens of the United Kingdom. Understand that the British Commonwealth is a family of nations and has an important role in promoting cultural understanding and the exchange of ideas

3.4.1 Understand the conditions which may lead to strain and conflict between communities in the UK.

National Curriculum programme of study, key stage 4
Key concepts 1.1 c; 1.3 b, c, d
Range and content 3 l, m

Q1 Agnieszka is almost certainly referring to a belief that is held that living standards in the UK are relatively high – for both the host and incoming populations.

In reality, however, newcomers may find that the accommodation and work that they obtain falls well below the standards that they had expected. Additionally, they may also face periods of isolation, and difficulties in becoming integrated with the host community.

Q2 The image of Britain that people develop overseas is likely to be shaped by:
- traditional views of British values, particularly a perceived concern for justice and fairness
- the perception, by some, of Britain as the 'mother country'
- the long-established nature of certain British institutions, such as the Royal Family and Parliament, and
- the portrayal of Britain in films and the media, which may be quite selective in the images that it presents, showing a country that many people may say no longer exists.

Q3 Option a) would arguably enable a larger number of people to work and settle in Britain than at present. This would almost certainly result in an increase in the size of the pool of available labour, which may be helpful to certain sectors of industry.

Fewer restrictions may also enable greater numbers to escape from difficult conditions in their home country, and may reduce the number of cases of apparent injustice, particularly for those who wish to make a positive contribution to British society, but are currently refused entry.

Possible drawbacks of a more open immigration system include excessive pressure on resources, such as education, housing and medical care, along with a certain amount of political discontent from some people believing that too many people were moving to Britain.

You may like to challenge those students who express fears that Britain is becoming 'full up' with the following points:
- many of the problems associated with our school, transport and health services are not associated with migration, but with under-investment
- many people like to live in crowded big cities, which they prefer to isolated country areas; large cities can provide people with an interesting and exciting life
- having new members in our society is likely to contribute new ideas and innovations that can improve people's lives
- although Britain has a number of large towns and cities, three quarters of the country is still agricultural.

Option b) may be beneficial to business and industry in helping to provide a skilled workforce and to meet labour shortages where they exist.

Critics of option b) may point to difficulties instigating and policing control of this kind. They may also question the ability of the authorities to distinguish between people making the right and wrong contribution to society. Again, it could be said that this may give rise to unfair decisions. For example, what should happen to migrants whose labour is no longer required, or who find themselves in trouble with the law. You may like to encourage students to discuss what they feel is a fair and reasonable way of dealing with these issues.

Students may suggest that the benefit of **option c)** include reducing further strain on housing and public services. Arguably it may also contribute to limiting population growth in a country where population numbers place a severe strain on the environment.

Some critics point to the difficulty in effectively implementing this strategy. They also say that discouraging certain groups of immigrants would damage our society by putting off talented workers from trying to move to Britain.

Seeking asylum, pages 104–105

In this first of three topics on asylum, students consider some of the reasons why people why people throughout the world may be forced to leave their home in search of safety, the impact this might have on them, and who is responsible for their care.

OCR GCSE Citizenship Studies

3.1.4 Explore connections between values, viewpoints and actions with respect to rights and responsibilities for individuals in national and global contexts.

3.2.1 Explore the diverse national, regional, ethnic and religious groups and communities in the United Kingdom and understand the different forces that bring about change in communities over time.

3.2.4 Understand that the United Kingdom … is committed to adhere to United Nations' agreements on human rights.

National Curriculum programme of study, key stage 4
Key concepts 1.1 c; 1.2 a; 1.3 b, c, d
Range and content 3 l, m, n

Q1 Answers from students may include violence, conflict, hunger, imprisonment, sadness, confusion, loss, isolation, etc.

Q2 Amongst the problems refugees are likely to face are:
- physical danger – as bystanders in a conflict, victims of persecution, or as a result of hunger or disease
- poverty – through the loss of their home or possessions, a lack of shelter, or the inability to find work
- isolation – through family break-up, living in an unfamiliar location, absence of contacts, ostracism, language or other difficulties limiting interaction with the host community, etc
- fear and despair – from the immediate danger that has driven them from their home, the human and material losses that they might have suffered, insecurity about the future, etc.

Q3 *Jingmei* left China to escape imprisonment for helping students who were demonstrating in opposition to the Chinese Government.

Benjamin left Chile as part of an international agreement with the Chilean Government to secure the release of prisoners held for their political opposition.

Majid claimed asylum in Hungary having fled to Pakistan to escape the fighting in Afghanistan, believing that it was still too dangerous to return to his home country.

Q4 The reference to *responsibility* in the question may be examined in two ways: referring to the *cause* of the refugees' plight and to the *duty* that a group or body may have for their welfare.

In certain circumstances, responsibility for the problems facing refugees may lie with their country of origin, and its failure to deal with such things as severe economic problems, warring factions, or the particular problem that has forced people to flee.

Responsibility to help refugees arguably lies with the international community, the country in which the refugee has sought asylum, and possibly with other countries also able to offer sanctuary and assistance.

Seeking asylum, pages 106–107

This topic introduces students to some of the more technical aspects of seeking refugee status in Britain and asks if the current employment restrictions on asylum seekers should be lifted.

OCR GCSE Citizenship Studies

3.2.1 Explore the diverse national, regional, ethnic and religious groups and communities in the United Kingdom and understand the different forces that bring about change in communities over time.

3.2.2 Know that international humanitarian law protects the human rights of individuals and communities in peace and conflict. Understand that individuals, organisations and governments have responsibility to ensure that rights are balanced, supported and protected.

3.2.4 Understand that the United Kingdom ... is committed to adhere to United Nations' agreements on human rights.

National Curriculum programme of study, key stage 4
Key concepts 1.1 b; 1.2 a; 1.3 b, c, d
Range and content 3 a, l, m, n

Q1 The outcome of the two cases was as follows:
- *Muna* was granted refugee status and allowed to stay in Britain.
- *Milan* was not granted asylum in Britain on the basis of the evidence that some degree of protection for Roma people like Milan is provided by the police in Slovakia.

Q2 This question is designed to examine the traditional distinction between economic migrants and political refugees.

Arguments in favour of removing this distinction tend to see it as artificial, asking why protection is available to people whose life is at risk from persecution, but not to those at risk from starvation. In a similar way, it may also be argued that a person who seeks to move elsewhere as a result of ethnic discrimination in education and employment in their home country is as much a refugee as an economic migrant.

However, those seeking not to blur the distinction may argue that the threat of injury or death from persecution is different (and more serious) than economic hardship, and that the removal of restrictions on economic migrants would be politically unacceptable.

Q3&Q4 Until 2002, asylum seekers who had not received an initial decision within six months of their application for asylum were able to apply for permission to work. However, this concession was abolished in July 2002, although some discretion to allow asylum seekers to work was retained.

In 2005, asylum seekers who had not had an initial decision on their application were allowed to apply to the Home Office for permission to work. This was the result of an EU directive on reception conditions, by which the UK is bound. Failed asylum seekers continued not to be allowed to work, even if they had previously been given permission to do so.

Arguments in favour of allowing asylum seekers to work include:
• employment enables them to support themselves and to make a contribution to society
• most expect and want to work
• not working deprives people of their dignity
• money would be saved by the state through the payment of fewer benefits
• work is good for community cohesion, increasing people's understanding of other groups
• it would allow asylum seekers to make use of their skills and education
• some refugees may become deskilled by remaining outside the labour market.

The primary reason for instigating this policy was the Government's wish to deter illegal immigrants from entering the county, believing that allowing asylum seekers to work attracted economic rather than political migrants.

Q4 For further information on this question, see the Refugee Council website, www.refugeecouncil.org.uk, in particular the section on *The truth about asylum.*

Seeking asylum, pages 108–109

This final topic looks at the portrayal of asylum seekers in parts of the media and attempts to provide students with more detail about the current numbers of people seeking asylum in Britain today.

OCR GCSE Citizenship Studies

3.1.4 Explore connections between values, viewpoints and actions with respect to rights and responsibilities for individuals in national and global contexts.

3.2.2 Know that international humanitarian law protects the human rights of individuals and communities in peace and conflict. Understand that individuals, organisations and governments have responsibility to ensure that rights are balanced, supported and protected.

3.2.4 Understand that the United Kingdom … is committed to adhere to United Nations' agreements on human rights.

National Curriculum programme of study, key stage 4
Key concepts 1.1 b; 1.2 a; 1.3 b, c, d
Range and content 3 a, l, m, n

Q1 The emotive words used in the reports include: *flooded, flooding, floodgates* and *inundated.* The reports fail to mention the reasons for the asylum seekers leaving their own country, and the conditions which they have had to endure.

Q2,Q3&Q4 JM Potton makes a number of points:
• that Britain has neither the space nor the economic capacity to admit refugees at the same rate as it has done over the past 40 years

- that there are a large number of refugees in London who beg with their young children, demanding money
- that refugees should be returned to their country of origin when it is safe for them to do so.

In reflecting on these various points, it may be helpful for students to consider how JM Potton's points relate to
a) current statistical data
b) students' personal experience
c) Britain's legal obligations
d) students' moral beliefs, and
e) their political judgment.

Identity

The two topics in this unit ask whether greater efforts should be made in Britain to give people a stronger sense of community and identity and, if so, what forms this might take.

Parallel lives, pages 110–111

This topic provides a very brief history of migration to the UK, indicating some of the main reasons why people seek to migrate.

OCR GCSE Citizenship Studies

3.2.1 Explore the diverse national, regional, ethnic and religious groups and communities in the United Kingdom and understand the different forces that bring about change in communities over time. Understand that the United Kingdom is a country with wide cultural diversity where people's sense of identity is often complex. Understand the interdependence of individuals, groups and communities, the need for mutual respect, and the importance of community cohesion

3.4.1 Understand the conditions that may lead to strain and conflict between communities in the UK. Understand successful strategies for developing more harmonious communities and societies.

National Curriculum programme of study, key stage 4
Key concepts 1.1 b, c; 1.2 b; 1.3 b, d
Range and content 3 d, h, l

Q1 Students' answers may include the following. Segregation may give rise to:
- significant differences in opportunities and life-chances, measured in life expectancy, employment rates, income, etc.
- a failure to understand other people's way of life, a lack of social and cultural awareness, leading to prejudice, fear and misunderstanding
- greater influence for extreme political parties.

Q2,Q3&Q4 Shortly after the riots of 2001, Oldham Council commissioned David Ritchie to conduct an independent review. In its published findings in 2002, the Ritchie report (entitled The Oldham Independent Review) criticised the Council for not doing enough to break down the long-established racial segregation in education and housing. It was also criticised for failing to employ more people from ethnic minorities in its own council workforce.

Many members of Oldham Council rejected these conclusions claiming that Mr Ritchie's enquiry had taken evidence from too small a sample and that the real causes of the troubles lay in poverty and social exclusion, made worse by a lack of government funding.

Opposing criticisms of segregation is the view that points to the difficulties and impracticalities of socially engineering people to live in certain areas or attend certain schools. 'Bussing,' they say, 'didn't work in America, and won't work here.' Instead they propose diverting money to separate communities in order to give all people the chance of a better education and the opportunity to move out of the ghetto.

Q5&Q6 The Ritchie report emphasised the importance of everyone being able to speak English as an essential part of creating mixed communities and ensuring that everyone can listen to and respond to other people's points of view.

It said that a failure to speak English acted as a barrier to integration. The need for interpreters and for certain documents to be translated, the report stated was 'an irritant to many, though not all, white and African-Caribbean people, because it undermines their deep feeling that 'English is the language of this town'.

Q7&Q8 The statement in Q7 was made by a second-generation British Asian man who believes that the community in which he lives is far preferable for a Muslim to an area on the other side of town where, as he says, he has little in common with the aspirations of people living in 'white working class estates'.

Being British, pages 112–113

This topic introduces a number of aspects of personal and social identity, and asks students to consider the value of proposed measures designed to strengthen national identity.

OCR GCSE Citizenship Studies

3.2.1 Understand the cultural traditions and value system that contribute to being British. Understand that the United Kingdom is a country with wide cultural diversity where people's sense of identity is often complex. Understand the interdependence of individuals, groups and communities, the need for mutual respect, and the importance of community cohesion

3.4.1 Understand successful strategies for developing more harmonious communities and societies.

National Curriculum programme of study, key stage 4
Key concepts 1.1 c; 1.2 b; 1.3 b, d
Range and content 3 d, l

Q1 You may wish to ask students to share some of the points they have written down. There is also an opportunity here, in the right circumstances and with a strong and supportive group, for students to share details of their personal identity to see if others can guess who it describes.

Q2 There is an opportunity here to list, group and question students on the general applicability of their suggestions. Do students feel their suggestions are only applicable to the UK (i.e. unique) or are they equally applicable to people living in Germany or France, etc.?

Q3,Q4&Q5 Developing a stronger sense of national identity may be seen as a means of:
- reducing social divisions and feelings of separateness
- reducing the likelihood that people build their identity on religion or ethnicity
- offering stability in periods of rapid change
- reducing the likelihood of extreme dissidence
- creating a more law-abiding population
- providing a sense of belonging.

In opposing this view, some people may argue that:
- the idea of national identity has become less appropriate in a world of globalisation and greater international mobility
- a sense of national identity cannot be manufactured in the way in which the Government has proposed
- a sense of national identity can be exclusive, as well as inclusive, particularly if certain groups within the population are perceived as lacking certain key 'national characteristics'
- it may give rise to undue separation, resulting, for example, in threats to the unity of the United Kingdom.

This question may be used, by those students taking the OCR examination, as a starting point for a citizenship campaign.

Q6 If time is available, this question can be used as the basis for further investigative work on the values and hopes for a class, school or community group. It may also be used for wider research into the future vision of political parties or other selected interest groups.

Unequal Britain

This unit looks at three areas of inequality in Britain: racism, sexual inequality and disability discrimination.

Racism, pages 114–115

This topic introduces students to the idea of institutional racism, based on the case of Zahid Mubarek who was murdered in prison by a fellow inmate.

> **OCR GCSE Citizenship Studies**
>
> **3.1.1** Understand the range and importance of fundamental human rights
> **3.2.1** Understand the interdependence of individual, groups and communities, the need for mutual respect and understanding
> **3.3.2** Understand the Government's role in … the planning and regulation of public services.
> **3.4.1** Understand the conditions which may lead to strain and conflict between communities in the UK.
>
> **National Curriculum programme of study, key stage 4**
> **Key concepts** 1.1 b, c; 1.2 a, b
> **Range and content** 3 a, b

Q1 As outlined in the next column, a public enquiry was held into the death of Zahid Mubarek. It opened in November 2004 and reported in June 2007, concluding that 19 members of the Prison Service played a role in the circumstances that led to the prisoner's death. These included medical and managerial staff, as well as prison officers. Also criticised were the lack of funding for the prison system, overcrowding, failures in the inspection of cells, and a failure at the prison to deal with racist behaviour, particularly racist language and banter.

Q2 In the final report, the chairman of the enquiry stated that his findings and recommendations were being published six years after the prisoner's murder and, as result, many of the proposals that he intended to make had already been implemented.

Among the report's recommendations were the following:
• ending of enforced cell-sharing
• greater consultation with prisoners over who they wish to share a cell with, when it is necessary to do so
• improvements in the way in which cells are searched for weapons
• improvements in the flow of information to prison staff concerning a prisoner's criminal convictions and outstanding charges
• greater efforts to identify prisoners with mental health problems, and
• more effective action to minimise the risk to inmates and staff posed by prisoners who are mentally disordered.

Q3&Q4 It is quite possible that the conductor had automatically jumped to the conclusion that, as a member of an ethnic minority, Mr Stemmet was unlikely to have a first-class railway ticket. When questioned about this later by Mr Stemmet, it appears that the conductor was unable to recognise or to admit that his action was discriminatory.

Q5&Q6 The tribunal ordered the train operator to pay Mr Stemmet £1,750 in compensation for the discrimination he had suffered. Mr Stemmet also received a letter apologising for the damage that the incident had caused.

The train operator agreed to draw up an equal opportunities policy, to be put into practice throughout the company. The then Commission for Racial Equality provided advice and assistance with this.

OCR Citizenship Studies Teacher's Resource Book for GCSE full and short course
© 2009 Hodder Education

The company also undertook to remind all employees of the importance of dealing with members of the public equally, and the conductor agreed to take further training.

Q7 This question may be used to generate a range of ideas from students about the actions that their own school might take to promote good race relations. These may be gathered and grouped together, with students in small groups taking one of these ideas and discussing and reporting back on how it might be developed. There is an opportunity here also to look at the school's race equality policy and for students to discuss their own ideas with a senior member of staff.

Students' suggestions for actions that schools might take may include the following:
- creating a welcoming and positive atmosphere in school
- valuing diversity
- promoting wider values of fairness and equal opportunity
- helping to prepare students for life in a multi-ethnic society
- challenging and refusing to tolerate racist behaviour in school
- monitoring the achievement levels and needs of different ethnic groups in the school, and taking action designed to remedy any shortcomings in attainment
- revising policies that might work against the needs of certain groups of students, such as those for whom English is not their first language
- establishing links with local ethnic communities
- encouraging involvement in the school of the parents and carers of children who are members of ethnic minorities.

Sexual equality, pages 116–117

This, the first of two topics on this subject, provides students with statistical data on female and male education and employment patterns, and asks them to consider what factors may limit the achievements of men and women.

OCR GCSE Citizenship Studies

3.1.1 Understand the moral and legal rights and responsibilities that apply to our interactions with others
3.1.2 Understand that employers and employees have rights and responsibilities
3.2.1 Understand … values of … equality of opportunity
3.2.3 Understand the development of, and struggle for different kinds of rights and freedoms
3.3.2 Understand the laws relating to employment

National Curriculum programme of study, key stage 4
Key concepts 1.1 b; 1.2 a, b
Range and content 3 a, k

Q1, Q2 & Q3 The statistical evidence on pages 116–117 suggests that, as a girl, Rosie is more likely to do well at school and at university than she would had she been a boy. In fact, the Higher Education Policy Institute reported in 2009 that this advantage is also likely to extend to Rosie's period in higher education. At every age, in every social and ethnic group, and in almost every subject, there are now more women than men gaining the best qualifications.

As for Rosie's remaining ambitions, her gender is unlikely to hold her back initially in her access to a caring profession but, as a woman, she is likely to face greater difficulties in reaching her goal of becoming an MP.

Q4 This question is designed to prompt discussion about the degree to which our behaviour is determined by our genes or our upbringing.

Q5 Suggestions that have been made over how this issue might be addressed include the following:
- more research to help understand why boys are now doing less well than girls
- increase the number of male teachers
- more disciplined regimes in schools
- introduce more 'boy-friendly' styles of teaching and assessment.

Two American researchers, William Draves and Julie Coates, have written that boys don't do as well as girls in school because they are graded on behaviour that is unrelated to what they have learnt. The researchers believe that test-scores are a better indicator of attainment by boys than grades or examination results.

Draves argues that when boys can do something, they want to move on. 'Boys are geared toward new challenges, and they're fine with being tested because they're fine with demonstrating what they know. But they are unwilling to do a repetitive, what is for them a boring task, over and over again when they could be learning something new.'

Sexual equality, pages 118–119

This topic provides a brief outline of the process by which women in Britain achieved the right to vote and stand as candidates in parliamentary elections. It goes on to ask students about their views on whether further measures are necessary to ensure more equal representation for women in Parliament.

OCR GCSE Citizenship Studies

3.2.3 Understand the development of, and struggle for different kinds of rights and freedoms

National Curriculum programme of study, key stage 4
Key concepts 1.1 b; 1.2 a, b
Range and content 3 a, k

Q1, Q2 & Q3 The key arguments in this debate are that women form more than half the population of Britain, but make up only 20 per cent of MPs, resulting in the under-representation of women in Parliament.

Those critical of this situation believe that men do not necessarily understand or represent women's interests, and that a more equal balance of the sexes in Parliament would contribute to better governance.

Further information on closing the gender gap may be found on the Fawcett Society website, www.fawcettsociety.org.uk. Putting the words 'Westminster' or 'politics' into the site's search engine should bring up a number of useful articles on this subject.

Challenging disability, pages 120–121

This topic introduces students to the Disability Discrimination Act 1995 with a case that may also be used to look at the further question of access to justice.

OCR GCSE Citizenship Studies

3.1.2 Understand that the rights of consumers and businesses can conflict but that both have legal rights and responsibilities to each other when items are bought and sold, and that rights are supported by statutory and non-statutory bodies.
3.2.1 Understand the interdependence of individuals, groups and communities
3.2.2 Understand the ways in which rights can compete and conflict. Understand the importance of the law in … resolving conflict and achieving just outcomes.
3.3.1 Evaluate the additional formal and independent support available to individuals requiring information and advice including that available from Government departments, agencies and official regulators, Citizens' Advice, consumer … or rights organisations and solicitors.
3.3.2 Understand the importance of ethical behaviour and social responsibility in enterprise and business including the moral and legal responsibilities businesses have towards each other and the wider community.

National Curriculum programme of study, key stage 4
Key concepts 1.1 b; 1.2 a, b, c
Range and content 3 a, h, k

Q1&Q4 This case hinges on the requirement in law for organisations such as banks to make 'reasonable adjustments' to ensure that all customers can use their services.

In this respect David clearly is unable to access the services offered by this particular branch of the bank and faces the unsatisfactory situation of having to be interviewed about opening a new account *outside* the building – treatment that no other customer would expect to receive.

The bank, on the other hand, claims that it has done everything that could *reasonably* be expected of it, namely providing:
• disabled access at three other branches in the city
• telephone and online banking services to which customers like David have easy access.

The bank also points out that the cost of installing full disabled access to the branch that David visited would be very high, and is a cost that they should not be expected to incur given the arrangements that they have already put in place.

You may also like to indicate to students that legal experts said that the court's decision set a legal precedent which other companies would be expected to follow. One barrister commented that companies could not assume that the provision of disabled access in some branches lighten their obligation to provided it in others.

Other comments at the time made reference to increased costs that small businesses were likely to face as a result of this decision. You may like to ask students whether they feel this is acceptable – particularly in times of economic difficulty.

Q3 As the text indicates, David's mother faced two difficult decisions – a) whether to go ahead with the case in the county court, where costs would be higher than under the small claims procedure, and b) whether to accept the bank's offer of settlement.

If the decision of the court favoured the bank, David's mother could be required to pay both her own legal costs and those of the bank (which are likely to be considerable). She also faced a further problem in her refusal to accept the bank's offer of £1,500 to drop the case. If, after hearing the evidence, the court decided that this was a reasonable settlement, David's mother could be required to pay the bank's costs as well as her own for, in effect, wasting the court's time.

Q5 The statement likening people's access to justice to the Ritz Hotel was made in the nineteenth century by an Irish judge, Justice Mathew, referring to the high costs that many people faced then of taking legal action through the court. As the question suggests, many people feel that this situation still applies, in certain circumstances, today – and raises the question of the strengths and weaknesses of extending access to justice to a much wider section of the population.

For more on this debate, see the Legal Action Group's website, www.lag.org.uk.

Older people

This unit raises a number of citizenship issues about the status and care of older people and outlines the legislation applying to age discrimination.

The future is grey, pages 122–123

In this topic, students discuss the capabilities of older people and the level of responsibility of the state for older people's welfare.

OCR GCSE Citizenship Studies

3.1.1 Understand the moral and legal rights and responsibilities that apply to our interactions with others.

3.3.2 Understand the Government's role in helping to manage the economy and the planning and regulation of public services.

3.4.1 Evaluate the role of governmental and non-governmental organisations to meet community needs, providing services and stimulation social change ... and promoting equal opportunity

National Curriculum programme of study, key stage 4
Key concepts 1.1 b; 1.2 a, b, c
Range and content 3 a

Q1–Q5 These questions are designed to encourage debate about common perceptions of older people, whether these are, in general, accurate, and the kinds of roles that older people can effectively play in society.

There are opportunities here for further research into these issues through students' own personal and family contacts, with the help of organisations such as Age Concern and Help the Aged, who lobby on behalf of older people, and by examining some of the circumstances of older people in the students' own locality.

Q6 This question may raise a number of issues which, if time is available, may merit further debate and investigation, including:
- Should the state retirement age be changed?
- What level of pension should be provided by the state?
- How much do people understand about the pension system in Britain?
- Do people make enough provision for their old age?

Q7 It may be helping in answering this question to ask students to discuss the criteria that they used for selecting their three favoured measures. For example, have they chosen the cheapest, the most effective, the easiest and quickest to implement, or perhaps those that might also benefit other groups in society.

An age-old problem, pages 124–125

This topic considers the arguments for rationing the healthcare of older people and asks whether the age discrimination law should be extended.

OCR GCSE Citizenship Studies

3.1.1 Understand the moral and legal rights and responsibilities that apply to our interactions with others.

3.1.2 Understand that the rights of consumers and businesses can conflict but that both have legal rights and responsibilities to each other when items are bought and sold, and that rights are supported by statutory and non-statutory bodies.

3.2.1 Understand the interdependence of individuals, groups and communities, the need for mutual respect, and the importance of community cohesion

3.3.2 Understand the Government's role in helping to manage the economy and the planning and regulation of public services.

3.4.1 Evaluate the role of governmental and non-governmental organisations to meet community needs, providing services and stimulating social change ... and promoting equal opportunity

National Curriculum programme of study, key stage 4
Key concepts 1.1 b; 1.2 a, b, c
Range and content 3 a

Q1 Students' observations about the care of the patients might include:
- the failure to ensure that the patients were suitably clothed for their transfer to the ambulance
- the demeaning way in which a patient was towed backwards by the porter

OCR Citizenship Studies Teacher's Resource Book for GCSE full and short course
© 2009 Hodder Education

- the failure to explain to patients what was happening, where they were going, and how long they would have to wait
- the clumsy and dangerous way in which the patients were moved about the hospital.

Q2 The hospital apologised to the two patients concerned and took disciplinary action against the staff involved. It also undertook to introduce training programmes to improve standards of care.

Q3&Q4 These questions are designed to encourage debate about the way in which medical care should be allocated. There are a number of criteria that may be used.

Access to medical treatment may be provided on the basis of
a) the position of a person on a waiting list, on the principle of first come, first served
b) the severity of the illness: patients with more serious illnesses receive greater priority
c) the likelihood of further deterioration, with higher priority being given to patients whose condition is likely to deteriorate rapidly
d) the availability of treatment, for example some parts of the country may not have provision for certain kinds of specialist treatment
e) the age of the patient: younger patients are given greater priority than those who are older
f) life style: patients who smoke or are addicted to other drugs are either given lower priority or required to wait for treatment until they have overcome their addiction
g) impact on quality of life: treatment that is likely to have a significant impact on one patient's quality of life can be given greater priority than another where it would have less impact.

Q5 If time is available there are opportunities here for students to investigate the adequacy of local facilities from the perspective of older people.

For more on this debate, see the Legal Action Group's website, www.lag.org.uk.

Housing

This unit introduces the main rights and responsibilities of tenants and landlords and outlines the main ways in which people can get further information and advice on these matters.

A place of your own, pages 126–127

In this topic, students are introduced to the law surrounding tenancy agreements and to the rights and responsibilities associated with the payment of rent and the maintenance and upkeep of a property.

OCR GCSE Citizenship Studies

3.1.2 Understand that landlords and tenants have legal rights and responsibilities in relations to **rents and deposits, health and safety, and the condition of the property.**

National Curriculum programme of study, key stage 4
Key concepts 1.1 b; 1.2 a, b
Range and content 3 a

Q1 There are a number of things in the tenancy agreement that are unclear:
a) the opening point concerning the right of the landlord to raise the rent is ambiguous. It is not clear whether the landlord reserves the right to raise the rent each year by £50 per month or only by £50 per year.
b) The fourth point requires the tenant to keep the interior of the premises 'clean and in good working order'. In fact, the upkeep of some parts of the interior is almost always the landlord's responsibility. This includes the structure of the building and essential services such as heating appliances, sinks, baths and toilets, and water, gas and electricity supplies. Under some tenancy agreements, the landlord may also be responsible for items such as the cooker, refrigerator and washing machine.

c) The use of the phrase 'emergency repairs' in the final clause is also open to interpretation. As the case studies show on pages 127 and 129, problems such as leaking pipes, faulty windows, a running toilet, etc., may all be considered, in certain circumstances, to be emergencies.

d) Finally, the agreement has a number of omissions which make it unfair and one-sided. It fails to list any of the landlord's responsibilities, for example responsibility for maintaining the external and internal structure, keeping key installations (e.g. a lift) in good working order, the maintenance and cleaning of common areas, ensuring that any furnishings provided are fit for purpose, notice periods to end the agreement, and the landlord's rights and duties of access to the tenants premises.

Q2 There are a number of courses of action open to Abyese and Michael. They can:

a) seek to negotiate an agreement with the landlord. They could point out that the charges are unreasonable as:
  • they were not consulted over the repairs and given the opportunity either to do the work themselves or to find someone else to do it who would charge less than the landlord
  • the landlord's labour charges seem very high; they should ask her to justify these rates and to supply receipts for the new materials that were purchased.
  • They can also obtain their own costings for the job by checking the price of materials required at a local DIY store and obtaining an estimate from someone who might carry out this kind of repair as part of their everyday business

b) seek advice from the CAB, local council housing department or other housing advice agency like Shelter to help them negotiate;

c) ask their landlord to use the free dispute resolution scheme operated by the tenancy deposit scheme they are using;

d) make a claim for their deposit in the small claims court; or

e) let the matter drop because they feel that they are unlikely to be successful or that the time taken to carry out the actions listed above would not be cost-effective.

Q3 Both Tom and Arjit should immediately contact the landlord, explaining that the leak had become much more serious and was now causing damage in both flats. In these circumstances it would be reasonable for Tom to request immediate action to effect repairs – i.e. that day, or by the following day at the latest. They should provide evidence of the problem (e.g. photographs or relevant medical evidence about the effect on their health). They should also seek advice about their legal position under the particular type of tenancy agreement.

If the landlord either rejects or fails to meet these demands, Tom has three further courses of action open to him. It would be sensible for him to take advice from, for example, the CAB or a specialist housing agency such as Shelter before taking any of these actions as the law is complicated and his tenancy could be put at risk in some cases.

The first is to begin proceedings against the landlord through a court order, which would require the landlord to carry out the necessary repairs. Tom may also be entitled to an order requiring the landlord to pay him compensation to cover his losses due to the landlord's failure to deal with the problem in a speedy and effective manner. However, going to court can be slow, expensive and time-consuming, and the landlord may well try and evict him by giving notice under the agreement. So Tom may prefer another course of action.

His second route is to report the matter to the local authority on the grounds that the leak poses an environmental or public health hazard. Although local authorities have a number of powers and duties in this respect, they are, in practice, reluctant to intervene in relatively minor cases in view of the financial outlay required.

Tom's third alternative is to arrange and pay for the repairs to be carried out and then to deduct the cost from his future payments of rent. However, in doing this, he runs the risk of the landlord seeking to evict him for failing to pay his rent in the required way. In order to avoid this problem, Tom should write to the landlord giving notice of his intention to arrange for the repairs to be carried out. He should then obtain more than one estimate for the cost of the work, and send these to the landlord, to give him or her a further chance to complete the work within a reasonable period. If the landlord again fails to meet this request, Tom may go ahead and arrange for the work to be done, withholding his rental payments until the cost of the work has been covered.

Whichever course of action Tom follows, it is important for him to keep records of all his telephone, meetings and correspondence surrounding the matter.

Q4 Gemma should seek advice on this matter as soon as possible.

It has already been noted that the terms of the tenancy agreement are ambiguous. With specialist help, Gemma may be able to establish that an increase of £50 per month is invalid. The rent rise may also be unlawful if it is the intention of the landlord to increase the rent within the current tenancy period. In these circumstances, a landlord cannot change the amount of rent payable without the agreement of the tenant, unless the terms of the tenancy allow the landlord to do so.

Gemma should also seek advice concerning any statutory benefits (e.g. housing benefit) to which she may be entitled in order to offset the cost of any additional rent that she may have to pay.

Dealing with problems, pages 128–129

This topic primarily outlines ways in which tenants may seek help and advice in the event of a problem with their landlord.

OCR GCSE Citizenship Studies

3.1.2 Understand that landlords and tenants have legal rights and responsibilities in relation to rents and deposits, health and safety, and the condition of the property, evaluate the extent to which rights are supported and protected by statutory and non-statutory bodies.

National Curriculum programme of study, key stage 4
Key concepts 1.1 b; 1.2 a, b
Range and content 3 a

Q1 Mari's main mistakes were:
- mismanagement of her finances
- her failure to deal with it
- her decision to withhold her rent, and
- her failure to inform or discuss the matter with her landlord or the landlord's agent.

The landlord's agent had no right, in these circumstances, to enter Mari's room, without her permission, to take her passport or to lock her room, denying her access. (Although taking her passport may be regarded as theft, the agent is likely to be able to maintain in his defence that he did not intend to keep it permanently.)

Q2 Mari should immediately contact the landlord's agent to demand that she be allowed readmission to her room. If she is not successful, she should seek advice from an agency or a solicitor with specialist knowledge of housing affairs, using all opportunities for them to intervene on her behalf.

Mari should also inform the college or university authorities about her situation (and, in particular, the actions of the landlord's agent) and take action to improve her current financial position.

In the longer term, Mari may also be able – with legal assistance and advice – to take action against the landlord's agent for unlawful eviction. If successful, Mari would be entitled to a sum in compensation, from either the landlord or the agent.

Q3 In both cases it is important to look at the terms of the agreement if there is one and to find out what type of tenancy it is. Most student tenancies are called 'assured short hold tenancies'. Under these:

Simone is quite entitled to ask the landlord not to come around to her flat unannounced, and to point out that he has no right check cupboards and drawers, etc., where her personal possessions are stored. She may also be able to use the wording of her tenancy agreement, if she has one, to strengthen her case.

She should also consider seeking legal advice and representation, for example a letter written to the landlord from a solicitor or with help from her local CAB will also considerably strengthen her case.

Harit must consider whether the open window poses a security risk or results in his discomfort. If not, arguably the landlord's decision to defer the repairs is reasonable.

If, however, it does seriously affect the security or comfort of the flat, Harit should repeat his request, in writing, to have the repairs dealt with immediately and like Simone, above, seek specialist legal advice with a view to getting help to negotiate with the landlord or as a last resort going to court.

Q4 This question provides opportunities for students to undertake some personal research on the strengths and weaknesses of housing information and advice services – either on a local or a national basis. The organisations mentioned all have information websites (www.advicenow.org.uk; www.shelter.org.uk etc) where students can begin their research.

In both respects, students might find it helpful to look at the services offered in terms of cost, accessibility, opening hours, waiting times and availability of specialist advice, and whether the individual or agency concerned is able to support or take action on a client's behalf.

The topic of access to legal information, advice and representation could form the basis of a *citizenship campaign* for students taking OCR GCSE Citizenship Studies. Evidence on this issue is available from a number of publications and organisations.

The need for greater legal understanding was investigated by the PLEAS (Public Legal Education and Support) task force, whose recommendations are available from its website, www.pleas.org.uk, and on www.plenet.org.uk. In 2006, the Dept for Constitutional Affairs (now the Ministry of Justice) published a report entitled *Getting Earlier, Better Advice to Vulnerable People*, setting out the consequences for people of getting into legal difficulties.

Students may also be able to obtain further information and guidance through local solicitor contacts, local law societies or community law services, or through national organisations such as Law Centres Federation, the Legal Action Group or Young Legal Aid Lawyers, again see websites for further details.

OCR Citizenship Studies Teacher's Resource Book for GCSE full and short course
© 2009 Hodder Education

Making a Difference

Voting and elections
- A problem for the council
- The right to vote
- Election to Parliament

Party politics
- Join the party
- Where do you stand?
- Newspapers

Campaigning
- Home alone
- We want our bus back!
- How far should you go?

Voting and elections

The three topics in this unit look at systems of voting in the UK.

A problem for the council, pages 130–131

This unit introduces the concept of democracy.

> **OCR GCSE Citizenship Studies**
>
> **3.2.3** Understand ways in which citizens can play an active part in the electoral process to influence decision-making through membership of political parties and participation in local and national elections. Evaluate the extent to which citizens can play an active part in the electoral process to influence decision-making and to hold decision-makers to account …
>
> **National Curriculum programme of study, key stage 4**
> **Key concepts** 1.1 a, d; 1.2 a
> **Range and content** 3 a, d, e

Q1 The City council could make these decisions by:
- a vote in council, without reference to any outside groups
- a vote in council, following local consultation or a public vote
- a public vote, i.e. a referendum, of all registered electors
- a limited public vote restricted, for example, to council tax payers or parents with children at school.

Q2 The main argument in support of the council's decision to hold a referendum is that it gave everyone an opportunity to register their view, ensuring that the will of the registered electors prevailed. It is, arguably, a very fair way to make the decision.

However, arguments against this measure include:
- 60 per cent of those eligible did not vote in the referendum, bringing into question whether the result was reflective of popular opinion
- voters included those who did not send their children to local state schools, perhaps bringing into question their right to vote on this matter.

Q3 Students' answers and reasoning are likely to be determined largely by the nature of the subject under consideration and the context in which the vote might take place.

For example, when citing direct democracy as the best option, students may argue that the issue is too important or too controversial for the government to make a decision on the nation's behalf. This is sometimes reflected in a country's decision to hold a referendum when changes to the constitution are being considered.

Sometimes a referendum may be more appropriate for issues that impact on personal behaviour. For example, New Zealand has in the past held referenda on the licensing and availability of alcohol.

The size of the country or community may also have some bearing on whether to invoke direct democracy. A referendum may be more appropriate (and easier to organise) in smaller relatively cohesive communities.

Some students may argue that representative democracy is more appropriate for complex issues on which it would be unreasonable to expect the general public to be able to make an informed decision. (It may be interesting here to explore arguments that run counter to this view.)

Finally, students may argue that certain issues may not merit the extra expenditure required to organise a referendum or may require a swift decision, making lengthy consultation inappropriate.

Q4 Direct democracy:
• gives people an opportunity to become directly involved in decisions about local community or national issues
• may not be appropriate for issues that are too complex, or cannot be reduced to one or two simple questions
• can work to the disadvantage of minority groups whose interests may not be addressed through a simple majority verdict.

Representative democracy:
• may largely reflect public opinion when representatives are elected
• may ensure a government response over a public outcry on a particular issue
• allows an elected government to be removed at the next election if it fails to meet public expectation
• offers an element of choice for the electorate between rival parties and programmes
• can offer a relatively swift, broad and considered level of decision-taking
• is able to protect the rights of individuals and minority groups.

However, governments based on representative democracy do not necessarily respond to public pressure and are not always reflective of opinion. It is also worth noting that certain conditions are required for the effective functioning of a representative democracy. These include regular and fair elections, with voting rights for all adults, offering an effective choice of candidates, with a free and diverse media.

Q5 In addition to those topics already listed in the materials, students' suggestions may include the detention of terror suspects, Britain's membership of the European Union, further devolution for Wales, Scotland and Northern Ireland, the provision of certain local services, and changes to the voting system.

This question may be used, by those students taking the OCR examination, as a starting point for a citizenship campaign.

The right to vote, pages 132–133

In this topic, students examine a number of issues associated with low voter turnout.

OCR GCSE Citizenship Studies

3.2.3 Understand ways in which citizens can play an active part in the electoral process to influence decision-making through membership of political parties and participation in local and national elections. Evaluate the extent to which citizens can play an active part in the electoral process to influence decision-making and to hold decision-makers to account …

National Curriculum programme of study, key stage 4
Key concepts 1.1 a, d; 1.2 a
Range and content 3 a, d, e

Q1 Natalie decided not to vote because she felt that none of the political parties truly represented her views.

Some students might argue that this was a good reason and that, by not voting, she indicated her disagreement with all the parties that were standing. Others might argue that she should still vote for the party that best reflects her views (even if this is not perfect). This is because of the unlikelihood of one party ever entirely reflecting her beliefs. They may add that by not voting, Natalie is exerting no influence at all in the outcome of the election.

Q2 In addition to the points listed in Q3, students may also argue that not voting doesn't matter because:
- one vote rarely counts among so many
- some people will vote, and a government will therefore always be chosen
- all parties are the same and therefore nothing will change.

On the other hand, it may also be argued that not voting means that:
- those who choose not to vote can have no say in who forms the government
- the government is not representative of the population as a whole.

Q3 Students can be asked in small groups, to rank these points, and any others of their own, as a stimulus for a discussion on the importance of voting in elections.

Q4 If time is available, students may wish to investigate these ideas further and to try to find out other measures that have been adopted by countries elsewhere in the world.

Further information on alternative voting methods is available from the Electoral Reform Society, www.electoral-reform.org.uk.

This question may be used, by those students taking the OCR examination, as a starting point for a citizenship campaign.

Q5 Some of the reasons might include:
- the impact of advertising and publicity campaigns deigned to encourage greater participation, such as those organised by the Electoral Commission, www.electoralcommission.org.uk
- less satisfaction with the Government than in 2001
- a wish by some people to register their opposition to controversial issues, such as the war in Iraq.

Election to Parliament, pages 134–135

This unit looks at recent general election results and alternative systems from first past the post.

OCR GCSE Citizenship Studies

3.2.4 Know in outline about our … political relationships with other countries in Europe
3.4.3 Evaluate the merits and demerits of the different voting systems operating within the United Kingdom.

National Curriculum programme of study, key stage 4
Key concepts 1.1 a, b, d; 1.2 a
Range and content 3 a, d, e

Q1 The Labour Party won the 2005 election

Q2 If seats had have been allocated according to the percentage of votes, the results would have been:
- Labour Party: 226 seats
- Conservative Party: 207 seats
- Liberal Democrats: 142 seats
- Others: 71 seats

Some criticisms of the first-past-the-post system are:
- the number of seats gained is not proportional to the number of votes
- smaller parties are at a disadvantage, as they often receive a smaller number of seats in proportion to their vote
- parties can win a lot of seats by a very small amount of votes.

Q3 This question could be used as the basis for a mock election which could run across a whole class or year group. Hansard's 'Y Vote' website is a useful source of information on this – www.mockelections.co.uk.

Q4 Students may notice that:
- the use of the single transferable vote (STV) means that the class ends up with several representatives, not just the one most popular
- the winners under STV and first-past-the-post vote might not be the same
- fewer students are dissatisfied with the result of the STV vote, although some might feel that this does not reflect the majority view.

Party politics

The three topics in this unit look at the nature and function of political parties and the impact of the media on the political process.

Join the party, pages 136–137

This topic provides students with a brief indication of the different political parties in England and Wales.

> **OCR GCSE Citizenship Studies**
>
> **3.2.3** Understand the ways in which citizens can play an active part in the electoral process to influence decision-making and to hold decision-makers to account locally, globally and nationally, including through membership of interest groups and pressure groups. Understand the importance of political parties, interest groups, pressure groups and the media in influencing public debate and policy formation.
>
> **National Curriculum programme of study, key stage 4**
> **Key concepts** 1.1 a, b, d; 1.2 a
> **Range and content** 3 a, d, e

Q1 Students might identify a range of local issues that are particular to their area. On a national and international level, potential issues include:
- reducing poverty
- action to prevent wars and conflict
- reducing taxes
- reducing debt for individuals and for nations
- improving services such as health and education.

Q2 In answering this question, students will need to consider how the support of individuals, communities and governments (possibly both at home and overseas) will be enlisted and maintained.

Q3 The best sources of information for this are the political party websites. If time is available, MPs, candidates or party representatives might be invited into school to explain their party's policies and to be questioned by students.

Q4 Students could record their findings to Q3 in the form of a table to make comparison easier. In identifying similarities and differences, it is probably helpful to ask them to concentrate on specific issues, such as the economy, health and education.

You may also wish to divide the class into groups to compare policies in different areas, and then to share their findings.

Q5 The strengths and weaknesses of single-issue parties include:
- they can be very effective in addressing specific issues that affect an area
- there is likely to be a strong awareness of the issue amongst the local community
- the party may not have well-developed policies covering matters outside the particular issue with which it is concerned
- it will probably be difficult for voters to gauge how the party will respond to other issues

OCR Citizenship Studies Teacher's Resource Book for GCSE full and short course
© 2009 Hodder Education

- even if successful, with just one MP a single-issue party may still find it difficult to achieve its main outcome unless it is able to forge alliances with one or more of the main parties.

Where do you stand? Pages 138–139

This topic examines the value of the terms left and right wing in describing and assessing political views.

OCR GCSE Citizenship Studies

3.2.3 Understand the ways in which citizens can play an active part in the electoral process to influence decision-making and to hold decision-makers to account locally, globally and nationally, including through membership of interest groups and pressure groups. Understand the importance of political parties, interest groups, pressure groups and the media in influencing public debate and policy formation.

National Curriculum programme of study, key stage 4
Key concepts 1.1 a, b, d; 1.2 a
Range and content 3 a, d, e

Q1 The political views broadly sit at the following ends of the political spectrum:
a) left wing
b) right wing
c) right wing
d) left wing
e) left wing
f) left wing
g) right wing.

Q2 This question might raise some difficulties if students have extreme views on particular issues. It may be advisable to ask students to complete this on the basis of specific areas, such as the economy and taxation, healthcare and education.

Q3 Students will find the research they did for Q3, page 137, helpful when answering this.

Most will probably come to the conclusion that the parties today are less strongly aligned to their traditional positions than they were in the past. If time is available, you could ask students to show on the political spectrum where each party stands on a limited number of issues.

Q4 Students will find their answer to Q4, page 137, helpful when answering this.

It can be argued that greater differences between parties would give more choice for voters, and perhaps raise voter turnout. On the other hand, it may be said that the similarities between parties represents greater social consensus than in the past.

Newspapers, pages 140–141

This topic looks at the influence of the media on political views.

OCR GCSE Citizenship Studies

3.2.3 Understand the ways in which citizens can play an active part in the electoral process to influence decision-making and to hold decision-makers to account locally, globally and nationally, including through membership of interest groups and pressure groups. Understand the importance of political parties, interest groups, pressure groups and the media in influencing public debate and policy formation.

National Curriculum programme of study, key stage 4
Key concepts 1.1 a, b, d; 1.2 a
Range and content 3 a, d, e

Q1 Factors influencing voting behaviour include:

- party policies
- the perception of the party leader
- the way each political party and leader is represented in the media
- the impact of recent events, working either in favour or against a political party
- their perception of the party that generally represents and supports their interests
- the party that they (or their family) have traditionally voted for.

Q2 The reporting of political issues in newspapers may reflect the political values of the newspapers, but also be shaped in way that is designed to maximise sales, by highlighting, for example, some of the more sensational aspects of a political party's plans or statements from their leader or MPs.

Radio and television reporting tends to be more neutral, although, at times, the broadcast media do find themselves censured for bias.

Some students may feel that the media often fail to provide a detailed insight into issues, with reports of limited length, giving no more than a brief overview.

To improve the situation, students might suggest:
- higher standards of citizenship or political education in schools
- stronger requirements for high-quality political programming in the broadcast media
- greater penalties for misleading reporting.

Q3 The representation given by the 3 different types of media could be as follows:
a) that only 40 per cent of people would vote against the currency
b) that well over half did not support the adoption of the euro
c) that the numbers supporting a move to the euro were marginally greater than those opposing it, but that almost one in six people remained uncertain about the issue.

Campaigning

The three topics in this unit are to explore a number of aspects of community action.

Home alone, pages 142–143

This topic asks students to consider the key factors in a successful campaign to prevent two people from being deported from the UK.

OCR GCSE Citizenship Studies

3.2.3 Understand the ways in which citizens can play an active part in the electoral process to influence decision-making and to hold decision-makers to account locally, globally and nationally, including through membership of interest groups and pressure groups.

National Curriculum programme of study, key stage 4
Key concepts 1.1 b,
Range and content 3 a, d, h

Q1 Students may suggest that Florence could:
- seek advice about her legal position from an organisation specialising in immigration affairs or from a solicitor with similar expertise.
- obtain statements from members of the local community, her daughters' school and possibly the church supporting her and her daughter's wish to stay in Britain
- seek publicity for the case from the local media
- approach local councillors and selected MPs for their support.

Q2 Students' answers may suggest that the school should show support for the girls by:
- writing letters to MPs and to the Home Secretary explaining why they think they should be allowed to remain in Britain
- gathering statements of support from students, parents, teachers and governors
- seeking assistance from other parts of the local community.

Q3 Important factors in the success of the campaign include:
- persistence: the campaign continued, even though leave to remain had twice been refused

- a range of methods: the campaign included lobbying, protests, public meeting, the use of the media and support of key local figures – as well as following the more formal appeals procedures
- the use of legal expertise.

Q4 The campaign clearly benefited the Okolo family, who were able to remain in Britain as they wished. Also, through their involvement in the campaign, benefits were almost certainly brought to the school and other parts of the local community involved in trying to persuade the authorities to overturn the original decision.

A Fight to Belong by Alan Gibbons, published by Save the Children, and accompanied by a teaching pack outlines the Okolo family campaign.

We want our bus back! Pages 144–145

This topic is based on a campaign led by young people to restore a bus service. It may be useful as a stimulus activity to help students begin planning their controlled assessment.

OCR GCSE Citizenship Studies

3.2.3 Understand the ways in which citizens can play an active part in the electoral process to influence decision-making and to hold decision-makers to account locally, globally and nationally, including through membership of interest groups and pressure groups. Understand the importance of political parties, interest groups, pressure groups and the media in influencing public debate and policy formation.
3.4.1 Understand the processes needed for successful community action.

National Curriculum programme of study, key stage 4
Key concepts 1.1 b
Range and content 3 a, d, h

Q1 All Lena's friends' comments are negative, indicating that they don't think there is much that can be done to stop the cancellation of the bus service.

You may wish to discuss this question as a whole after students have had the opportunity to discuss and respond to (say) three of the statements in small groups.

Q2 Suggestions for what to do next might include:
- organise a petition to reinstate the bus service
- discuss the matter with senior staff at school and seek the school's help to take up the matter with the local authority and the bus company
- seek support from local councillors and MPs
- invite the local media to write a story about their campaign.

Q3 The tactics used by the students in their campaign were:
- writing a letter to the bus company, pointing out their concern
- organising a petition signed by those who used the existing bus service
- gaining publicity in the local press, and providing them with photographs and material for articles
- making posters for display in the local area
- seeking help and advice from the school
- meeting a local councillor
- writing to their local MP.

Q4 Probably the most significant measure was to persuade the local council to begin discussions with the bus company about ways of retaining the service.

Q5 Pressure groups identified in each category could include those listed below:
Sectional: National Union of Teachers, British Medical Association, Confederation of British Industry, Unison.
Cause: Greenpeace, Countryside Alliance, Liberty, Friends of the Earth.
Insider: Confederation of British Industry, Trade Unions (although they have less influence now than they once did).
Outsider: Greenpeace, Fathers for Justice groups

How far should you go? Pages 146–147

This topic, centred on protests to close a farm breeding animals for scientific experimentation, asks whether illegal action by campaigners can be justified. It may also be used as part of a wider study on the arguments surrounding the use of animals in scientific research.

OCR GCSE Citizenship Studies

3.2.2 Understand ways in which rights can compete and conflict and how the law is used to resolve these issues justly

3.2.3 Understand the ways in which citizens can play an active part in the electoral process to influence decision-making and to hold decision-makers to account locally, globally and nationally, including through membership of interest groups and pressure groups. Understand the importance of political parties, interest groups, pressure groups and the media in influencing public debate and policy formation.

3.4.2 Evaluate the justifications people give for breaking the law, including to bring about change, and understand the reasons for upholding the rule of law.

National Curriculum programme of study, key stage 4
Key concepts 1.1 b; 1.2 a, b, c
Range and content 3 a, b d, h

Q1 You could present this question by asking students for general comments on the use of animals in scientific experiments. These can be sorted into broadly positive and negative and the arguments developed – with the support of the information on these, and available elsewhere.

There are obviously opportunities for further research if time is available.

Q2 Students might argue that the protestors were right to use force because
• the breeding of cats for use in medical research is entirely unacceptable, and
• earlier, more lawful efforts to stop the breeding had been unsuccessful.

Others might argue that:
• violent actions of this kind are wrong, regardless of how the protestors might have felt about the animal breeding programme
• even if the protests stop Mr Brown from breeding cats for research, it will still be possible to obtain them from elsewhere
• violent action of this kind is costly and disruptive to the wider community.

These, and the remaining questions in this section, provide a useful opportunity to discuss with students the question of the rule of law with students. Is it ever acceptable to break the law – even for a just cause – or should protest be entirely within the law?

Q3&Q4 Before setting these final questions, and if time is available, it may be helpful to widen this question by looking at other examples of active campaigning and protest. These might include actions taken by Fathers 4 Justice, Greenpeace and groups campaigning against the expansion of airports/widening of roads/housing developments. There may be also be local examples to draw upon.

Alternatively, if the facilities are available, students could be asked to research and identify a campaign fitting one or more of the statements.

Government

> **National government**
> - Governing Britain
> - Controlling the government
>
> **Devolution**
> - Governing ourselves
>
> **Local government**
> - Local councils
>
> **European government**
> - Governing Europe
>
> **Forms of government**
> - The power to govern

National government

The two topics units in this unit outline the role of MPs and how the power of government is kept in check.

Governing Britain, pages 148–149

This unit examines some of the roles and responsibilities of MPs.

> **OCR GCSE Citizenship Studies**
>
> **3.2.3** Understand ways in which citizens can play an active part in the electoral process to influence decision-making through membership of political parties and participation in local and national elections. Evaluate the extent to which citizens can play an active part in the electoral process to influence decision-making and to hold decision-makers to account …
> **3.4.3** Understand the role of a Member of Parliament (MP) and how they exercise responsibility for constituents.
>
> **National Curriculum programme of study, key stage 4**
> **Key concepts** 1.1 a, b, d; 1.2 a, c
> **Range and content** 3 a, c, d, e

Q1 a) The main types of work undertaken by the MP in the week in question are as follows:
- dealing with constituency matters: reading and replying to correspondence from constituents; listening to constituents concerns, and advising and helping, where appropriate; attending functions in the constituency; acting on behalf of constituents
- attending Parliament: taking part in debates and Prime Minister's Question Time
- dealing with party matters: in his own constituency and meeting in Westminster with other Conservative MPs to discuss the week's business in Parliament
- dealing with special Parliamentary interests.

b) The MP's special areas of interest are: children's issues (e.g. poverty, social services) and the environment.

Q2 There is a strong argument that Mr Mandelson should represent the views of his constituents, regardless of his own personal thoughts on the matter. As an elected representative, he has a duty to speak on their behalf on the issue.

However, in opposing this, some students may argue that Mr Mandelson also has a duty to take decisions in what he regards as the best interests of his constituency – even if this does not always reflect the opinions of the majority of his constituents. They may add that Mr Mandelson also has to recognise that many constituents will not have the full facts of the case available to them.

You may wish to continue the discussion by giving students further instances of this kind of dilemma, perhaps encouraging them to draw up criteria that might determine or shape the position an MP might take on other controversial issues, such as abortion or fox hunting.

Q3 Legally, car park tickets are usually non-transferable. This means that they have no validity in law if passed from one user to the next, even if there is time remaining. Despite this, however, it is a common practice amongst the public.

This dilemma was taken from the website of John Redwood MP, who was offered a ticket by one of his constituents just as he was about to pay his parking fee. The offer was one of kindness and there was no chance that anyone would find out about it. The MP had three choices to:
- accept the ticket and save money
- avoid the dilemma by telling the constituent that he needed to buy a ticket for more than an hour, or
- explain that (particularly as an MP) he had a duty not to break the law and should pay for a ticket.

Mr Redwood decided to refuse the offer and buy a ticket, feeling that he could not break the rules, even though it was unlikely that anyone would ever find out.

The case was put up on Mr Redwood's website, and selected for *Citizenship Studies*, before the public controversy surrounding MPs' claims and expenses. Although of a relatively trivial nature, it may be used to raise a more general question about the standards of probity that should be followed by MPs – and others.

You may find the following viewpoints useful in a discussion:
- if people don't like the rules, they shouldn't break them, but should seek to change them; this is the basis of democracy
- we cannot be selective about the law, cherry-picking those we agree with and ignoring those that we don't
- as lawmakers, MPs have a greater duty than others not to be lawbreakers.

This final point can be summarised in a quotation from Chaucer's *Canterbury Tales*, 'if gold rusts what will iron do?'

Controlling the government, pages 150–151

This topic discusses a number of ways in which the power of a government may be kept in check.

OCR GCSE Citizenship Studies

3.2.3 Evaluate Parliament's role in holding the Government to account in a representative democracy. Understand that non-democratic forms of government are likely to infringe human rights. Evaluate the extent to which citizens can play an active part in the electoral process to influence decision-making and to hold decision-makers to account …

3.4.3 Understand the role of a Member of Parliament (MP) and how they exercise responsibility for constituents.

National Curriculum programme of study, key stage 4
Key concepts 1.1 a, b, d; 1.2 a, b
Range and content 3 a, c, d, e

Q1 There are obviously a wide range of issues on which students could draw to answer this question. For example, they might relate to problems surrounding:
- the quality of health care or education
- childcare or other social service provision
- the release and supervision of offenders
- transport policy
- economic issues
- migration policy
- crime reduction
- protection of the environment
- preparations for the Olympic Games.

It is important here for students to identify national, rather than local, issues that are of concern to the government in Westminster. Local issues, such as reducing litter or providing more facilities for young people, are the responsibility of the local council, although students could consider what national government could do to improve local government and local right across the country.

This question may be used, by those students taking the OCR examination, as a starting point for a citizenship campaign.

Q2 The release of the minutes of Cabinet meetings held in the run up to the Iraq War in 2003 was vetoed by Justice Secretary Jack Straw in February 2009 using a clause in the *Freedom of Information Act*. This followed a decision by the Information Tribunal in January 2009 that they should be published.

The government argued that the release of the minutes would do 'serious damage' to Cabinet government by making ministers reluctant to discuss such controversial issues in the future, making decision-making more difficult.

The Information Tribunal ruled that the papers should be released in the public interest because of the significance of this particular decision and the questions surrounding the legality of the war in Iraq. Some argued that refusal to do so added to the perception that the government had something to hide.

In June 2009, the Government announced plans for an independent Committee of Inquiry into the Iraq War, with evidence being heard in private. The Prime Minister explained to the House of Commons that the Committee of Inquiry will have access to the full range of information, including secret information, and will be able to see any British document and to ask for any British citizen to appear before it. He added that the Committee will publish its findings in as full a form as possible, and that they will then be debated in both the House of Commons and the House of Lords.

Devolution

This unit gives details of the Scottish Parliament and the Northern Ireland and Welsh assemblies, and asks whether greater independence should be given to people in Scotland and Wales.

Governing ourselves, pages 152–153

OCR GCSE Citizenship Studies

3.2.1 Explore the diverse national, regional … communities in the United Kingdom and understand the different forces that bring about change in communities over time. Understand that the United Kingdom is a country with wide cultural diversity where people's sense of identity is often complex.

3.4.3 Understand the changing relationships in the United Kingdom between England, Scotland, Wales and Northern Ireland, and the role of national assemblies/parliaments in establishing different laws and policies in the four nations.

National Curriculum programme of study, key stage 4
Key concepts 1.1 b, c; 1.2 c; 1.3 a, b, d
Range and content 3 a, c, d, e, l

Q1&Q2 Arguments in favour of independence include the following:
- it is the only way in which both countries can take control of their own affairs
- both countries lack real power in the current situation
- the current allocation of funding under the Barnett Formula is unfair
- both countries have extensive natural resources, from which they do not currently fully benefit, but which could be used to secure economic survival under independence
- the needs and interests of Welsh and Scottish people cannot be met by the government at Westminster, because of the domination of English MPs
- Scotland and Wales have a distinct culture and history that is different from England and that Scotland, at one time, existed as an independent kingdom.

Some of the arguments against independence are that:
- it will bring about the break-up of the United Kingdom – something that will work to the disadvantage of all UK citizens
- contrary to those in favour of independence, critics argue that Scotland and Wales do particularly well under the Barnett Formula
- independence would damage, rather than improve, the economic position of Scotland and Wales
- as small independent countries, Scotland and Wales would become marginalised on the European and world stage.

The Barnett Formula is the name given to a mechanism used to determine the budgets of the Welsh, Scottish and Northern Ireland Offices.

Named after the former Chief Secretary, Joel Barnett, the Formula automatically adjusts the amount of money available to the devolved countries, based on population level, when changes in funding levels are made in England. Under this arrangement, the devolved governments have considerable discretion in how this money is allocated.

Q3 Students' suggestions may include:
- to provide England with its own Parliament to decide on matters affecting England alone. This could be either a distinct body, or simply those Westminster MPs representing English constituencies
- remove the voting rights of Scottish MPs on matters that purely affect England
- remove all Scottish MPs from the Commons, giving Scotland its own Parliament and, therefore, independence.

Local government

This unit outlines the work of local government and asks whether there should be any changes in the way in which local services are paid for.

Local councils, pages 154–155

OCR GCSE Citizenship Studies

3.2.3 Understand ways in which citizens can play an active part in the electoral process to influence decision-making through membership of political parties and participation in local and national elections. Evaluate the extent to which citizens can play an active part in the electoral process to influence decision-making and to hold decision-makers to account …

3.4.1 Understand that different groups may hold differing views on the nature of the community's needs and the best ways to meet these needs.

3.4.3 Understand the process through which candidates are nominated for local … elections

National Curriculum programme of study, key stage 4
Key concepts 1.1 a, b, d; 1.2 a
Range and content 3 a, d, e, m

Q1 The following services are made reference to in the passage:
- refuse collection and recycling
- public transport
- education
- highway maintenance and safety
- public libraries
- recreation and leisure services
- social services and care for the elderly
- planning.

Q2 A *local income tax* would probably work through the Inland Revenue, much like income tax. Those people who support the idea believe that it would avoid the great variation that currently exists in council tax levels from one part of the country to another, and would ensure that people are taxed on the value of their income, rather than

OCR Citizenship Studies Teacher's Resource Book for GCSE full and short course
© 2009 Hodder Education

the value of the property. Council tax rates are the same for the rich and the poor, who live in a particular area, and are not dependent on a person's ability to pay.

Charging for local services would have some benefit of equity or fairness, and may ensure an improvement in service delivery. It may also serve to change people's behaviour in a positive way. For example, charging people to collect their rubbish may encourage people to waste less and to recycle more (or to drive out of town and dump it on the roadside). Critics may also argue that some services bringing a relatively low income, perhaps libraries or museums, are likely to be lost under such an arrangement. It may also be pointed out that some people would be reluctant to have to begin paying for services that are currently included within the general council tax payment.

A population tax was the basis of the community charge, or poll tax, introduced in 1989 in Scotland, and in 1990 in England and Wales. Tax rates in some areas were higher than anticipated, and the tax became widely unpopular. It was also a tax that was not always paid – owner-occupiers were easy to identify, but it was difficult to collect from those who frequently changed their accommodation. Many people also refused to pay their tax on principal, believing it to be fundamentally unjust.

Q3&Q4 Reasons for low turnout in local elections include the following:
- the perception of local government as lacking importance in people's lives
- the failure of some people to register to vote
- the recent perceived decline in the status of political parties and politicians
- disengagement of certain groups of people from politics
- insufficient campaigning by the political parties

European government

The unit is designed to provide a simple outline of the structure of government in the European Union, and asks students to consider how it could be made more democratic.

Governing Europe, pages 156–157

OCR GCSE Citizenship Studies

3.2.4 Know, in outline, about our economic, political, legal and cultural relationships with other countries in Europe. Evaluate the implications of the United Kingdom's membership of the European Union and that European Union decisions have an impact upon citizens of the United Kingdom.

National Curriculum programme of study, key stage 4
Key concepts 1.1 d
Range and content 3 c, d, e, m

Q1 The following websites may be helpful for research, although, with some, students may need guidance on finding the appropriate pages:
- the official gateway to the European Union, http://europa.eu
- the Directgov website, www.direct.gov.uk – click on the links to Government, citizens and rights, UK Government, UK and the World, and then the European Union
- the BBC News Inside Europe, accessible via the BBC News website, http://news.bbc.co.uk
- the website of the European Parliament, www.europarl.europa.eu
- the UK Office of the European Parliament, www.europarl.org.uk.

Q2 For this question, it would be helpful to split local and national government into their constituent parts, similar to Q1. For local government this could include: parish, district/borough, metropolitan or county councils depending on the area. For national government this could include: House of Commons, House of Lords, Monarchy, Government, Prime Minister and the Cabinet.

Students might need to research the powers of each institution and how representatives are chosen more thoroughly.

Section 6: Answers to questions in the Student's Book

For information on local government, students can refer to pp.154–155 of the student's book and the websites of their own local authority. Information is also available from the Directgov website, www.direct.gov.uk, clicking on Government, citizens and rights, and then local government.

Information about the UK national government can be found in the student material on pp. 148–151 and on the website for the UK Parliament Education Service, at www.parliament.uk/education/index.htm.

Forms of government

This unit uses the example of a former dictatorship to ask students to consider the question of how a country should be governed.

The power to govern, pages 158–159

OCR GCSE Citizenship Studies

3.1.4 Explore connections between values, viewpoints and actions with respect to rights and responsibilities for individuals in national and global contexts

3.2.1 Understand the interdependence of individuals, groups and communities, the need for mutual respect and understand and the importance of community cohesion.

3.2.2 Understand that organisations and governments have responsibility to ensure that rights are balanced, supported and protected.

3.2.3 Understand the different operation of power and authority in democratic and non-democratic forms of government, historically and across the world today. Understand that non-democratic forms of government are likely to infringe human rights.

National Curriculum programme of study, key stage 4
Key concepts 1.1 b, d; 1.2 b
Range and content 3 a, e

Q1&Q2 If time is available, you may wish to provide or help students find more information on some of the events surrounding this issue.

The election of President Allende in 1970 was subject to close scrutiny and involvement by the American CIA and the Russian KGB, with both organisations trying to influence its outcome, with a view to retaining influence in the area.

The US Government had particular concerns over the establishment of a *Marxist* government in Chile, whose proposals included the nationalisation of US interests in the country. The US Government became actively involved in trying to defeat Salvador Allende in the election and imposed economic sanctions on Chile immediately after the election result.

In the short run, President Allende's economic policies of price freezes, wage increases and state intervention met with some success, helping to redistribute income, reduce unemployment and curb inflation. However, within two years, serious problems had returned. Inflation had reached 140 per cent, private investment was being withdrawn and there were acute shortages in the shops.

Q3 Some students might suggest that it is acceptable to overthrow a government when it is:
- seriously abusing its power by, for example, committing major human rights atrocities
- facing serious and widespread outbreaks of crime and disorder
- creating serious and widespread economic problems through its management of the economy

Again, if time permits, it be would be instructive for students to try to link their suggestions to real-life events.

Q4&Q5 Students may suggest that the following practices are unacceptable:
- the widespread detention of President Allende's supporters
- their torture and murder of more than 3,000 people
- the imposition of military rule

- becoming President of Chile, and appointing others in position of power, without an electoral mandate
- suppressing political debate and opposition
- the persecution of political opponents
- heavy censorship of the press
- forbidding workers from going on strike
- the unilateral creation of a new national constitution that would ensure that President Pinochet would remain in power, regardless of the will of the electorate.

Q6 A simple way of answering this question is for students to supply words or phrases describing qualities that governments should show: for example, fairness, support for the weak, leadership, strength, a willingness to tackle difficult problems, listening to the views of the people.

Q7 The case for the *gradual* introduction of liberal democracy is made in the question. Students who oppose this view may argue that
- it is a recipe for things to stay the same and for dictatorships to remain in place
- the introduction of democracy may give people the feeling that they have more of a stake in their nation's future, resulting in more participation and enterprise
- it is incorrect (and patronising) to argue that uneducated people cannot determine what their country's interests are
- allowing free discussion and debate, with equal access to the media, should allow people to listen to the full-range of political views, and enable them to come to a reasoned judgement.

Media

The power of the media
- The front page
- Managing the news
- Freedom to publish

The power of the media

This unit looks at the influence of the media on our lives and asks whether there should be any changes in the way that it operates.

The front page, pages 160–161

This topic outlines the significance of the print and broadcast media in Britain today.

OCR GCSE Citizenship Studies

3.3.3 Understand the role of the media, the internet and other new communication technologies, in international affairs, in providing information and affecting opinion.

National Curriculum programme of study, key stage 4
Key concepts 1.2 c
Range and content 3 g

Q1&Q2 Each of the headlines was placed on the front page of the following papers:

Headline	Newspaper
The last few hours of the US presidential election campaign	*Daily Mail* *Daily Telegraph* The *Guardian* The *Independent* The *Sun* The *Times*
Banks charging borrowers too much	*Daily Express*
Schools breaking guidelines for pupil admissions	*Daily Telegraph*
Terminally ill patients more likely to get drugs to give them an extra month or two of life	*Daily Telegraph*
Claims that Lewis Hamilton's winning race was fixed	*Daily Express* *Daily Star*
Call to reduce the amount of swearing on television	*Daily Mirror*
Scientists create clones of a mouse that has been dead and frozen for 16 years	*Daily Mail*
Don't stretch before taking exercise	*Daily Telegraph*
Presidential candidate's grandmother dies on eve of presidential election	The *Sun*

Q3 You may wish to ask students to look at this question from a number of different perspectives, for example from that of:

the reader: to update, to inform, to entertain, to explore certain issues more deeply, as reference, to confirm or support their own views

the newspaper: to sell newspapers, to develop a loyal readership base, to promote a particular political perspective, to gain support for a particular cause

interest groups, political parties, etc: for these groups, newspapers have a purpose in informing the public, disseminating ideas, encouraging discussion and debate, which arguably contributes to a more informed and literate society, and one which democratic values are more likely to pervade.

Q4 The *advantages* of access to multi-channel television lie in the access to the huge store of information that it provides. The accessibility, quantity and (generally speaking) quality of this information exceed anything that has been available in the past.

It also, arguably, provides more rounded coverage of international events than would be available through just a small number of channels. For those who choose to take advantage of it, viewers are now able to have a number of perspectives (e.g. from the US, Europe and the Middle East) on certain international issues.

The *disadvantages* of multi-channel access may be seen in terms of questions of the quality and reliability of reporting. Stations on a limited budget may be largely reliant on outside sources for their information, resulting in possibly simplified or limited content, or in presentational formats that are designed primarily to entertain, rather than inform.

Q5 Students may point out that the consolidation of the media into a smaller number of groups enables companies to share resources and benefit from economies of scale. This may be of particular value to those companies that are suffering from loss of income through declining advertising sales.

The drawbacks of larger and fewer businesses controlling the media include:
- the risk that it poses for local newspapers and broadcasting stations. Some may be unable to compete with rivals that have taken over by major organisations, and those that come under new ownership may lose their community function in the pursuit of company profits.
- local programming and features may not be maintained under multinational ownership, resulting in less diverse and sometimes lower quality programmes or features.

More information on this question is available in the First Report of the House of Lords Communications Committee, Session 2007–8, www.publications.parliament.uk/pa/ld200708/ldselect/ldcomuni/122/12202.htm

Managing the news, pages 162–163

This topic looks at the presentation of the news in the media, and asks students to discuss the acceptability of news management.

OCR GCSE Citizenship Studies

3.3.3 Understand the role of the media, the internet and other new communication technologies, in international affairs, in providing information and affecting opinion.
3.4.3 Understand, by studying examples, the way in which the media exert power through the use of editorials, headlines and the selection and presentation of news.

National Curriculum programme of study, key stage 4
Key concepts 1.1 b, c, d; 1.2 a, b, c
Range and content 3 g

Q1 This question is designed to draw out discussion on the degree to which the wishes, views and statements of proscribed groups should be placed in the public domain. This question is not dissimilar from the one that is raised about the strengths and weakness of providing members of the British National Party with opportunities to write, broadcast or respond to questions in the media.

Q2 Most students will probably suggest that the media should provide accurate and up-to-date information to the public, without placing the armed forces or the nation's military strategy at risk.

There may be more disagreement, however, over whether there should be news of
- the enemy's successes

- casualties suffered by the home nation
- voices of opposition to the conflict, or
- criticism of current strategies.

The same question may be raised in a slightly different way by asking students what broadcasting strategy they would recommend if they were a government minister responsible for the decision to go to war in controversial circumstances.

Q3 It is generally agreed that the government adviser believed that the extensive news coverage following the tragedy in New York would allow the Government to release unnoticed, or with very little public discussion, some potentially unpopular or controversial news items.

Q4 The key issue in this question probably concerns the degree to which a government 'spins' a press release. Students may wish to discuss whether governments should be expected to provide open or balanced appraisals of their work knowing that their political opponents will almost certainly try to capitalise on government shortcomings. It may not be unreasonable to argue that it is the job of the Opposition and media to provide this counterbalance. A further view that may be put forward is that a government that is generally open and honestly critical of itself may inspire more confidence from the electorate.

Q5 The authors feel that their underlying message in this unit is that there is a tendency for governments to try to influence the media – and they would like to encourage students to be critically aware of this.

Other sections of the unit suggest that, in reporting certain issues and events, newspapers and broadcasters also have a political agenda that they try to impose on their readers. Again the authors would like students to be aware of this and to ask certain critical questions about the style and content of certain reports.

Freedom to publish, pages 164–165

Students discuss a number of issues relating to the censorship of the media.

OCR GCSE Citizenship Studies

3.2.3 Understand the importance of a free press in a democracy by knowing that, in the United Kingdom, the media have the right to investigate, and to report upon, issues of public interest, subject to the need for accuracy and respect for people's privacy and dignity.

National Curriculum programme of study, key stage 4
Key concepts 1.1 b, c; 1.2 a, b, c
Range and content 3 f, g

Q1 Discussion of whether the singer should be censored provoked many responses on the BBC News website; most of them were in support of Eminem. These statements give an idea of the views of those who opposed censorship:
- if people don't like it, they shouldn't listen
- people have a right to free speech
- the singer has a lot of talent
- banning singers does not stop people listening to them, but has the opposite effect
- what he talks about happens every day
- a person doesn't advocate violence by singing about it
- kids are smart, they know the difference between right and wrong
- you can't ban him, because so many people like him.

If time is available, you may wish to write some or all of these on card (plus suggestions from students), asking students to assess what they feel are the strongest and weakest arguments that are being made.

Q2 To some extent, the argument that a person can switch off any television programme they find offensive is perfectly valid, but it doesn't address all situations. It does not apply to children or young people who are watching a programme alone or not in the company of an adult, nor does it apply to actions or statements made on television or radio that may cause damage or offence to someone other than the viewer. This was the case surrounding the controversial broadcast by Jonathan Ross and Russell Brand.

More information on the procedures that are followed to deal with complaints about broadcasts can be found on the Ofcom site, www.ofcom.org.uk, by clicking on the Complaints button.

Q3 The *Coronation Street star* complained about the article to the Press Complaints Commission, which investigated the case and found that the content of the article was an unreasonable intrusion into the actress's private life. It found that the intimate details contained in the article were 'salacious and intrusive' and that there was no public interest in such revelations.

The *Premiership footballer* was unable to persuade the court that the newspaper should not publish his name and details of his affairs. In explaining the court's decision the judge said that, although public figures had a right to a private life, they should recognise that their actions will be more closely scrutinised because of their public position.

The *radio presenter* took her complaint to the Press Complaints Commission and, as a result, received an apology from the newspaper. She also sued the paper, complaining of an invasion of her right to privacy, and was awarded £50,000 in damages. The defendants were required to pay costs estimated at £50,000.

The *television personality* was unable to prevent the press from publishing details of his visit to a brothel because, the judge ruled, there is nothing in the relationship between a prostitute and client that requires any kind of confidentiality on either part.

Environment

> **Climate change**
> • The problem
> • The solution
>
> **Choices for the future**
> • Powering the nation

Climate change

This unit asks students to consider what action should be taken in view of what we know about changes in the world's climate.

The problem, pages 166–167

This topic outlines some of the evidence for climate change.

> **OCR GCSE Citizenship Studies**
>
> **3.1.3** Understand the interdependence of individuals, groups and communities, and assess critically the impact of their own actions on communities and the wider world now and in the future. Make recommendations to others for action and change. Evaluate, with reference to one topical global issue, the ways in which individuals, organisations, businesses and governments promote sustainable development through policies and practices, including agenda 21.
>
> **National Curriculum programme of study, key stage 4**
> **Key concepts** 1.2 a, c
> **Range and content** 3 i, m, n

Q1 Included amongst the observations students may make are the following:
• There has been a general rise in observed global average surface temperature since 1860 – and particularly since 1950
• The average surface temperature has varied from year to year
• A steady increase in temperature change took place between 1910 and 1940 and between 1980 and 2005.

Q2 Arguments in favour of taking steps immediately to reduce global warming include:
• they will increase the likelihood of a slow-down in global warming, and therefore reduce some of the problems associated with it
• the problems associated with global warming are potentially so serious that immediate action is vital
• governments today have a duty to take whatever action they can to protect the interests of future generations
• it is inevitable that some form of action will need to be taken. By taking action sooner, rather than later, a country is more likely to reap any associated economic benefits
• immediate action increases the likelihood of saving many people's lives, and this places a moral duty on nations to act as soon as possible.

Opposing arguments include the following:
• it is difficult for us to have any impact on global warming; we should try instead to invest in measures to protect people from its most serious effects
• immediate action, such as replacing fossil fuels, cannot be done instantly – large sections of the economy will be damaged by over-hasty action
• there are more immediate concerns for government expenditure, such as healthcare and education
• we should wait for more data before we take action
• not all scientists agree that global warming is caused by human activities; some argue that it is a cyclical phenomena – and, if this is the case, there is little point in attempting to stop something beyond human control.

This question may be used, by those students taking the OCR examination, as a starting point for a citizenship campaign.

The solution, pages 168–169

This topic outlines some of the steps that have already been taken by world governments to deal with the threat of climate change, and asks students to consider where the responsibility lies for further action.

OCR GCSE Citizenship Studies

3.1.3 Understand the interdependence of individuals, groups and communities, and assess critically the impact of their own actions on communities and the wider world now and in the future. Make recommendations to others for action and change. Evaluate, with reference to one topical global issue, the ways in which individuals, organisations, businesses and governments promote sustainable development through policies and practices, including agenda 21.

3.2.4 Understand the United Nation's role in helping to resolve international disagreements… Understand that the United Kingdom, as a member country, is committed to adhere to the United Nation's agreements on … the environment.

3.3.3 Understand the implications of Agenda 21 for promoting sustainable development on local, national and global scales, together with the constraints limiting the extent of its implementation.

National Curriculum programme of study, key stage 4
Key concepts 1.1 b; 1.2 a, c
Range and content 3 i, m, n

Q1 The table below illustrates how the problems might be tackled:

	Local	National	International
Short supply	• Local media campaigns encouraging people to use less water, and more education on the importance of saving water • Compulsory use of water metering • Giving greater powers to local government to limit the use of water, particularly in times of shortage • A free distribution of low-cost water-saving devices	• National support for implementing local strategies, including financial incentives for individuals and organisations to use less water • A national focus on ways to use less water in manufacturing, and on devices that will enable people to use less water in the home	• The transfer of water-saving technologies to help countries with short supplies • Greater funding from developed countries to bring a regular and reliable supply of water to all countries
Polluted	• More effective monitoring for pollution in waterways and rivers	• Amending the law to require high standards of water purity in the manufacturing process • Greater penalties for companies causing the pollution	• The creation of more stringent international rules and laws limiting pollution levels • A requirement for multinational companies to observe the same water-purification standards in all countries in which they trade
Costly			• International cooperation to reduce the cost of domestic supplies of water to communities without a sufficient and reliable supply

Q2 It could be argued that long-established industrialised countries, such as the UK, the USA and Germany have a greater responsibility to reduce their carbon emissions because of their greater financial resources and their responsibility for carbon emissions in the 19th and early 20th centuries.

However, it may also be argued that it is only in the last 30 years that these countries have become aware of the impact on the environment of these emissions, and therefore cannot be expected to take full responsibility for the damage caused.

Perhaps the widespread current awareness of the impact carbon emissions places a responsibility on all nations to pursue more environmentally friendly policies in the interests of communities throughout the world.

Q3 Some students might argue that China should take the responsibility because the consumer has no control over the amount of emissions produced during manufacture.

However, a small environmental levy on the price paid for the goods in the country where they are purchased could perhaps be used to fund some kind of carbon offset programme.

Choices for the future

This unit examines the question of how Britain should obtain its energy supplies over the next 30–40 years.

Powering the nation, pages 170–171

OCR GCSE Citizenship Studies

3.1.3 Understand the interdependence of individuals, groups and communities, and assess critically the impact of their own actions on communities and the wider world now and in the future. Make recommendations to others for action and change. Evaluate, with reference to one topical global issue, the ways in which individuals, organisations, businesses and governments promote sustainable development through policies and practices, including agenda 21.

3.3.3 Understand the implications of Agenda 21 for promoting sustainable development on local, national and global scales, together with the constraints limiting the extent of its implementation.

National Curriculum programme of study, key stage 4
Key concepts 1.2 a, c
Range and content 3 i, m, n,

Q1 Students should select their arguments for and against the development of wind power from those given on page 170.

Students may be able to relate to this issue more closely by linking this question to any proposals for wind farms in the local area.

Q2 This comment was made by Edward Miliband at the screening of a documentary on climate change in March 2009. The comment is in line with the Government's commitment to meet EU targets to produce one-fifth of all energy through renewable sources by 2020.

Some might agree with his comments and argue that many of the disadvantages of wind turbines – such as noise, damage to the local landscape and lack of benefit to the local community – only impact on a small number of people, and do not outweigh the advantages.

Others may feel that local people have every right to be angry as they are the people who have to face and deal with the drawbacks of the scheme.

Although people, arguably, have the right to voice their opposition to changes in their local area, appeals against planning decisions of this kind may cause considerable delay, and the Government has announced that it is considering measures to speed up the process of planning enquiries.

Q3&Q4 There is potential to extend this activity through further research and contact with organisations either promoting or opposing various of the measures listed on page 171.

If time allowed, it could be interesting for students to interview representatives from some of these bodies and to develop an action based on their findings.

(This may require considerable organisation – this kind of activity is appropriate for full or half days on a suspended timetable with students interrogating experts using a carousel format, followed by the presentation of their proposals or a parliamentary-style debate, perhaps chaired by the local MP.)

Justice

> **Civil law**
> - Taking a case to court
> - The county court
>
> **Criminal law**
> - Arrest and charge
> - Inside a magistrates' court
> - In court
> - Crown Court
> - Cause of death
> - Prisons and sentencing

Civil law

This unit outlines the way in which a case may be dealt with in the civil court.

Taking a case to court, pages 172–173

This topic outlines the steps that a person might take who is considering making a claim for damages.

> **OCR GCSE Citizenship Studies**
>
> **3.2.2** Understand the importance of law in maintaining order, resolving conflict and achieving just outcomes, and understand that the law places a responsibility on all members of society to conform to a common code of behaviour, including obedience to … civil law. Know how legal advice and support may be obtained.
> **3.3.1** Evaluate the additional formal and independent support available to individuals requiring information and advice including that available from Government departments, agencies, and official regulators, Citizens Advice, consumer protection or rights organisations and solicitors.
> **3.4.2** Understand the role of individuals, lawyers and courts in the civil legal and justice system.
>
> **National Curriculum programme of study, key stage 4**
> **Key concepts** 1.2 a, b, c
> **Range and content** 3 a, b

Q1 You may find it helpful to list the various parties on sets of cards or slips, for each small group of students to sort and arrange, according to the level of responsibility that they feel each one has for the accident. In brief:
- The *leisure centre* is responsible for providing a facility that is safe for players and spectators to use.
- Members of the *trampoline club* have a duty to leave the hall at, or before, a set time and not to delay the activities of other clubs.
- *Mark and the other footballers* have a duty to take action over anything in the playing area that they believe is unsafe. (Although *we* know that Mark had recognised the hazard quite early on, this fact will not necessarily have been revealed in Mark's statements concerning the accident that followed.)

Q2&Q3 Mark faces a number of options. He may decide to take his solicitor's advice to pursue a claim for damages, trying to seek an out-of-court settlement with the local authority. If he does not succeed in this (or finds that the local authority's offer is unacceptably low), he will then have to decide whether to proceed further and take his claim to court.

Alternatively he may decide not to take any further action, believing that he is unlikely to succeed or that the potential cost, stress and disruption of the case would not be worthwhile.

The county court, pages 174–175

In this topic, students are introduced to the procedure that may be followed by someone pursuing a claim for damages in the county court.

OCR GCSE Citizenship Studies

3.2.2 Understand the importance of law in maintaining order, resolving conflict and achieving just outcomes, and understand that the law places a responsibility on all members of society to conform to a common code of behaviour, including obedience to … civil law. Know how legal advice and support may be obtained.

3.4.2 Understand the role of individuals, lawyers and courts in the civil legal and justice system.

National Curriculum programme of study, key stage 4
Key concepts 1.1 b; 1.2 a, b, c
Range and content 3 a, b

Q1 The lawyer for the *plaintiff* (Mark) may argue that:

- the management of the leisure centre (in this case, the local authority) has a duty to ensure that the premises and facilities it provides are safe for normal use (i.e. five-a-side football)
- that, perhaps because of the late-running of the previous club, the staff had either overlooked or chosen to ignore the bench that had been left by the wall on one side of the hall
- this oversight indicates that the leisure centre management clearly failed in their duty of care and, as a result, Mark suffered a serious injury, with consequences for both his personal and working lives.

Counsel for the defendant will almost certainly acknowledge the duty of care that the leisure centre has to members of the public who use the facilities, but may argue that the one remaining bench by the wall was clearly visible to both team's players – and any one of these people could and should have noticed (particularly after playing for 20 minutes) that it had not been put away.

Q2&Q3 This particular case is fictional, but an experienced lawyer's opinion is that it would not be easy to say who would succeed and that different courts might well reach different decisions.

In her own judgement, the lawyer suggested that a judge would probably decide that, although leisure centre staff have a duty to provide a safe environment, which includes removing potentially dangerous objects from the playing area, Mark was also, in this situation, responsible for his own safety. Even if he hadn't told his solicitor about already seeing the bench, the judge might well decide that Mark some of the other footballers *should* have seen it and moved it to a safer position.

The lawyer suggested that Mark's swift return to work indicates that he did not suffer long-term damage in the accident and that compensation would be at the lower end of the guidelines for a simple fracture, which are £3,250–£10,000 (2008). Mark would also be entitled to special damages of £2,490. However, the lawyer suggested that the judge might then deduct a proportion of the total award to reflect Mark's role in the accident – perhaps awarding him 50 per cent of the value of his claim.

Criminal law

This unit covers a number of aspects of criminal law, including police powers and the work of the magistrates' court and the Crown Court. The final topic raises the question of whether offenders sentenced to a period of custody should be required to serve their full term.

Arrest and charge, pages 176–177

This, the first section of a two-part topic, uses an important case to indicate the current law relating to the powers and duties of the police when arresting and questioning a suspect.

OCR GCSE Citizenship Studies

3.2.2 Understand the different roles of the police, Crown Prosecution Service, criminal courts, including judges and juries, in upholding the law, dealing with criminals and attempting to secure fairness and justice within our democracy. Understand the ways in which rights can compete and conflict and how the law is used to resolve these issues justly. Understand the importance of the law in maintaining order, resolving conflict and achieving just outcomes, and understand that the law places a responsibility on all members of society to conform to a common code of behaviour, including obedience to criminal and civil law

3.3.1 Evaluate the additional formal and independent support available to individuals requiring information and advice including that available from … solicitors.

3.4.2 Understand the role of individuals, lawyers and courts in the civil legal and justice system.

National Curriculum programme of study, key stage 4
Key concepts 1.1 b, 1.2 a, b, c
Range and content 3 a, b, f

Q1 The following are among the points that students may raise:
- two relatively young boys were questioned by the police alone and without access to a solicitor
- the third suspect, who was older, had severe learning difficulties, and again was questioned by the police without anyone present to support him or represent his interests
- all three suspects alleged they had been assaulted by the police during questioning.

None of these situations are acceptable today. Further details are given on page 177 in the student's book, and in the section on *Police and courts* in the *Young Citizens Passport*, published by Hodder Education.

Q2 The police should not normally interview anyone under 17 (or ask them to sign a statement), without a parent or other 'appropriate adult' being present. This applies whether the young person is a suspect or a witness to a crime.

The presence of a familiar adult is designed to calm and reassure the young person, in the event of what may be a very stressful interview, to advise the young person and to do their best to make sure that the interview is conducted fairly.

Q3 Although it may be argued that an innocent person has nothing to hide, as the example in this topic shows, there have been occasions in which statements and confessions have been obtained by the police which have later proved to be untrue.

The presence and assistance of a legal representative at an interview is designed to minimise the possibility of undue police oppression or of a confession being elicited from a 'suggestible' witness.

The implementation of clearly defined procedures during an interview (the right to advice, the tape recording of interviews, etc.) is likely to ensure that, in the event of the prosecution going ahead, any evidence that is obtained is reliable and robust.

Arrest and charge, pages 178–179

This topic outlines the origins and nature of the Crown Prosecution Service, and provides a case study for students to decide how it might be dealt with.

OCR GCSE Citizenship Studies

3.2.2 Understand the different roles of the police, Crown Prosecution Service, criminal courts, including judges and juries, in upholding the law, dealing with criminals and attempting to secure fairness and justice within our democracy. Understand the ways in which rights can compete and conflict and how the law is used to resolve these issues justly. Understand the importance of the law in maintaining order, resolving conflict and achieving just outcomes, and understand that the law places a responsibility on all members of society to conform to a common code of behaviour, including obedience to criminal and civil law

National Curriculum programme of study, key stage 4
Key concepts 1.1 b, 1.2 a, b, c
Range and content 3 a, b

Q1 The police officers are likely to ask the store manager for evidence concerning the theft. This is likely to concern:
- evidence from counter and security staff
- evidence from CCTV footage
- further evidence relating to records of sales.

They are also likely to question Sophie and Lauren about:
- their reasons for being in the store
- purchases they made there and elsewhere
- how Lauren obtained the perfume that was found in her pocket.

Q2 All this information is provided on page 177 of the student's book.

Q3 In a similar case a woman from Staffordshire was prosecuted for taking two small relatively inexpensive items in similar circumstances.

The scenario on which this case is based would result in arrest and would be passed to the CPS for vetting. Shoplifting is contrary to the *Theft Act 1968* and viewed sufficiently seriously for those arrested to be brought before a court. It is likely that both girls would get bail unless the police had clear evidence that they were likely to abscond.

Q4 For the CPS to bring a case, the evidence must fall within the Attorney General's guidelines; i.e. there must be a better than 50/50 chance of the evidence presented producing a conviction. The guidelines were introduced early in the CPS's history to try to bring some national coherence to what had been a county by county approach and as a means of reducing expenditure when hopeless cases were pursued.

As the question implies, there has been some criticism of the failure of the CPS for a failure to prosecute certain cases, leading to a belief that too few 'guilty' people are being sent to court because the CPS is setting the bar too high. The Nottinghamshire Chief Constable is reported to have said that the public doesn't get the protection it deserves because the CPS is playing too safe.

Inside a magistrates' court, pages 180–181

In this topic, students are provided with a basic outline of a magistrates' court and a description of the process of arrest and charge.

OCR GCSE Citizenship Studies

3.2.2 Understand the different roles of the police, Crown Prosecution Service, criminal courts, including judges and juries, in upholding the law, dealing with criminals and attempting to secure fairness and justice within our democracy. Understand the ways in which … the law is used to resolve these issues justly. Understand the importance of the law in maintaining order, resolving conflict and achieving just outcomes, and understand that the law places a responsibility on all members of society to conform to a common code of behaviour, including obedience to criminal and civil law

3.4.2 Understand the role of individuals, lawyers and courts in the civil legal and justice system.

National Curriculum programme of study, key stage 4
Key concepts 1.1 b, 1.2 a, b, c
Range and content 3 a, b

In court, pages 182–183

This topic outlines the workings and powers of magistrates' courts and asks students to consider what kind of person makes a good magistrate.

OCR GCSE Citizenship Studies

3.2.2 Understand the different roles of the police, Crown Prosecution Service, criminal courts, including judges and juries, in upholding the law, dealing with criminals and attempting to secure fairness and justice within our democracy. Understand the ways in which rights can compete and conflict and how the law is used to resolve these issues justly. Understand the importance of the law in maintaining order, resolving conflict and achieving just outcomes, and understand that the law places a responsibility on all members of society to conform to a common code of behaviour, including obedience to criminal and civil law

3.4.2 Understand the role of individuals, lawyers and courts in the civil legal and justice system.

National Curriculum programme of study, key stage 4
Key concepts 1.1 b, 1.2 a, b, c
Range and content 3 a, b

Q1

	Advantages	Disadvantages
Local	• Magistrates are familiar with aspects of the social, economic and cultural life of the area • Arguably engenders a greater sense of responsibility in magistrates who know that some of their decisions may have a direct impact on the area in which they live	• Familiarity may lead to a lack of objectivity in taking certain decisions
Unpaid	• This may increase the likelihood that the people offering themselves as magistrates are doing so in order to make a contribution to society, rather than for reasons of personal gain.	• May limit the recruitment of magistrates to certain socio-economic sectors. For example, some employees may not be able to undertake the work because of their employer's reluctance or difficulty to pay them whilst they are not at work. The recruitment of magistrates from certain sections of the self-employed may be similarly difficult.
Without legal training	• This may allow magistrates to take a broader perspective on cases and, where appropriate, to adopt a common-sense perspective instead of one entirely fashioned by legal rules.	• Although all magistrates receive extensive training, a stronger legal background could arguably enable them to deal with cases more quickly and more reliably and with cases of a more complex legal nature.

Q2 After listening to the case, the magistrates would want to know any mitigating or aggravating features of the case. For example, had Rhys Hughes done this before or had he committed any other offences?

Q3 The magistrates would then retire and go through the key decisions involved in the sentencing process:
a) assessing the seriousness of the offence: magistrates would identify an appropriate starting point using their latest sentencing guidelines
b) form a preliminary idea of the appropriate sentence and then consider mitigation
c) consider a reduction in sentence for a guilty plea
d) consider what are known as ancillary orders, including compensation and costs
e) decide the sentence, and clarify their reasoning.

In this case, the court's decision may be announced in the following way:

'In reaching our decision, we have taken into account your guilty plea and the fact that this is your first time in court. For driving with excess alcohol, the reading being twice the legal limit, you will be disqualified from driving for 24 months. You will also pay a fine of £750, costs of £60 and a victim surcharge of £15.

We will offer you the drink drivers' rehabilitation course, and, if you are successful, your disqualification period will be reduced by a quarter.

How can the fine, costs, and victim surcharge be paid?'

Since April 2007, anyone who is given a fine after being convicted of a criminal offence has been required to pay a £15 surcharge. This is a fixed charge and does not depend on the severity of the offence. The money goes towards improving services for victims of crime.

Under the Code of Practice for Victims of Crime, victims are entitled to details from the police about whether an investigation will take place and, if so, how it is progressing, and whether anyone has been charged. Victims who are called upon to give evidence in court should be given help to minimise the difficulties that they might face in attending. Victims should also be informed about the offender's sentence and, if the offence was serious, be given the opportunity to express their views and concerns about licensing conditions or supervision for the offender on his or her release from prison.

Victims may now opt to make a personal statement, which may include details of the impact that the crime has had on their life. This statement becomes part of the case and may be used as evidence in court.

Q4 The Ministry of Justice sets a number of key qualities that magistrates should possess:
- *aged 18–70*: a person must be at least 18 years old to apply to be a magistrate, and an applicant over the age of 65 would not normally be appointed. Magistrates retire from the bench at 70 years of age.
- good character: to have personal integrity, enjoy the trust of others and be able to maintain confidences. There should be nothing in their private or working lives, which, if it became generally known, might bring them or the Magistracy into disrepute
- *understanding and communication*: to be able to understand documents, identify and understand relevant facts and follow evidence and arguments. They must be able to communicate effectively with colleagues, court staff and court users, including defendants
- *social awareness*: to appreciate and accept the need for the rule of law in society and should display an understanding of their local community, society in general and of the causes and effects of crime. An awareness of life beyond their immediate circle of family, friends and work is highly desirable.
- *maturity and sound temperament*: to have an awareness and understanding of people and a sense of fairness
- *sound judgement*: to be able to think logically, weigh arguments and to reach a sound decision
- *commitment and reliability*: to be committed to serving the community, to be willing to undertake training and to be fit enough to carry out their duties on a regular basis.

Q5 In answer to this question, one magistrate wrote: 'People become magistrates because they want to serve the community. It may be that the community has given them a career and they want to use their expertise on behalf of that community. They certainly don't do it for the glory.'

Q6 There is a strong argument to say that local benches should be representative of the community in which they operate. However, with 90.9 per cent of magistrates being from a white ethnic background, there is an ethnic imbalance in many areas, particularly in parts of large conurbations.

The Advisory Committees that select magistrates have carried out several measure to try to rectify this:
- open days at courts
- talking to bodies representing the interests of black and Asian people
- giving talks to Asian and black communities to encourage people to apply
- talking to employees.

Crown Court, pages 184–185

In this topic, students are introduced to the work of the Crown Court through the experience of someone called for jury service.

OCR GCSE Citizenship Studies

3.2.2 Understand the different roles of the police, Crown Prosecution Service, criminal courts, including judges and juries, in upholding the law, dealing with criminals and attempting to secure fairness and justice within our democracy. Understand the ways in which rights can compete and conflict and how the law is used to resolve these issues justly. Understand the importance of the law in maintaining order, resolving conflict and achieving just outcomes, and understand that the law places a responsibility on all members of society to conform to a common code of behaviour, including obedience to criminal and civil law

3.4.2 Understand the role of individuals, lawyers and courts in the civil legal and justice system.

National Curriculum programme of study, key stage 4
Key concepts 1.1 b, 1.2 a, b, c
Range and content 3 a, b

Q1 It is the job of a jury to listen to the facts of a case and to decide on the guilt or innocence of the accused. By long tradition and experience, it is generally recognised that one of the best ways of doing this job is to select at random twelve ordinary people.

Although it may be inconvenient or uncomfortable for Tessa, arguably as a citizen of the state (and a beneficiary of the protection that it provides) she has a duty to play her part in the maintenance of justice and the rule of law.

Q2 Arguably, members of a jury representing a relatively narrow cross-section of society (e.g. older people, those retired or not working, and those from white, rather than black or Asian, communities) will have less understanding or insight than a more heterogeneous group, and is less likely to reach a fair and just decision.

It may also be argued that people's perception of the justice administered by the Courts may decline if juries are not seen as being representative of society as a whole.

Q3&Q4 The rules on jury service were reformed under the *Criminal Justice Act 2003*, with judges, vicars, doctors, midwives and police all having their exemption removed.

Q5 In 2009, the maximum allowance for jurors, for the first ten days of service, was £58.38 per day. This rises to £116.78 per day for jury service lasting more than ten days, and to £205 for those extending beyond 201 days – which is very rare. The allowances paid for most people's jury service is well below the national average wage for full-time workers.

Larger businesses and organisations are likely to continue to pay their employees at their normal rate during jury service (though it is not a legal requirement). Those who are self-employed or involved with small businesses arguably face the greatest financial penalties from jury service.

The Courts Service explains the limits on allowances in terms of its duties to spend public money wisely and to encourage the widest possible participation in jury service.

Cause of death, pages 186–187

This topic is designed to provide students with further understanding of the work of the Crown Court, drawing on a real case study.

OCR GCSE Citizenship Studies

3.2.2 Understand the different roles of the police, Crown Prosecution Service, criminal courts, including judges and juries, in upholding the law, dealing with criminals and attempting to secure fairness and justice within our democracy. Understand the ways in which rights can compete and conflict and how the law is used to resolve these issues justly. Understand the importance of the law in maintaining order, resolving conflict and achieving just outcomes, and understand that the law places a responsibility on all members of society to conform to a common code of behaviour, including obedience to criminal and civil law

3.4.2 Understand the role of individuals, lawyers and courts in the civil legal and justice system.

National Curriculum programme of study, key stage 4
Key concepts 1.1 b, 1.2 a, b, c
Range and content 3 a, b

Q1 This story is loosely based on a case that came before the courts in 1989 – recorded as *R v Watson [1989] 1WLR 684 (CA)*.

In *R v Watson* it appears that the jury were of the opinion that the elderly man's heart rate had returned to normal about 20 minutes after the burglary, but that medical problems returned with the arrival of the police and the council workmen – and that it was one, or other, or both of these incidents that was the cause of death.

They found the accused guilty of murder, presumably concluding that the burglary triggered off this series of events and was the cause of the elderly man's subsequent death.

Q2 Students may raise the following points surrounding the question of whether juries should give reasons for their verdicts. Those *in favour* may include:
- that a defendant is being denied justice if he or she is not told the reason for their conviction
- an explanation by the jury might also help victims of crime to understand why the accused was not found guilty
- it is already customary for magistrates to give reasons in court for their decisions.

Those *against* may argue that requiring a jury to give reasons for its decision may:
- limit the frankness of jurors' debates and discussions
- have some impact on the secrecy and sanctity of the jury room and require a change in the law
- leave jurors more open to criticism, harassment and reprisals
- reduce the finality of a jury's verdict
- prevent juries from reaching perverse decisions when, for example, they recognise that the accused may have broken the law, but believe that the circumstances surrounding the case do not merit a conviction.

Prisons and sentencing, pages 188–189

This topic provides a basic outline of one aspect of the sentencing system (that of parole), and raises a number of questions surrounding the current practice of sending offenders to prison and then releasing most prisoners under licence halfway through their sentence.

OCR GCSE Citizenship Studies

3.2.2 Understand the importance of the law in maintaining order, resolving conflict and achieving just outcomes, and understand that the law places a responsibility on all members of society to conform to a common code of behaviour, including obedience to criminal and civil law.

3.4.2 Evaluate the role and effectiveness of the police, probation service and prison service in reducing crime and rates of reoffending including by punishing and rehabilitating people who disobey the law.

National Curriculum programme of study, key stage 4
Key concepts 1.1 b, 1.2 a, b, c
Range and content 3 a, b

Q1 Students may suggest the following reasons for the purpose of prison:
- as a *deterrent* against crime for both offenders and members of wider society
- as a *punishment* for crime
- as *retribution*, pay back or vengeance against wrongdoing
- as *reform*, by helping the offender to not commit similar acts in the future
- as *protection* for the public, particularly from dangerous or persistent offenders.

Having elicited these answers, it may be useful to go back and ask students, 'Yes, but what *is* the purpose of prison?', because a multiple answer to this question does not really define what prisons should be doing. You may like to encourage students to select the most important function from the list above, and then ask them to think about the implications of their decision on the nature of the prison system in this country.

Q2 The following points may be among students' suggestions:
- prison is expensive; as a rule of thumb, the cost of keeping someone in prison for a year is at least equivalent to the average national full-time wage. The figure is up to twice this level for prisoners held under special conditions.
- the prisoner is removed from society, losing income, work and possibly friends and social acquaintances
- in prisons, prisoners may become more criminally socialised through contact with other offenders, particularly those involved in more serious crimes.

Q3,Q4&Q5 One of the main arguments in favour of prisoners serving their full sentence is that early release reduces prison's deterrent effect. It may also be damaging to a victim or their family, who may well regard a shortened sentence as a 'let-off', and something that completely fails to address the seriousness of the crime or the impact that it had on others.

Without early release, our prisons would almost certainly, under present policies, be more overcrowded than they are at present. Arguably, the prospect of early release acts, in general, as an incentive for prisoners to keep to the rules and behave in the required way. An automatic requirement for prisoners to serve their full sentence would remove this incentive and may, in some cases, lead to a deterioration in behaviour.

Indeterminate sentences were designed as a means of detaining a small number of dangerous offenders, but critics complain that they have committed several thousand people to an unjust sentence and further contributed to the problem of prison overcrowding. Prisoners state that it is not fair or just for someone not to know the maximum amount of time that they will be held.

As explained in the student text, prisoners with an indeterminate sentence must remain in prison until the Parole Board is satisfied that they may be safely released. One of the ways in which this might be achieved is through a prisoner's satisfactory completion of certain courses. However, the government has been heavily criticised for failing to provide these and therefore not giving such prisoners a chance for their sentence to be ended. In 2008, the Court of Appeal found that the Justice Secretary acted unlawfully by failing to provide some inmates with access to courses needed for parole.

Further information on the prison system may be found on the following websites:
- The Howard League for Penal Reform: www.howardleague.org
- HM Prison Service: www.hmprisonservice.gov.uk
- The Prison Reform Trust: www.prisonreformtrust.org.uk.

Section 7: Further resources

There are many useful sites providing further information on the topics covered in *Citizenship Studies*. The following list contains those that the authors have found most useful. Inevitably, some sites and addresses change over time – so please accept our apologies if any of these are unavailable. Further guidance and sources are available in the section on Links with outside agencies, pages 35–41.

Chapter and unit	Organisations and publications
General	Each of the following covers many aspects of the OCR GCSE Citizenship Studies specification
Advice Guide	The Citizens Advice Bureau's online guide: www.adviceguide.org.uk
Advice Now	An independent advice service providing on a wide range of topics: www.advicenow.org.uk
Ask the police	A legal question and answer data base, focusing – but not entirely – on criminal issues: www.askthe.police.uk
BBC News	A very useful source of reference on current and controversial issues: www.bbc.co.uk
Community Legal Advice	The Community Legal Advice site provides information on a wide range of civil and criminal issues: www.communitylegaladvice.org.uk
Directgov	The official website for citizens in the United Kingdom, www.direct.gov.uk
The Young Citizen's Passport	A pocket guide to the law, updated each year and published by Hodder Education; also available online by subscription: www.ycponline.co.uk.
Rules and laws	
The European Commission	An outline of EU terminology – treaties, directives etc: http://ec.europa.eu/community_law/introduction/treaty_en.htm
Parliament UK	The official UK Parliament contains a wide range of information on many aspects of Parliament, including the legislative process: www.parliament.uk
Youth Citizenship Commission	The YCC has published a list of the main ages at which young people assume adult responsibility: www.ycc.uk.net/votes/clp
Human rights	
Inside Britain: a guide to the UK constitution	A guide to the rules and workings of government, setting out many of the rights and duties of government. Produced by the Citizenship Foundation, and published by Hodder Education
Liberty	A well-established organisation promoting civil liberties and human rights: www.liberty-human-rights.org.uk
Family and school	
Advisory Centre for Education	A national charity providing information to parents and carers on a wide range of school-based issues: www.ace-ed.org.uk
Children's Legal Centre	Providing legal advice, information and representation for children and young people: www.childrenslegalcentre.com
Consumer law	
Consumer Direct	The government-funded telephone and online service offering information and advice on consumer issues: www.consumerdirect.gov.uk

Chapter and unit	Organisations and publications
Moneymadeclear	Information on many aspects of finance from the Financial Services Authority: www.moneymadeclear.fsa.gov.uk/home.html
Employment	
Equality and Human Rights Commission	The official body promoting equality and human rights: www.equalityhumanrights.com/our-job
Economy	
The Dept for International Development	The Dept for International Development (DfID) is the government department managing aid and working to eradicate extreme poverty. The site provides useful on a range of topics, including Millennium Development Goals and fighting poverty: www.dfid.gov.uk/Global-Issues
HM Revenue & Customs	Basic information about tax is available from: www.hmrc.gov.uk/index.htm
HM Treasury	Wide range of financial information, with an accessible micro site on the Budget: www.hm-treasury.gov.uk
Community	
Commonwealth Secretariat	For summaries of the work and history of the Commonwealth, click on Take a tour, Timeline, and History: www.thecommonwealth.org
Equality and Human Rights Commission	The official body promoting equality and human rights: www.equalityhumanrights.com/our-job
Moving Here	A database of migration history: www.movinghere.org.uk
Refugee Council	For an overview of the asylum system see: www.refugeecouncil.org.uk/practice
Shelter	Shelter, the housing and homeless charity, provides a great deal of further information on tenancies, eviction and repossession etc. Access to the main UK portal via: www.shelter.org.uk
Making a difference	
About My Vote	A public site, produced by the Electoral Commission designed to answer questions about elections and the voting system: www.aboutmyvote.co.uk/default.aspx
Giving Nation	Summary information on a large number of charities is available from G-Nation's database, accessible via the Charities link: www.g-nation.co.uk
Parliament UK	The official UK Parliament contains a wide range of information on many aspects of Parliament, including useful explanatory sheets on particular subjects, voting systems: www.parliament.uk
Political parties	Details of party policies are available on each party's own website
Government	
Dept of Communities and Local Government	For information on the work of local government and how to become a councillor, see: www.communities.gov.uk/localgovernment
Inside Britain: a guide to the UK constitution	A guide to the rules and workings of government, produced by the Citizenship Foundation, and published by Hodder Education
Number 10	For historical information on Number 10 Downing Street, past prime ministers and the Cabinet, see www.number10.gov.uk

OCR Citizenship Studies Teacher's Resource Book for GCSE full and short course
© 2009 Hodder Education

Chapter and unit	Organisations and publications
Media	
Ofcom	Ofcom is the main regulatory body set up to maintain and monitor standards in the communications industries. It is independent of government, but answerable to Parliament: www.ofcom.org.uk
Press Complaints Commission	The PCC is the independent body that deals with complaints about the content of newspaper and magazine articles. The site gives details of how to make a complaint along with details of cases recently heard by the Commission: www.pcc.org.uk/index.html
Environment	
Environment Agency	The Environment Agency is a public body responsible, in England, to the Dept of the Environment and, in Wales, to the National Assembly for Wales. The site map gives access to explanatory sections on pollution, climate change, waste and recycling: www.environment-agency.gov.uk
Pressure groups	Main pressure group websites, such as www.foe.co.uk; www.greenpeace.org.uk; www.wwf.org.uk can provided a useful first-reference point for key environmental issues
Justice	
Criminal Justice System	CJS online provides detailed information about the court system for witnesses, victims, defendants and for prisoners: www.cjsonline.gov.uk
HMCS	Background information on many aspects of the Court Service is available from the Court Service website via Information on: www.hmcourts-service.gov.uk/index.htm
Youth Justice Board	The youth justice system in England and Wales is overseen by the Youth Justice Board. The public section of the site outlines the way in which the youth justice system works: www.yjb.gov.uk/en-gb

Mapping the specification to the Student's Book

Below are four grids that map the pages and content in the Student's Book to the different units in the OCR GCSE in Citizenship Studies specification. This gives you an at-a-glance view of where the content is covered.

Unit A341: Rights and Responsibilities – Getting Started as an Active Citizen		
Specification content	**Student's Book topic**	**Student's Book page**
3.1.1 Our rights and responsibilities to each other, within families and within the wider community		
Understand the ways in which moral and legal rights and responsibilities develop with maturity and age.	It's the rule: Legal rights and responsibilities It's the rule: Criminal responsibility	14–15 12–13
Understand the moral and legal rights and responsibilities that apply to our interactions with others and know that members of families have responsibilities (moral and legal) as well as rights.	It's the rule: Home time It's the rule: Legal rights and responsibilities Family: Changing times Family: Parents' rights and responsibilities Family: Parents' rights and wrongs Consumer rights: Borrowing money Consumer rights: Selling old as new Consumer complaints: Taking action Looking for work: Equal opportunities: Car Crazy Looking for work: Train departure Looking for work: Race discrimination Fairness at work: Religious discrimination Fairness at work: Sexuality and age discrimination Fairness at work: Disability discrimination Losing your job: Fired! Losing your job: Claiming unfair dismissal Losing your job: The employment tribunal Unequal Britain: Sexual equality Older people: The future is grey Older people: An age-old problem	6–7 14–15 36–37 38–39 40–41 54–55 56–57 58–59 62–63 64–65 66–67 68–69 70–71 72–73 80–81 82–83 84–85 116–117 122–123 124–125
Understand the range and importance of fundamental human rights and their impact on national and international law. Identify and debate cases where different human rights may be in conflict.	What are human rights?: The abuse of power Human rights law: Protecting human rights Human rights law: The European Convention on Human Rights Human rights law: Rights and freedoms in Britain Human rights law: Held in detention Unequal Britain: Racism	24–25 26–27 28–29 30–31 32–33 114–115
Engage in responsible action to develop the school community, including understanding the benefits of an active School Council or Student Council.	School: Student voice Campaigning: We want our bus back!	48–49 144–145

Specification content	Student's Book topic	Student's Book page
3.1.2 Our rights and responsibilities as citizens within the economy and welfare systems		
Understand their responsibility for participation in the economy through employment and understand how, and for what purposes, taxes are raised (locally and nationally).	Managing the economy: Taxation	88–89
Understand that the rights of consumers and businesses can compete and conflict but that both have legal rights and responsibilities to each other when items are bought and sold, and that rights are supported and protected by statutory and non-statutory bodies.	Consumer rights: Contract Consumer rights: When things go wrong Consumer rights: Borrowing money Consumer rights: Selling old as new Consumer complaints: Taking action Consumer complaints: Problem solving – a guide Unequal Britain: Challenging disability Older people: An age-old problem	50–51 52–53 54–55 56–57 58–59 60–61 120–121 124–125
Understand that employers and employees have rights and responsibilities that can compete and conflict and that employees can be supported by trade unions.	Looking for work: Equal opportunities: Car crazy Looking for work: Equal opportunities: Train departure Looking for work: Race discrimination Fairness at work: Religious discrimination Fairness at work: Sexuality and age discrimination Fairness at work: Disability discrimination Working for a living: In work Working for a living: Working life Trade unions: Trade unions Losing your job: Fired! Losing your job: Claiming unfair dismissal Losing your job: The employment tribunal Unequal Britain: Sexual equality	62–63 64–65 66–67 68–69 70–71 72–73 74–75 76–77 78–79 80–81 82–83 84–85 116–117
Understand that landlords and tenants have legal rights and responsibilities in relation to rents and deposits, health and safety and the condition of the property, evaluate the extent to which rights are supported and protected by statutory and non-statutory bodies.	Housing: A place of your own Housing: Dealing with problems	126–127 128–129
3.1.3 Our rights and responsibilities as global citizens		
Understand the interdependence of individuals, groups and communities, and assess critically the impact of their own actions on communities and the wider world now and in the future. Make recommendations to others for action and change.	Managing the economy: All Change World trade: Globalisation World trade: Anti-globalisation World trade: A fair price to pay? World trade: Ironing out the highs and lows Poverty: Foreign aid Climate change: The problem Climate change: The solution Choices for the future: Powering the nation	86–87 90–91 92–93 94–95 96–97 98–99 166–167 168–169 170–171

Specification content	Student's Book topic	Student's Book page
Understand that the world's resources are scarce but that demand for them is increasing and that this can lead to the need to make just decisions about fair distribution and use.	Climate change: The solution Choices for the future: Powering the nation	168–169 170–171
3.1.4 Campaigning to raise awareness and advocate action within the community		
Research and present a convincing argument in the context of our rights and responsibilities by critically interpreting and analysing information from different sources, including ICT-based sources, showing an awareness of different values, viewpoints and bias.	Family: Parents' rights and responsibilities Family: Parents' rights and wrongs	38–39 40–41
Enlist support for a viewpoint and organise a campaign to promote it within a school, college or local community by negotiating with others and managing time and resources appropriately.	There are a number of questions throughout the book that could be used as a starting point for a citizenship campaign. These are identified in Section 6.	
Express, explain and critically evaluate different viewpoints, including those with which they do not agree, as part of a formal debate at which a vote is taken.	Most units provide material through which this can be undertaken.	
Explore connections between values, viewpoints and actions with respect to rights and responsibilities for individuals in national and global contexts.	Coming to Britain: Seeking asylum Coming to Britain: Seeking asylum Forms of government: The power to govern	104–105 108–109 158–159

Unit A342: Identity, Democracy and Justice – Understanding our Role as Citizens		
Specification content	**Student's Book topic**	**Student's Book page**
3.2.1 Citizenship, identity and community in the United Kingdom		
Understand the cultural traditions and value system that contribute to being British.	Human rights law: Rights and freedoms in Britain Identity: Being British Unequal Britain: Sexual equality	30–31 112–113 116–117
Explore the diverse national, regional, ethnic and religious groups and communities in the United Kingdom and understand the different forces that bring about change in communities over time.	School: A matter of faith Coming to Britain: Migration Coming to Britain: Migration Coming to Britain: Seeking asylum Coming to Britain: Seeking asylum Identity: Parallel lives Devolution: Governing ourselves	44–45 100–101 102–103 104–105 106–107 110–111 152–153
Understand that the United Kingdom is a country with wide cultural diversity where people's sense of identity is often complex.	Family: Changing times Coming to Britain: Migration Identity: Parallel lives Identity: Being British	36–37 100–101 110–111 112–113

Specification content	Student's Book topic	Student's Book page
Understand the interdependence of individuals, groups and communities, the need for mutual respect and understanding and the importance of community cohesion.	Looking for work: Race discrimination Unequal Britain: Racism Unequal Britain: Challenging disability Older people: An age-old problem Forms of government: The power to govern	66–67 114–115 120–121 124–125 158–159
3.2.2 Fairness and justice in decision-making and the law		
Understand the different roles of the police, Crown Prosecution Service, criminal courts, including judges and juries, as part of the justice system in upholding the law, dealing with criminals and attempting to secure fairness and justice within our democracy. Understand that criminal activity can threaten human rights.	It's the rule: What is law? It's the rule: Criminal responsibility Criminal law: Arrest and charge Criminal law: Arrest and charge Criminal law: Inside a magistrates' court Criminal law: In court Criminal law: Crown Court Criminal law: Cause of death	10–11 12–13 176–177 178–179 180–181 182–183 184–185 186–187
Know that International Humanitarian Law protects the human rights of individuals and communities in peace and in conflict. Understand that individuals, organisations and governments have responsibility to ensure that rights are balanced, supported and protected.	The law machine: Law makers Human rights law: The European Convention on Human Rights Human rights law: Rights and freedoms in Britain Human rights law: Held in detention International human rights: The United Nations Coming to Britain: Seeking asylum Coming to Britain: Seeking asylum Forms of government: The power to govern	16–17 28–29 30–31 32–33 34–34 106–107 108–109 158–159
Understand ways in which rights can compete and conflict and how the law is used to resolve these issues justly.	It's the rule: Home time Human rights law: Protecting human rights School: A right to education? Losing your job: Fired! Losing your job: Claiming unfair dismissal Losing your job: The employment tribunal Unequal Britain: Challenging disability Campaigning: How far should you go?	6–7 26–27 42–43 80–81 82–83 84–85 120–121 146–147
Understand the importance of the law in maintaining order, resolving conflict and achieving just outcomes, and understand that the law places a responsibility on all members of society to conform to a common code of behaviour, including obedience to criminal and civil law.	It's the rule: Home time It's the rule: What is law? It's the rule: Criminal responsibility Looking for work: Equal opportunities: Car crazy Looking for work: Equal opportunities: Train departure Looking for work: Race discrimination Fairness at work: Religious discrimination Fairness at work: Sexuality and age discrimination Fairness at work: Disability discrimination Working for a living: In work Working for a living: Working life Civil law: Taking a case to court Civil law: The county court Criminal law: Prisons and sentencing	6–7 10–11 12–13 62–63 64–65 66–67 68–69 70–71 72–73 74–75 76–77 172–173 174–175 188–189
Understand how a Bill passes through the UK Parliament to become an Act, which is then law.	The law machine: Law makers The law machine: Parliamentary process	16–17 18–19

Specification content	Student's Book topic	Student's Book page
Know how legal advice and support may be obtained.	Consumer rights: Selling old as new Consumer complaints: Problem solving – a guide Looking for work: Race discrimination Fairness at work: Disability discrimination Civil law: Taking a case to court Criminal law: Arrest and charge	56–57 60–61 66–67 72–73 172–173 176–177
3.2.3 Democracy and voting		
Engage in different democratic decision-making exercises that have an influence on school or community life.	School: Student voice	48–49
Understand the development of, and struggle for, different kinds of rights and freedoms (speech, opinion, association and the right to vote) in the United Kingdom as part of securing a representative democracy. Understand the different operation of power and authority in democratic and non-democratic forms of government, historically and across the world today. Evaluate Parliament's role in holding the Government to account in a representative democracy. Understand that non-democratic forms of government are likely to infringe human rights.	Human rights law: Rights and freedoms in Britain Unequal Britain: Sexual Equality Unequal Britain: Sexual Equality National government: Controlling the government Forms of government: The power to govern	30–31 116–117 118–119 150–151 158–159
Understand ways in which citizens can play an active part in the electoral process to influence decision making through membership of political parties and through participation in local and national elections.	Voting and elections: A problem for the council Voting and elections: The right to vote Party politics: Join the party Party politics: Where do you stand? Party politics: Newspapers Campaigning: Home alone Campaigning: We want our bus back! National government: Governing Britain Local government: Local councils	130–131 132–133 136–137 138–139 140–141 142–143 144–145 148–149 154–155
Evaluate the extent to which citizens can play an active part in the democratic process to influence decision making and to hold decision makers to account locally, nationally and globally, including through membership of interest groups and pressure groups.	Campaigning: How far should you go?	146–147
Understand the importance of political parties, interest groups, including religious organisations, pressure groups and the media in influencing public debate and policy formation.	Party politics: Join the party National government: Governing Britain	136–137 148–149

OCR Citizenship Studies Teacher's Resource Book for GCSE full and short course
© 2009 Hodder Education

Specification content	Student's Book topic	Student's Book page
Understand the importance of a free press in a democracy by knowing that, in the United Kingdom, the media have the right to investigate, and to report upon, issues of public interest, subject to the need for accuracy and respect for people's privacy and dignity. Understand the use politicians make of the media in communicating with the public. Understand how the media influence the decision-making process through the use of information, by affecting public opinion, and by exerting pressure on local and national governments.	The power of the media: Freedom to publish	164–165
3.2.4 The United Kingdom's relationships in Europe, including the European Union (EU), and relationships with the Commonwealth and United Nations (UN)		
Know, in outline, about our economic, political, legal and cultural relationships with other countries in Europe. Evaluate the implications of the United Kingdom's membership of the European Union and that European Union decisions have an impact upon citizens of the United Kingdom.	The law machine: Law makers The law machine: European law Trade unions: Trade unions Coming to Britain: Migration Coming to Britain: Migration Voting and elections: Election to Parliament European government: Governing Europe	16–17 22–23 78–79 100–101 102–103 134–135 156–157
Understand that the British Commonwealth is a family of nations and has an important role in promoting cultural understanding and the exchange of ideas.	Coming to Britain: Migration	100–101
Understand the United Nations' role in helping to resolve international disagreements and conflict. Understand that the United Kingdom, as a member country, is committed to adhere to the United Nations' agreements on human rights, international relations and the environment. Evaluate the role and effectiveness of the United Nations in one international issue, emergency or dispute.	International human rights: The United Nations Coming to Britain: Seeking asylum Coming to Britain: Seeking asylum Coming to Britain: Seeking asylum Climate change: The solution	34–35 104–105 106–107 108–109 168–169

Unit A343: Rights and Responsibilities – Extending our Knowledge and Understanding		
Specification content	**Student's Book topic**	**Student's Book page**
3.3.1 Our rights and responsibilities at school/college and within the wider community		
Know that members of the school/college community have responsibilities (moral and legal) as well as rights.	School: A right to education? School: Student voice	42–43 48–49

Specification content	Student's Book topic	Student's Book page
Understand the formal (legal) and informal means through which rights and responsibilities can be balanced, supported and safeguarded in schools.	School: School choice	46–47
Evaluate the additional formal and independent support available to individuals requiring information and advice, including that available from: Government departments, agencies and official regulators; Citizens' Advice, consumer protection or rights organisations and solicitors.	Unequal Britain: Challenging disability Civil Law: Taking a case to court Criminal law: Arrest and charge	120–121 172–173 176–177
Evaluate the additional formal and independent support available to individuals requiring information and advice, including that available from: Government departments, agencies and official regulators; Citizens' Advice, consumer protection or rights organisations and solicitors.	Consumer complaints: Problem-solving: a guide	60–61
Analyse the Universal Declaration of Human Rights, the European Convention on Human Rights and the Human Rights Act. With reference to these documents, evaluate possible infringements of human rights in the UK and elsewhere.	Human rights law: Protecting Human Rights Human rights law: The European Convention on Human Rights	26–27 28–29
3.3.2 Our rights and responsibilities as citizens within the economy and welfare systems		
Understand the role of trade unions and employers' associations in supporting and representing their members.	Trade unions: Trade unions	78–79
Understand that laws relating to employment and the production, taxation and sale of goods need to recognise the interests of employers, employees, buyers, sellers and the environmental impact of production. Understand how these interests can compete and conflict.	Consumer rights: Contract Consumer rights: When things go wrong Consumer rights: Borrowing money Consumer rights: Selling old as new Consumer complaints: Taking action Looking for work: Equal opportunities: Car crazy Looking for work: Equal opportunities: Train departure Looking for work: Race discrimination Fairness at work: Religious discrimination Fairness at work: Sexuality and age discrimination Fairness at work: Disability discrimination Working for a living: In work Working for a living: A working life Losing your job: Fired! Losing your job: Claiming unfair dismissal Losing your job: The employment tribunal Managing the economy: Taxation World trade: Anti-globalisation Unequal Britain: Sexual equality	50–51 52–53 54–55 56–57 58–59 62–63 64–65 66–67 68–69 70–71 72–73 74–75 76–77 80–81 82–83 84–85 88–89 92–93 116–117

Appendix 1

Specification content	Student's Book topic	Student's Book page
Understand the Government's role in helping to manage the economy and the planning and regulation of public services. Evaluate and debate the different opinions on how far the state or individuals should take responsibility for the provision of income protection, health and education.	School: A matter of faith School: School choice Managing the economy: All change Unequal Britain: Racism Older people: The future is grey Older people: An age-old problem	44–45 46–47 86–87 114–115 122–123 124–125
Understand the importance of ethical behaviour and social responsibility in enterprise and business, including the moral and legal responsibilities businesses have towards each other and the wider community.	World trade: Globalisation Unequal Britain: Challenging disability	90–91 120–121
3.3.3 Extending understanding of a global citizen's rights and responsibilities		
Understand the implications of Agenda 21 for promoting sustainable development on local, national and global scales, together with the constraints limiting the extent of its implementation.	Climate change: The solution Choices for the future: Powering the nation	168–169 170–171
Understand the differences between fair and unfair trade and the role of traders' organisations, pressure groups and governments in bringing about change.	World trade: Anti-globalisation World trade: A fair price to pay? World trade: Ironing out the highs and lows Poverty: Foreign aid	92–93 94–95 96–97 98–99
Evaluate the different types of aid that may be offered to Less Economically Developed Countries (LEDCs) and the relative merits of these for people in the donor and recipient countries.	Poverty: Foreign aid	98–99
Understand the role of the media, the internet and other new communications technologies, in international affairs, in providing information and affecting opinion, and how they may be used to attempt to bring about change, in democratic and non-democratic societies.	The power of the media: The front page The power of the media: Managing the news	160–161 162–163
Evaluate the key points of one international citizenship issue related to trade or aid.	World trade: Globalisation World trade: Anti-globalisation World trade: A fair price to pay? World trade: Ironing out the highs and lows Poverty: Foreign aid	90–91 92–93 94–95 96–97 98–99

Unit A344: Identity, Democracy and Justice – Leading the Way as an Active Citizen		
Specification content	Student's Book topic	Student's Book page
3.4.1 Citizenship, identity and community cohesion in the United Kingdom		
Understand the specific contributions of at least two different cultural traditions to the richness of life in the UK.	Coming to Britain: Migration Identity: Being British	100–101 112–113
Research the needs of different groups in their local community by using a simple but valid social survey. Understand that different groups may hold differing views on the nature of the community's needs and the best ways to meet these needs.	Local government: Local councils	154–155
Understand the conditions which may lead to strain and conflict between communities in the UK.	School: A matter of faith Coming to Britain: Migration Identity: Parallel lives Unequal Britain: Racism	44–45 102–103 110–111 114–115
Engage with and evaluate the effectiveness of informal and formal community leaders (small business owners, councillors, youth workers, media workers, etc), community groups and non-governmental organisations (such as community groups, charities and special interest groups) in addressing and supporting community needs, providing services, promoting community cohesion and bringing about social change.	Identity: Being British Older people: The future is grey Older people: An age-old problem	112–113 122–123 124–125
Evaluate the effectiveness of the law in discouraging unfair discrimination.	Looking for work: Equal opportunities: Car crazy Looking for work: Equal opportunities: Train departure Looking for work: Race discrimination Fairness at work: Religious discrimination Fairness at work: Sexuality and age discrimination Fairness at work: Disability discrimination	62–63 64–65 66–67 68–69 70–71 72–73
With reference to the above, actively engage in and understand the processes needed for successful community action designed to have an impact in the school, college and/or wider community: researching the background (including identification of key decision-makers); negotiating responsibility within a team; finding sources of information and support; engaging in community action; reflecting on the process of participating and, if appropriate, consolidating or extending the project.	Campaigning: We want our bus back!	144–145

OCR Citizenship Studies Teacher's Resource Book for GCSE full and short course
© 2009 Hodder Education

Appendix 1

Specification content	Student's Book topic	Student's Book page
3.4.2 Extending understanding of the legal and justice system		
Understand, through the study of suitable examples, that the courts are charged with responsibility to interpret the law in reaching judgements and that this creates a precedent for future judgements and to judge-made case law.	The law machine: Law makers The law machine: Judge-made law	16–17 20–21
Understand the importance of supporting victims of crime and the processes involved.	Criminal law: In court (see also p. 171 of this teacher's book)	182–183
Evaluate the role and effectiveness of the police, probation service and prison service in reducing crime and rates of re-offending, including by punishing and rehabilitating people who disobey the law.	Criminal law: Prisons and sentencing	188–189
Understand the role of individuals, lawyers and courts in the civil legal and justice system.	It's the rule: What is law? Looking for work: Race discrimination Losing your job: Claiming unfair dismissal Losing your job: The employment tribunal Civil law: Taking a case to court Civil law: The county court Criminal law: Arrest and charge Criminal law: Inside a magistrates' court Criminal law: In court Criminal law: Crown Court Criminal law: Cause of death	10–11 66–67 82–83 84–85 172–173 174–175 176–177 180–181 182–183 184–185 186–187
Evaluate the justifications people give for breaking the law, including to bring about change, and understand the reasons for upholding the rule of law.	It's the rule: Breaking the law. Campaigning: How far should you go?	8–9 146–147
3.4.3 Democracy and voting		
Understand the processes through which candidates are nominated for local, national and European elections.	Local government: Local councils	154–155
Understand the role of a Member of Parliament (MP) and how they exercise responsibility for constituents.	National government: Governing Britain National government: Controlling the government	148–149 150–151
Evaluate the merits and demerits of the different voting systems operating within the United Kingdom.	Voting and elections: Election to Parliament	134–135
Understand the changing relationships in the United Kingdom between England, Scotland, Wales and Northern Ireland, and the role of national assemblies/parliaments in establishing different laws and policies in the four nations.	Devolution: Governing ourselves	152–153
Understand, by studying examples, the way in which the media exert power through the use of editorials, headlines and the selection and presentation of news.	The power of the media: Managing the news	162–163

Mapping the Student's Book to the Key Stage 4 Programme of Study

The grid below maps the pages and content in the Student's Book to the Citizenship Key Stage 4 Programme of Study. This gives you an at-a-glance view of where the content is covered.

Programme of Study content	Student's Book topic	Student's Book page
Key concept 1.1 Democracy and justice		
a. Participating actively in different kinds of decision-making and voting in order to influence public life.	School: Student voice	48–49
	Managing the economy: Taxation	88–89
	Voting and elections: A problem for the council	130–131
	Voting and elections: The right to vote	132–133
	Voting and elections: Election to Parliament	134–135
	Party politics: Join the party	136–137
	Party politics: Where do you stand?	138–139
	Party politics: Newspapers	140–141
	National government: Governing Britain	148–149
	National government: Controlling the government	150–151
	Local government: Local councils	154–155
b. Weighing up what is fair and unfair in different situations, understanding that justice is fundamental to a democratic society and exploring the role of law in maintaining order and resolving conflict.	It's the rule: Home time	6–7
	It's the rule: Breaking the law	8–9
	It's the rule: What is law?	10–11
	It's the rule: Criminal responsibility	12–13
	It's the rule: Legal rights and responsibilities	14–15
	The law machine: Law makers	16–17
	The law machine: Judge-made law	20–21
	What are human rights? The abuse of power	24–25
	Human rights law: Protecting human rights	26–27
	Human rights law: The European Convention on Human Rights	28–29
	Human rights law: Rights and freedoms in Britain	30–31
	Human rights law: Held in detention	32–33
	International human rights: The United Nations	34–35
	School: A right to education?	42–43
	School: School choice	46–47
	School: Student voice	48–49
	Looking for work: Equal opportunities: Car Crazy	62–63
	Looking for work: Equal opportunities: Train departure	64–65
	Consumer rights: Selling old as new	56–57
	Looking for work: Race discrimination	66–67
	Fairness at work: Religious discrimination	68–69
	Fairness at work: Sexuality and Age discrimination	70–71
	Fairness at work: Disability discrimination	72–73
	Working for a living: In work	74–75
	Working for a living: A working life	76–77
	Trade unions: Trade Unions	78–79
	Losing your job: Fired!	80–81
	Losing your job: Claiming unfair dismissal	82–83
	Losing your job: The employment tribunal	84–85
	Managing the economy: All change	86–87

OCR Citizenship Studies Teacher's Resource Book for GCSE full and short course
© 2009 Hodder Education

Programme of Study content	Student's Book topic	Student's Book page
b. *continued*	World trade: Globalisation	90–91
	World trade: Anti-globalisation	92–93
	World trade: A fair price to pay?	94–95
	World trade: Ironing out the highs and lows	96–97
	Poverty: Foreign Aid	98–99
	Coming to Britain: Seeking asylum	106–107
	Coming to Britain: Seeking asylum	108–109
	Identity: Parallel lives	110–111
	Unequal Britain: Racism	114–115
	Unequal Britain: Sexual equality	116–117
	Unequal Britain: Sexual equality	118–119
	Unequal Britain: Challenging disability	120–121
	Older people: The future is grey	122–123
	Older people: An age-old problem	124–125
	Housing: A place of your own	126–127
	Housing: Dealing with problems	128–129
	Party politics: Join the party	136–137
	Party politics: Where do you stand?	138–139
	Party politics: Newspapers	140–141
	Campaigning: Home alone	142–143
	Campaigning: We want our bus back!	144–145
	Campaigning: How far should you go?	146–147
	National government: Governing Britain	148–149
	National government: Controlling the government	150–151
	Devolution: Governing ourselves	152–153
	Local government: Local councils	154–155
	Forms of government: The power to govern	158–159
	The power of the media: Managing the news	162–163
	The power of the media: Freedom to publish	164–165
	Climate change: The solution	168–169
	Civil law: The county court	174–175
	Criminal law: Arrest and charge	176–177
	Criminal law: Arrest and charge	178–179
	Criminal law: Inside a magistrates' court	180–181
	Criminal law: In court	182–183
	Criminal law: Crown Court	184–185
	Criminal law: Cause of death	186–187
	Criminal law: Prisons and sentencing	188–189
c. Considering how democracy, justice, diversity, toleration, respect and freedom are valued by people with different beliefs, backgrounds and traditions within a changing democratic society.	The law machine: European law	22–23
	What are human rights? The abuse of power	24–25
	Human rights law: Protecting human rights	26–27
	Fairness at work: Religious discrimination	68–69
	Fairness at work: Sexuality and Age discrimination	70–71
	Coming to Britain: Migration	100–101
	Coming to Britain: Migration	102–103
	Coming to Britain: Seeking asylum	104–105
	Identity: Parallel lives	110–111
	Identity: Being British	112–113
	Unequal Britain: Racism	114–115
	Devolution: Governing ourselves	152–153
	The power of the media: Managing the news	162–163
	The power of the media: Freedom to publish	164–165

Programme of Study content	Student's Book topic	Student's Book page
d. Understanding and exploring the roles of citizens and parliament in holding government and those in power to account.	The law machine: Law makers	16–17
	The law machine: Parliamentary process	18–19
	Human rights law: Protecting human rights	26–27
	Human rights law: Rights and freedoms in Britain	30–31
	Human rights law: Held in detention	32–33
	School: School choice	46–47
	Managing the economy: All change	86–87
	Voting and elections: A problem for the council	130–131
	Voting and elections: The right to vote	132–133
	Voting and elections: Election to Parliament	134–135
	Party politics: Join the party	136–137
	Party politics: Where do you stand?	138–139
	Party politics: Newspapers	140–141
	National government: Governing Britain	148–149
	National government: Controlling the government	150–151
	Local government: Local councils	154–155
	European government: Governing Europe	156–157
	Forms of government: The power to govern	158–159
	The power of the media: Managing the news	162–163
Key concept 1.2 Rights and responsibilities		
a. Exploring different kinds of rights and obligations and how these affect both individuals and communities.	It's the rule: Home time	6–7
	It's the rule: Criminal responsibility	12–13
	It's the rule: Legal rights and responsibilities	14–15
	The law machine: Law makers	16–17
	What are human rights? The abuse of power	24–25
	Human rights law: Protecting human rights	26–27
	International human rights: The United Nations	34–35
	Family: Changing times	36–37
	Family: Parents' rights and responsibilities	38–39
	Family: Parents' rights and wrongs	40–41
	School: A right to education?	42–43
	School: School choice	46–47
	Consumer rights: contract	50–51
	Consumer rights: When things go wrong	52–53
	Consumer complaints: Taking action	58–59
	Consumer complaints: Problem solving – a guide	60–61
	Looking for work: Equal opportunities: Car crazy	62–63
	Looking for work: Equal opportunities: Train departure	64–65
	Looking for work: Race discrimination	66–67
	Fairness at work: Religious discrimination	68–69
	Fairness at work: Sexuality and Age discrimination	70–71
	Fairness at work: Disability discrimination	72–73
	Working for a living: In work	74–75
	Working for a living: A working life	76–77
	Trade unions: Trade unions	78–79
	Losing your job: Fired!	80–81
	Losing your job: Unfair dismissal	82–83
	Losing your job: The employment tribunal	84–85
	Managing the economy: All change	86–87
	Managing the economy: Taxation	88–89
	Coming to Britain: Seeking asylum	104–105
	Coming to Britain: Seeking asylum	106–107

OCR Citizenship Studies Teacher's Resource Book for GCSE full and short course
© 2009 Hodder Education

Programme of Study content	Student's Book topic	Student's Book page
a. *continued*	Coming to Britain: Seeking asylum	108–109
	Unequal Britain: Racism	114–115
	Unequal Britain: Sexual equality	116–117
	Unequal Britain: Sexual equality	118–119
	Unequal Britain: Challenging Disability	120–121
	Older people: The future is grey	122–123
	Older people: An age-old problem	124–125
	Housing: A place of your own	126–127
	Housing: Dealing with problems	128–129
	Voting and elections: A problem for the council	130–131
	Voting and elections: The right to vote	132–133
	Voting and elections: Election to Parliament	134–135
	Party politics: Join the party	136–137
	Party politics: Where do you stand?	138–139
	Party politics: Newspapers	140–141
	Campaigning: How far should you go?	146–147
	National government: Governing Britain	148–149
	National government: Controlling the government	150–151
	Local government: Local councils	154–155
	The power of the media: Managing the news	162–163
	The power of the media: Freedom to publish	164–165
	Climate change: The problem	166–167
	Climate change: The solution	168–169
	Choices for the future: Powering the nation	170–171
	Civil law: Taking a case to court	172–173
	Civil law: The county court	174–175
	Criminal law: Arrest and charge	176–177
	Criminal law: Arrest and charge	178–179
	Criminal law: Inside a magistrates' court	180–181
	Criminal law: In court	182–183
	Criminal law: Crown Court	184–185
	Criminal law: Cause of death	186–187
	Criminal law: Prisons and sentencing	188–189
b. Understanding that individuals, organisations and governments have responsibilities to ensure that rights are balanced, supported and protected.	The law machine: Parliamentary process	18–19
	The law machine: Judge-made law	20–21
	What are human rights? The abuse of power	24–25
	Human rights law: Protecting human rights	26–27
	Human rights law: The European Convention on Human Rights	28–29
	Human rights law: Rights and freedoms in Britain	30–31
	Human rights law: Held in detention	32–33
	Family: Parents' rights and responsibilities	38–39
	Family: Parents' rights and wrongs	40–41
	School: A right to education?	42–43
	School: A matter of faith	44–45
	School: School choice	46–47
	School: Student voice	48–49
	Consumer rights: When things go wrong	52–53
	Consumer rights: Borrowing money	54–55
	Working for a living: In work	74–75
	Working for a living: A working life	76–77
	Trade unions: Trade unions	78–79
	Managing the economy: Taxation	88–89

Programme of Study content	Student's Book topic	Student's Book page
b. *continued*	World trade: Globalisation	90–91
	World trade: Anti-globalisation	92–93
	World trade: A fair price to pay?	94–95
	World trade: Ironing out the highs and lows	96–97
	Poverty: Foreign aid	98–99
	Identity: Parallel lives	110–111
	Identity: Being British	112–113
	Unequal Britain: Racism	114–115
	Unequal Britain: Sexual equality	116–117
	Unequal Britain: Sexual equality	118–119
	Unequal Britain: Challenging disability	120–121
	Older people: The future is grey	122–123
	Older people: An age-old problem	124–125
	Housing: A place of your own	126–127
	Housing: Dealing with problems	128–129
	Campaigning: How far should you go?	146–147
	National government: Controlling the government	150–151
	Forms of government: The power to govern	158–159
	The power of the media: Managing the news	162–163
	The power of the media: Freedom to publish	164–165
	Civil Law: Taking a case to court	172–173
	Civil Law: The county court	174–175
	Criminal law: Arrest and charge	176–177
	Criminal law: Arrest and charge	178–179
	Criminal law: Inside a magistrates' court	180–181
	Criminal law: In court	182–183
	Criminal law: Crown Court	184–185
	Criminal law: Cause of death	186–187
	Criminal law: Prisons and sentencing	188–189
c. Investigating ways in which rights can compete and conflict, and understanding that hard decisions have to be made to try to balance these.	It's the rule: Home time	6–7
	The law machine: Law makers	16–17
	What are human rights? The abuse of power	24–25
	Human rights law: Protecting human rights	26–27
	School: A right to education?	42–43
	School: Student voice	48–49
	Consumer rights: Contract	50–51
	Looking for work: Equal opportunities: Car crazy	62–63
	Looking for work: Equal opportunities: Train departure	64–65
	Looking for work: Race discrimination	66–67
	Fairness at work: Religious discrimination	68–69
	Fairness at work: Sexuality and Age discrimination	70–71
	Fairness at work: Disability discrimination	72–73
	Losing your job: Fired!	80–81
	Losing your job: Unfair dismissal	82–83
	Losing your job: The employment tribunal	84–85
	Unequal Britain: Challenging disability	120–121
	Older people: The future is grey	122–123
	Older people: An age-old problem	124–125
	Campaigning: How far should you go?	146–147
	National government: Governing Britain	148–149
	Devolution: Governing ourselves	152–153
	The power of the media: The front page	160–161
	The power of the media: Managing the news	162–163

OCR Citizenship Studies Teacher's Resource Book for GCSE full and short course
© 2009 Hodder Education

Programme of Study content	Student's Book topic	Student's Book page
c. *continued*	The power of the media: Freedom to publish	164–165
	Climate change: The problem	166–167
	Climate change: The solution	168–169
	Choices for the future: Powering the nation	170–171
	Civil law: Taking a case to court	172–173
	Civil law: The county court	174–175
	Criminal law: Arrest and charge	176–177
	Criminal law: Arrest and charge	178–179
	Criminal law: Inside a magistrates' court	180–181
	Criminal law: In court	182–183
	Criminal law: Crown Court	184–185
	Criminal law: Cause of death	186–187
	Criminal law: Prisons and sentencing	188–189
Key concept 1.3 Identities and diversity: living together in the UK		
a. Appreciating that identities are complex, can change over time and are informed by different understandings of what it means to be a citizen in the UK.	It's the rule: Home time	6–7
	Family: Changing times	36–37
	Fairness at work: Religious discrimination	68–69
	Devolution: Governing ourselves	152–153
	Forms of government: The power to govern	158–159
b. Exploring the diverse national, regional, ethnic and religious cultures, groups and communities in the UK and the connections between them.	It's the rule: Home time	6–7
	School: A matter of faith	44–45
	Fairness at work: Religious discrimination	68–69
	Coming to Britain: Migration	100–101
	Coming to Britain: Migration	102–103
	Coming to Britain: Seeking asylum	104–105
	Coming to Britain: Seeking asylum	106–107
	Coming to Britain: Seeking asylum	108–109
	Identity: Parallel lives	110–111
	Identity: Being British	112–113
	Devolution: Governing ourselves	152–153
c. Considering the interconnections between the UK and the rest of Europe and the wider world.	International human rights: The United Nations	34–35
	Managing the economy: All change	86–87
	World trade: Globalisation	90–91
	World trade: Anti-globalisation	92–93
	World trade: A fair price to pay?	94–95
	World trade: Ironing out the highs and lows	96–97
	Poverty: Foreign Aid	98–99
	Coming to Britain: Migration	100–101
	Coming to Britain: Migration	102–103
	Coming to Britain: Seeking asylum	104–105
	Coming to Britain: Seeking asylum	106–107
	Coming to Britain: Seeking asylum	108–109
d. Exploring community cohesion and the different forces that bring about change in communities over time.	Coming to Britain: Migration	100–101
	Coming to Britain: Migration	102–103
	Coming to Britain: Seeking asylum	104–105
	Coming to Britain: Seeking asylum	106–107
	Coming to Britain: Seeking asylum	108–109
	Identity: Parallel lives	110–111
	Identity: Being British	112–113
	Devolution: Governing ourselves	152–153

Programme of Study content	Student's Book topic	Student's Book page
3 Range and content The study of citizenship should include:		
a. political, legal and human rights and freedoms in a range of contexts from local to global.	It's the rule: Home time	6–7
	It's the rule: Breaking the law	8–9
	It's the rule: What is law?	10–11
	It's the rule: Criminal responsibility	12–13
	What are human rights? The abuse of power	24–25
	Human rights law: Protecting human rights	26–27
	Human rights law: The European Convention on Human Rights	28–29
	Human rights law: Rights and freedoms in Britain	30–31
	Human rights law: Held in detention	32–33
	International human rights: The United Nations	34–35
	Family: Changing times	36–37
	Family: Parents' rights and responsibilities	38–39
	Family: Parents' rights and wrongs	40–41
	School: A right to education?	42–43
	School: School choice	46–47
	Consumer rights: Contract	50–51
	Consumer rights: When things go wrong	52–53
	Consumer rights: Borrowing money	54–55
	Consumer rights: Selling old as new	56–57
	Consumer complaints: Taking action	58–59
	Consumer complaints: Problem solving – a guide	60–61
	Looking for work: Equal opportunities: Car crazy	62–63
	Looking for work: Equal opportunities: Train departure	64–65
	Looking for work: Race discrimination	66–67
	Fairness at work: Religious discrimination	68–69
	Fairness at work: Sexuality and Age discrimination	70–71
	Fairness at work: Disability discrimination	72–73
	Working for a living: In work	74–75
	Working for a living: A working life	76–77
	Trade unions: Trade unions	78–79
	Losing your job: Fired!	80–81
	Losing your job: Unfair dismissal	82–83
	Losing your job: The employment tribunal	84–85
	Coming to Britain: Seeking asylum	106–107
	Coming to Britain: Seeking asylum	108–109
	Unequal Britain: Racism	114–115
	Unequal Britain: Sexual equality	116–117
	Unequal Britain: Sexual equality	118–119
	Unequal Britain: Challenging disability	120–121
	Older people: The future is grey	122–123
	Older people: An age-old problem	124–125
	Housing: A place of your own	126–127
	Housing: Dealing with problems	128–129
	Voting and elections: A problem for the council	130–131
	Voting and elections: Right to vote	132–133
	Voting and elections: Election to Parliament	134–135
	Party politics: Join the party	136–137
	Party politics: Where do you stand?	138–139
	Party politics: Newspapers	140–141

Appendix 2

Programme of Study content	Student's Book topic	Student's Book page
a. *continued*	Campaigning: Home alone	142–143
	Campaigning: We want our bus back!	144–145
	Campaigning: How far should you go?	146–147
	National government: Governing Britain	148–149
	Devolution: Governing ourselves	152–153
	National government: Controlling the government	150–151
	Local government: Local councils	154–155
	Forms of government: The power to govern	158–159
	Civil law: Taking a case to court	172–173
	Civil law: The county court	174–175
	Criminal law: Arrest and charge	176–177
	Criminal law: Arrest and charge	178–179
	Criminal law: Inside a magistrates' court	180–181
	Criminal law: In court	182–183
	Criminal law: Crown Court	184–185
	Criminal law: Cause of death	186–187
	Criminal law: Prisons and sentencing	188–189
b. the roles and operation of civil and criminal law and the justice system.	It's the rule: Home time	6–7
	It's the rule: What is law?	10–11
	It's the rule: Criminal responsibility	12–13
	Looking for work: Equal opportunities: Car crazy	62–63
	Looking for work: Equal opportunities: Train departure	64–65
	Looking for work: Race discrimination	66–67
	Fairness at work: Religious discrimination	68–69
	Fairness at work: Sexuality and Age discrimination	70–71
	Fairness at work: Disability discrimination	72–73
	Unequal Britain: Racism	114–115
	Campaigning: How far should you go?	146–147
	Civil law: Taking a case to court	172–173
	Civil law: The county court	174–175
	Criminal law: Arrest and charge	176–177
	Criminal law: Arrest and charge	178–179
	Criminal law: Inside a magistrates' court	180–181
	Criminal law: In court	182–183
	Criminal law: Crown Court	184–185
	Criminal law: Cause of death	186–187
	Criminal law: Prisons and sentencing	188–189
c. how laws are made and shaped by people and processes, including the work of parliament, government and the courts.	The law machine: Law makers	16–17
	The law machine: Parliamentary process	18–19
	The law machine: Judge-made law	20–21
	The law machine: European law	22–23
	Human rights law: Rights and freedoms in Britain	30–31
	Managing the economy: Taxation	88–89
	National government: Governing Britain	148–149
	National government: Controlling the government	150–151
	Devolution: Governing ourselves	152–153
	European government: Governing Europe	156–157
d. actions citizens can take in democratic and electoral processes to influence decisions locally, nationally and beyond.	School: Student voice	48–49
	World trade: Globalisation	90–91
	World trade: Anti-globalisation	92–93
	World trade: A fair price to pay?	94–95
	World trade: Ironing out the highs and lows	96–97

Programme of Study content	Student's Book topic	Student's Book page
d. *continued*	Poverty: Foreign aid	98–99
	Identity: Parallel lives	110–111
	Identity: Being British	112–113
	Voting and elections: A problem for the council	130–131
	Voting and elections: The right to vote	132–133
	Voting and elections: Election to Parliament	134–135
	Party politics: Join the party	136–137
	Party politics: Where do you stand?	138–139
	Party politics: Newspapers	140–141
	Campaigning: Home alone	142–143
	Campaigning: We want our bus back!	144–145
	Campaigning: How far should you go?	146–147
	National government: Governing Britain	148–149
	National government: Controlling the government	150–151
	Devolution: Governing ourselves	152–153
	Local government: Local councils	154–155
	European government: Governing Europe	156–157
e. the operation of parliamentary democracy within the UK and of other forms of government, both democratic and non-democratic, beyond the UK.	International human rights: The United Nations	34–35
	Looking for work: Equal opportunities: Train departure	64–65
	Looking for work: Race discrimination	66–67
	Fairness at work: Religious discrimination	68–69
	Voting and elections: A problem for the council	130–131
	Voting and elections: The right to vote	132–133
	Voting and elections: Election to Parliament	134–135
	Party politics: Join the party	136–137
	Party politics: Where do you stand?	138–139
	Party politics: Newspapers	140–141
	National government: Governing Britain	148–149
	National government: Controlling the government	150–151
	Devolution: Governing ourselves	152–153
	Local government: Local councils	154–155
	European government: Governing Europe	156–157
	Forms of government: The power to govern	158–159
f. the development of, and struggle for, different kinds of rights and freedoms (speech, opinion, association and the vote) in the UK.	What are human rights? The abuse of power	24–25
	Human rights law: Protecting human rights	26–27
	Human rights law: Rights and freedoms in Britain	30–31
	Family: Parents' rights and wrongs	40–41
	The power of the media: Freedom to publish	164–165
	Criminal law: Arrest and charge	176–177
g. how information is used in public debate and policy formation, including information from the media and from pressure and interest groups.	The power of the media: The front page	160–161
	The power of the media: Managing the news	162–163
	The power of the media: Freedom to publish	164–165
h. the impact and consequences of individual and collective actions on communities, including the work of the voluntary sector.	School: Student voice	48–49
	World trade: A fair price to pay?	94–95
	World trade: Ironing out the highs and lows	96–97
	Identity: Parallel lives	110–111
	Unequal Britain: Challenging disability	120–121
	Campaigning: Home alone	142–143
	Campaigning: We want our bus back!	144–145
	Campaigning: How far should you go?	146–147

Programme of Study content	Student's Book topic	Student's Book page
i. policies and practices for sustainable development and their impact on the environment.	Climate change: The problem Climate change: The solution Choices for the future: Powering the nation	166–167 168–169 170–171
j. the economy in relation to citizenship, including decisions about the collection and allocation of public money.	Trade unions: Trade unions Managing the economy: All change Managing the economy: Taxation	78–79 86–87 88–89
k. the rights and responsibilities of consumers, employers and employees.	Consumer rights: Contract Consumer rights: When things go wrong Consumer rights: Borrowing money Consumer rights: Selling old as new Consumer complaints: Taking action Consumer complaints: Problem solving – a guide Looking for work: Equal opportunities: Car crazy Looking for work: Equal opportunities: Train departure Looking for work: Race discrimination Fairness at work: Religious discrimination Fairness at work: Sexuality and Age discrimination Fairness at work: Disability discrimination Working for a living: In work Working for a living: A working life Trade unions: Trade unions Losing your job: Fired! Losing your job: Unfair dismissal Losing your job: The employment tribunal World trade: A fair price to pay? World trade: Ironing out the highs and lows Unequal Britain: Sexual equality Unequal Britain: Sexual equality Unequal Britain: Challenging disability	50–51 52–53 54–55 56–57 58–59 60–61 62–63 64–65 66–67 68–69 70–71 72–73 74–75 76–77 78–79 80–81 82–83 84–85 94–95 96–97 116–117 118–119 120–121
l. the origins and implications of diversity and the changing nature of society in the UK, including the perspectives and values that are shared or common, and the impact of migration and integration on identities, groups and communities.	Family: Changing times School: A matter of faith Fairness at work: Religious discrimination Coming to Britain: Migration Coming to Britain: Migration Coming to Britain: Seeking asylum Coming to Britain: Seeking asylum Coming to Britain: Seeking asylum Identity: Parallel lives Identity: Being British Devolution: Governing ourselves	36–37 44–45 68–69 100–101 102–103 104–105 106–107 108–109 110–111 112–113 152–153
m. the UK's role in the world, including in Europe, the European Union, the Commonwealth and the United Nations.	The law machine: Law makers The law machine: European law Human rights law: Protecting human rights Human rights law: The European Convention on Human Rights International human rights: The United Nations Trade unions: Trade unions Managing the economy: All change Coming to Britain: Migration Coming to Britain: Migration Coming to Britain: Seeking asylum	16–17 22–23 26–27 28–29 34–35 78–79 86–87 100–101 102–103 104–105

Programme of Study content	Student's Book topic	Student's Book page
m. *continued*	Coming to Britain: Seeking asylum	106–107
	Coming to Britain: Seeking asylum	108–109
	Local government: Local councils	154–155
	European government: Governing Europe	156–157
	Climate change: The problem	166–167
	Climate change: The solution	168–169
	Choices for the future: Powering the nation	170–171
n. the challenges facing the global community, including international disagreements and conflict, and debates about inequalities, sustainability and use of the world's resources.	Managing the economy: All change	86–87
	World trade: Globalisation	90–91
	World trade: Anti-globalisation	92–93
	World trade: A fair price to pay?	94–95
	World trade: Ironing out the highs and lows	96–97
	Poverty: Foreign aid	98–99
	Coming to Britain: Seeking asylum	104–105
	Coming to Britain: Seeking asylum	106–107
	Coming to Britain: Seeking asylum	108–109
	Climate change: The problem	166–167
	Climate change: The solution	168–169
	Choices for the future: Powering the nation	170–171